OIL PAINT AND GREECE

PETER HEMMING

Cover Painting: Myrtos Beach, oil on canvas by Peter Hemming

www.oilpaintandgreece.com
email: oilpaintandgreece@yahoo.com

ISBN: 1481891723
ISBN-13: 978-1481891721

DEDICATION

This book is dedicated to Stathis and Irini, and
Spyros and Connie.

They came up trumps when we needed a winning
hand.

ACKNOWLEDGMENTS

The technical 'behind the scenes' work that Pam sweated over has been monumental. She not only wore her fingers to the bone at the computer, but she was also my prop at times when inspiration failed me. Thanks Pam, because without you this book could never have come to fruition.

There is a special thank you to Makis and Soula who treated us not only as tenants, but as friends, Pam and I will never forget you.

I would also like to thank the many other Kefalonians (and non Kefalonian Greeks) who took us to their hearts. It's impossible to mention them all by name because there would be so many Makis's, Costas's, Spyros's, Maria's, Irini's, Eleni's and others to include.

It wasn't only Greek friendships that blossomed on the island because Kefalonia welcomes visitors from around the world. Some of you are mentioned by name in the following pages, but once again many of you are not. Without you there would have been no Gallery, no exhibitions, and ultimately no Oil Paint and Greece. You read the diary, you visited The Gallery, and the Bell Tower, and in turn became patrons of the arts. You know who you are, here's a big thank you to you all.

And finally, thanks to everyone who gave me permission to use photographs... *Yiammas*!

Late October 2007

The Departure

It was one of those beautiful Kefalonian mornings when the light was soft and the air still, and frankly I still wasn't sure if the decision we'd made had been the right one, but now it was too late, there was no turning back. The sun, which was slowly rising above the distant horizon had turned the sky from a translucent blue to a dreamy lilac, and the sea below to a blinding shimmering silver. The island itself was slipping away in slow motion, appearing not to move, instead, it lay dark and sombre, yet still as enchanting and inviting as it had ever been, then gradually as we gained height the dawn approached. Yes, it really was paradise and I was leaving it forever.

It had been almost six and a half years to the day since I'd first arrived for what was to have been a summer painting holiday, and living there for any longer had never been part of the plan (if there had ever been one), but there was something magnetic and magical about Kefalonia and in the end I had no other choice than to stay. Once in a lifetime experiences like that sometimes happen and I'm glad mine did, because during those years my life changed in a way I could never have imagined, nor will ever forget.

We, that's my partner Pam and I, had made the decision some years ago to live there but knowing it wouldn't be forever, and because we'd talked about it often, leaving, although emotional was never difficult. It was just a question of timing the departure, and that time had finally arrived.

The Lithostroto, Argostoli

2001 – A Six Month Painting Holiday

April - The Arrival

Spring arrived early in Kefalonia and so did the morning flight from Athens; very early, at about seven o'clock, give or take a few minutes. Since leaving the UK a couple of days earlier I'd lost a lot of sleep due to late night flights and lousy connections, and as a consequence spent a day and night in Glyfada (pronounced gleefatha) on the coast south of Athens. Although not seeing much of it, I did at least get some artwork done along the waterfront in between the sun and the showers.

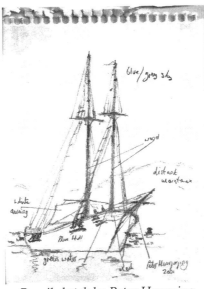

Pencil sketch by Peter Hemming

It was from Glyfada that I posted the first diary. My intention was to send The Diary every week by email as a

3

way of keeping family and a few friends in touch with my 'dream' while I was away, putting them in the picture so to speak.

During an early evening stroll I found an internet café that had all the hallmarks of a modern glitzy Greek palace; the rapper's Acropolis. Chrome and glass sparkled under the over-the-top lighting, and as is the custom, there was the heavy throbbing bass lines of the latest music sounds; very loud music sounds. Having been shown upstairs to the computers I eventually logged on, albeit with the help of one of the 'palace guards' who couldn't hide his amusement as I fumbled with the keyboard. And neither would it be the last time I was to be seen fumbling with a Greek keyboard. The first diary went like this:

"hi everzone, zes I have landed in greece and tomorrow I flz on to kefalonia and hopefullz some nice weather. The weather might dampen mz hair but it won't dampen mz spirits. bze for now......peter"

I'd been unlucky enough to have picked a dodgy keyboard which printed z's instead of y's, and notice the lack of capitals which for a while would become my email trademark. Logging on was stressful enough, so hitting 'caps lock' would have been taking too big a chance, because all I wanted to do was send the message without losing it, any further cock ups would have been disastrous.

The direct flight from Athens to Kefalonia takes less than an hour, and as the plane banked for the final approach, the morning sun lit the dark slopes of Mount Aenos, reaching up to what was left of the winter snow. The Ionian Sea was a patchwork of cobalt, turquoise and viridian, and although I was tired, euphoria and adrenaline kicked in as the runway of Kefalonia airport rushed up to meet us.

4

Within minutes of landing I was strolling towards the terminal building which looked so familiar, while at the same time thinking, 'Is this really happening, am I really walking towards a new life?' People back home in the UK had said I was 'living the dream', but I wasn't quite sure what they meant, after all, it was only going to be a summer painting holiday.

Once inside the airport I was greeted by Dimitris. The handshake was firm and the smile, stretching from ear to ear was as welcoming as ever; he was, after all a professional smiler. The mixture of Greek and Canadian in his deep voice was as I remembered it, and the twinkle in his dark brown eyes was enough to charm the knickers off a nun; Pam and I didn't call him The Smooth Operator for nothing. He had greeted us often as tourists the previous summer at the Phaedra taverna in Lassi, and it was good to see him again, especially so early in the morning.

We hadn't waited long before the flashing lights indicated that the carousel was about to start another monotonous, rhythmic journey, delivering an assortment of baggage from the depths. My battered suitcase was easy enough to spot and so too was the large studio easel, protected by layers of corrugated cardboard and bubble wrap.

As it appeared Dimitris completely lost his smile, then turning to me with a grimace and a groan, half knowing what the answer would be, asked in almost inaudible tones, 'Yours?'

'Yes,' I replied, then it was my turn to smile.

'But it'll never fit in the car.' His protest fell on deaf ears.

'My friend, in the last two days that easel has been in a Fiat Punto, two planes, a coach, and a yellow taxi, I don't think we'll have too much trouble squeezing it into a

Mercedes, do you?' And with that he groaned a little more.

The only alternative to the taxi ride would have been to have carried it from the airport to Argostoli, a distance of about four miles, and he certainly wasn't up for that; come to think of it, neither was I. Ten minutes later we off-loaded it along with everything else into his studio flat close to the Kefalos Theatre in Argostoli.

On that first morning I took him to the central square, or should I say he took me, and because he'd paid for the cab I stood the cost of breakfast, although I wasn't quite sure who got the best deal, because the cafés in the square were expensive then; they still are.

Dimitris was a tailor by trade and worked during the winter months in what he simply referred to as 'The Tailor's'. After breakfast he headed off there while I strolled into the bright morning sunshine to sit in the square, quietly exploring my thoughts. It was then, and only then that I realised I was on my own, and for the first time since leaving the UK, which seemed like an eternity ago, I felt very vulnerable.

Making Tea

As I soaked up the warmth of the sun, it dawned on me that my immediate priority was to find somewhere to live for a few days. A friend of Dimitris's girlfriend (his ex-girlfriend by the time I arrived) had a spare room in her apartment and wanted to rent it out. I was interested, but until I'd made contact I had to find somewhere else quick. I trawled the waterfront hotels before eventually booking into the Cephalonia Star, close to the Lixouri ferry port. My room on the top floor, although basic, was spotlessly clean with a clear view of the mountains and everything in between, which included the port authority and dock area.

Clara, the owner's wife cooked a wonderful breakfast

but couldn't understand why I didn't eat meat, and more than once said in her Brooklyn drawl (that's Brooklyn, New York), 'Peter, you're so thin, you should eat more,' and she made sure I did.

Although her breakfasts were legendary, being an American living in Greece she wasn't quite up to making tea the way the British like it. I gave her a crash course in how to make it the British way, pointing out that the water should be on the boil as it's poured over the tea bag, which is either in a pot or cup, and that the tea bag should never sit in the saucer as the water cools in the cup, which was how Clara had originally made mine, thus giving iced tea a whole new meaning. Wisely, I didn't try explaining the intricacies of brewing up with loose tea as Clara was struggling to understand the concept of bags and boiling water. Other than that I couldn't have been in better hands, and because of her motherly fussing The Star felt very much like home. I was almost one of the family, and after all, like most businesses in Kefalonia, it was a family affair.

Clara's pregnant daughter-in-law, Marina, spoke excellent English and had welcomed me with a big smile from behind the reception desk, while Aleckos, her husband, helped out generally around the hotel. Panagis (pronounced 'pana geese'), the owner, appeared every so often but spent most of his time across the road fishing near the ferry port which was a favourite meeting place for locals who gathered in all weathers, all year round, to enjoy their relaxing pastime and to catch up with the latest gossip.

Prue

A couple of evenings after booking into The Star I was sitting having a quiet drink and watching the world go by through the huge front windows that looked out onto the street. I hadn't been there long when an English couple came

7

in and sat at the next table, then after dragging me into their conversation I was invited to join them. There were introductions of a sort; it was Prue and two Petes, the two Petes being me and the other bloke.

Prue had features you don't forget in a hurry. Her weathered face was etched with the odd line or two, making it difficult to guess her age, not that that was important. The thick lenses of her glasses made her eyes appear smaller than they actually were, while her cropped greying hair (which never appeared to get any greyer, or longer) was striking, and although she spoke with an accent that bordered on being 'posh', it was something she always denied (being posh that is), albeit with a smile.

As the evening slipped cheerfully away I soon began to realise I was the only coherent one of the trio. A collection of empty beer bottles was filling the table, like skittles in a bowling alley, resembling a sort of drinkers' battleground. I made no attempt to match the pace of their drinking because they were in alcoholic free-fall, making it almost impossible for me to follow the thread of the conversation which I was supposed to be part of, whereas they were communicating by drunk speak. Eventually, just when I thought one of them might pass out, the other Pete stood up, put his hand in his pocket, scattered some loose change, without counting it, on the table, then rather unsteadily and not being too sure about it, left.

As he staggered across the road and fell into his car I asked Prue, 'Where's he going?'

'Oh he's off to a business meeting in Poros,' she said, or rather poshly slurred. He had a job to walk, never mind discussing business; and drive? The road south from Argostoli isn't exactly straight or flat, so for someone as drunk as he was it must have been an important meeting.

Although I'd been on the calm side of a seismic

drinking session it had been a great evening, so much so that Prue and I met later in the week to chat over a meal at the 'Palia Plaka' taverna, which was close to the small marina in the area of the town known as Maistrato. This time the conversation was on more of an even keel. She was good company and had some interesting stories about her life in Greece, now, and over the past few years. Despite our different lifestyles we had a lot in common, because as well as being an artist she too was a published writer.

Prue

A few weeks after that first meeting Prue and a crew of one sailed her catamaran 'Tom Tom' back from Chania (pronounced han ya), Crete, to Argostoli. She lived on it for a while moored up along the quayside with her animals - a crazy half breed puppy dog named Lizzie, and a cat that she called, of all things, Pussy Cat. Whereas Pussy Cat was relatively docile, Lizzie was as wild as ten, and like most puppies needed the training and discipline that Prue never gave her.

Pam and I told her more than once, 'You'll have to show that dog who's master, otherwise she'll be leading you the dog's life.'

'Oh, but she's only a puppy and she'll learn as she gets older,' was her usual reply; but of course it didn't work that way and Lizzie just got more crazy.

After spending most of the summer on Tom Tom, Prue moved to the comfort of a single storey house in Lixouri and moored the boat up in the marina there. In her former life she'd lived in caves, travelled with the circus and run a kafeneion in Chania with her German partner, another Peter, who had since died. So compared to some of her previous homes the house really was a luxury which she sometimes found hard to cope with. There was too, the added bonus of a garden that was big enough for Lizzie to be as mad as she wanted. Despite being moderately eccentric, Prue was a lovely person and great fun to be with, and became a close friend of ours for the rest of her life.

Argostoli

I'd decided to live in Argostoli because it was the island's capital and at the cutting edge of all that was happening on it! Not having a car wasn't a problem, and because I was only going to be there for a few months it was pointless buying one, and besides, the town was small enough for everything to be within easy walking distance.

Becoming a 'Townie' again appealed to me, because having lived in London and Swindon for the past twenty six years, I'd grown used to the high life and culture in its many different forms, so I was determined to do the same in Argostoli. There were three museums, a theatre, which doubled up as the cinema, a philharmonic hall, a small outdoor cinema called 'The Anny' which only opened in the summer, an English bar, and an old pub! Tavernas, kafeneions, coffee shops and pavement cafés were scattered around the town like confetti at a wedding, so it seemed like the place to be for a hungry culture-vulture.

To the Kefalonians, Argostoli is the centre of the universe, and as well as the entertainment venues, everything else, well almost everything, was conveniently close at hand. The island's main hospital was there, as was an abundance of professional services, mainly lawyers, accountants and the over populated Government offices, and, oddly enough, more than enough hairdressers and shoe shops.

The town of course had other extras to offer as one would expect from the capital of the largest of the Ionian islands. The pedestrianised Lithostroto Street was lined with a selection of shops offering everything from newspapers (local and national), to fashion clothing and expensive jewellery. The main, and only Post Office in the town was there too. But it was at the beginning of May when the Lithostroto really came to life, as the summer season slowly woke from its winter slumber. That was when a multitude of gift shops re-opened, appearing like mushrooms in the early morning mist, and adding a bazaar-like atmosphere to the town's main street.

Despite the variety of shops in Argostoli, there was, to my delight, no picture shop or art gallery selling original artwork of the island. Great news because it was my intention to open one where I would paint and exhibit my work. Opening one would be easy, at least that's what I thought.

Getting Started

I've always believed that to get on in life contacts are important; the old saying, 'It's not what you know, it's who you know' is often true, and because I was getting started it was important to make as many as I could, as soon as I could. One of the first was Len, the landlord of the popular two-in-one establishment, an English Bar and Indian Restaurant: The Queen Vic or Indian Queen, depending on which side of the sign you were looking at. Len's place was a popular watering hole for the island's British ex-pats, which was where I hoped to make most of my contacts, at least to start with.

After telling Len about my plan for the coming summer he said, or rather warned, 'Peter, the first thing you'll need to do is find an accountant, because to work here you have to be legal, there's no such thing as casual work, you really do have to become part of the system. An accountant will sort you out with a tax number and a licence, because you can't work without either.'

I understood the need for having a tax number, but a licence; what next!

He recommended an accountant, although oddly enough didn't use him himself, but insisted that he was good, with the following assurance, 'A lot of Greeks use him.' I still wasn't sure, and because the Greeks used him, did that really make him good? Anyway, Len gave me the bloke's name and address and like a lamb to the slaughter that's where I went; there was no other choice. I'd got six months which really wasn't long enough to compare notes.

After weeks of frustration and stress I eventually got a tax number and licence, but it was an experience I'd gladly have done without; legal or not. The most annoying part of that whole 'getting legal' chapter was the number of unnecessary visits I had to make to the accountant's office, because instead of giving me a comprehensive list of all his requirements, he asked for each item separately. There's no doubt in my mind that I was being charged for each visit, but because there were never any invoices or receipts I'll never know.

Equally stressful were the times I had to go to the tax office; the epitome of Greek bureaucracy and home to the pro-smoking lobby. In addition to the Greek documents that I was signing trustingly and blindly, there were various official English papers the accountant said he had to have.

They included tax records, proof of earnings, and bizarrely, a letter from the Wiltshire Constabulary (Wiltshire being the county where I lived in the UK) to prove I was a law abiding citizen.

And then, just when I thought things couldn't get any worse, they did.

'You must go to Athens to get your licence, because they are not issued here in Kefalonia, it's a special one for artists,' he told me, grinning from ear to ear.

'Oh yes? Me go to Athens, like hell I am.' Then I read the riot act, pointing out that so far I'd paid him thousands of drachmas and was getting nothing back other than stress and frustration. Sensing my anger rising the grin returned, before saying there was probably a way round it and that I shouldn't worry. Of course there was a way round it and within a couple of days my licence documents appeared on his desk, as if by magic. 'Great,' I thought.

However, the feel good factor didn't last long because a few days later he dropped another bombshell and took great delight in telling me, with the same sickly grin, that I had to pay a fine because I'd missed a deadline for submitting a tax form. For goodness sake, I was paying him to look after all that stuff, and there he was pointing the finger at me. It was the straw that broke the camel's back, and as the grin returned I exploded, got to my feet, leant across his desk and pointed the finger right back at him.

'OK,' I said, 'I've had enough of being ripped off by you, you will give me all of my documents now.' And surprisingly he did.

Taking my business elsewhere meant nothing to him, but I was glad the whole episode was over. It had taken over two months to 'get legal' and in the heat of that moment the euphoria of early April evaporated in the Kefalonian sun. On my way out of the office that morning I met another frustrated Englishman who was suffering as I was and willingly confided his tales of woe.

As we exchanged phone numbers he said, 'If you're ever in Fiskardo give me a ring and we'll meet up.'

'Thanks Christian I might just take you up on that.'

Back to Square One

That whole accountant fiasco had drained me physically and mentally and now I was back to square one, well almost, but at least I had a tax number and I was licensed, even if it was as a painter and decorator. But I didn't have an accountant. Nevertheless, with Len's help I found another, and that time it was the one he used. After the recent experience I was apprehensive and it took a lot of convincing by him to bring me round. He was adamant that his guy was sound, and after all, what had I got to lose? All the hard work had been done back at the other place.

The new accountant's name was Dimitris (who, by the way, had Greek clients so he must have been good) but I dealt mainly with his wife and able assistant Eleni. Over the years she guided me through the maze of bureaucracy of which there was much, and generally calmed me in times of stress, of which there were many. Len's recommendation seemed to be spot on the second time round.

Pub Old House

Whereas the Queen Vic was popular with the British, at Pub Old House they were conspicuous by their absence, and although it was called a pub there was little resemblance to any I'd ever seen or used in the UK. 'Alternative' summed up the Argostoli equivalent nicely.

On my first visit, which was the evening after meeting Prue and Pete (going there was her idea), walking through the door into the semi darkness of the bar completely knocked me out.

Before going in I'd looked at the building from the outside and thought, 'Well at least they've got the name right, because it certainly looks old.'

Replacing the thatch or tiles of a traditional English country pub were steel rods that pointed skyward from the flat concrete roof and rustic wooden shutters protected the windows. Directors' chairs, tables, sun umbrellas and firewood were stacked haphazardly in an outside yard, partly visible through the bushes growing over the black wrought iron fence. That yard, I discovered later was 'The Garden', which, like the pub was totally different to any English pub garden I'd been in.

It was about 9 o'clock. Early - at least by Greek standards - when I arrived and there were only two people sitting at the bar. The room, although dimly lit, was not dark. There was music playing, but not loud. There was a wood burner, but it wasn't too hot. There were artefacts on the walls, but they weren't too cluttered, and like most other bars in Kefalonia there was a television; and then there was Lefteris… he owned the pub.

He was big… fat… big, oh, what's the difference? A full beard covered his chubby face and thick lips. Long black hair snaked down his back in a pony tail that he habitually played with by continually wrapping it round his fingers. To say he was casually dressed would be an understatement; tee shirt, jogging leggings and deck shoes were standard issue, at least during the winter. Like most Kefalonians he hid a warm smile behind the serious façade and facial growth, and I saw more of the smile as I got to know him better.

Just inside the door of the bar was where Lefteris held court and played on the computer engulfed in a fog of cigarette smoke. It was rare to see him behind the bar because that would have meant working, so he left that to his live-in girlfriend Linda.

Linda, like Lefteris had long black hair but without the facial growth, and she didn't play with hers, she didn't have time. Like him she spoke good English, but that was where any similarity between them ended, because she was pretty, and even when she dressed casually there was something classy about her; like a pearl in a pawn shop window. On that first evening in Pub Old House my drinking habits were changed forever, and as things turned out the place would have a lasting effect on my life.

The couple at the bar were Colin and Jan. Lefteris introduced Colin as, 'My English brother', but he didn't introduce Jan, so Colin did. That was something I soon got used to in Kefalonia; formal introductions were rare.

As I left Pub Old House that night I noticed an empty building next door. The sign on the wall read, 'Café Mystique'.

On The Move

The first few days in Argostoli passed quickly and at the end of the week I moved out of The Star and into the spare room of Jean, the friend of Dimitris's ex girlfriend. The apartment was conveniently close to the town centre and overlooked the street known as 'Vyronos' (Byron Street), named after Lord Byron, who had lived on the island in the village of Metaxata.

Jean was friendly and a real mine of information, a 'Rough Guide' on legs who gave me advice on all sorts of things, especially where the best places were to shop. One valuable tip I've never forgotten, and she was very specific, 'Peter when you're vegetable shopping, check everything carefully and make sure your onions are hard.'

16

Well, well, how come I'd never checked that my onions were hard before!

Having lived in the town for some time she'd become part of the 'in crowd' and clubbing scene, an essential part of Argostoli night-life, but as far as I was concerned Jean's frequent 'early mornings' had their drawbacks. I was often woken in the early hours by the banging of doors and other more passionate noises of the night as she dragged herself, and anyone else she had in tow, back from another hectic session on the dance floor.

There was one particular time when I was startled by the sound of my bedroom door opening, and in the darkness I couldn't be sure what was happening. Then the light came on. I looked up sleepily to see a bloke standing over me with not a stitch on, and when I say standing, I mean standing proud, he was huge and ready for action.

Realising he was in the wrong room he muttered the word '*Signomi*' (sorry), then trying, without much luck to cover himself with his hands backed out wearing nothing but a huge grin.

Behind him a voice from the darkness whispered, 'I'm over here.' Living there with the unexpected was only transitory, and almost immediately after moving in I began looking elsewhere for a place of my own, which, I was told, was impossible due to the imminent start to the season which was less than 3 weeks away.

I was using the internet café Exelixis almost on a daily basis, and asked Costas if he knew anyone that might have accommodation to rent, and without hesitating he picked up the phone and made a call which I didn't understand much of.

That was when fate dealt me an ace, because minutes later, and with the help of Costas's scribbled map I was introducing myself to Makis, his wife Soula and their two adult children, Athena, and the English speaking Minas. I was given a guided viewing there and then of a studio apartment they were renting. They also asked me to stay for lunch, but, because I'd already eaten, I politely refused. I hoped Makis and Soula hadn't been offended by me turning down their offer, but they smiled as Minas explained why; I sighed a sigh of relief. After a handshake to seal the deal there were more smiles, and it was agreed, I would move in at the beginning of May.

The apartment was compact and functional with a kitchen big enough to eat in, and eye watering bright yellow and white patterned wall tiles as decoration. They must have been a job lot because the bathroom was done out the same. The kitchen door opened out onto a typically tiled Greek patio, but those tiles weren't the yellow and white variety. The bedroom was big and had recently been decorated by Makis's brother Panagis, my future neighbour next door, who, unlike Makis and Soula, spoke good English which he'd learnt while living in the United States. As well as sleeping in it, the bedroom was utilised to become the lounge, living room, study, and most importantly a painting studio.

Looking out of the large window, views stretched from the towering Kastro in the south to the distant mountains that dropped down to the gulf of Argostoli in the north. Closer were neighbouring roofscapes and glimpses of Napier's Garden through the giant eucalyptus trees; it was worth living there just for the views.

Although the apartment was let furnished, when I'd viewed it there hadn't been a bed (the previous tenant had slept in a sleeping bag on the floor), but Minas was in control of the situation and had since bought a new double one. I'd dreaded the thought of two singles, which was common in some Kefalonian holiday apartments, because they would have taken up so much of the room, leaving me with very little studio space to work in.

On the early May Bank Holiday and with a little help from Christos, the man with a van, I moved into my new home in Piniatorou Street.

Air

In the short time between my arrival and the start of the season Dimitris and Antonia had been more than helpful, but I knew once they started their summer jobs I'd be on my own and there really was so much to do, with so little time in which to do it.

Antonia, originally from Sunderland, on the north east coast of England, worked as a tour guide during the season which was how I'd got to know her. She had guided the excursions that Pam and I went on the previous year, and when I told her I was thinking of coming to Kefalonia for the summer she offered to help once I'd arrived. Over the course of the summer she met scores of people who had the same idea as me, and to her I was just another 'dreamer', someone else who had been seduced by the island's special charm, looking to swap the toil and stress of the UK for a chunk of 'Ionian paradise'. It was quite a surprise for her then when I actually turned up; but she was as good as her word.

There were a lot of things I needed to know and do, and one in particular was to open a bank account, so she directed me to the Alpha Bank while at the same time warning, 'Whatever you do, don't forget to take your passport,' and although I wasn't travelling anywhere it turned out to be sound advice. Carrying it was vital as it was the substitute for the European identity card and had to be shown on demand anywhere, especially in government offices, and of course Banks.

Dimitris was great. He spoke Greek and arranged meetings with local property owners who were usually Greek speakers, so his role as interpreter was crucial. I became single minded in the search for a business premises, and in my anxiety to start selling pictures and making money I went about it like a bull in a china shop, but getting that together turned out to be as frustrating as getting legal had been.

'*Siga siga*,' (slowly slowly), Dimitris cautioned as my frustration started to boil over, so I slowed down, but I had a long way to go before mastering '*Siga siga*' to perfection… the way the Kefalonians did. After the first of Dimitris's arranged meetings he gave me a good telling-off for dressing too smartly. What? Apparently, wearing casual trousers, a blue shirt and contrasting silk tie was a signal to any Greek property owner that I was loaded with money, and justified demanding a rent way above the already high levels.

'The next time you turn up for a meeting, wear jeans and a tee shirt,' he said. It seemed to me that even without any extra hike the rents were outrageously high for what was on offer, which in most cases was nothing more than a shell, four walls, a door, a window, no fixtures, no fittings; no nothing.

There was one particular property close to the square which had a huge basement, and as a way of subsidising the high rent Dimitris suggested sub-letting it to migrant Albanian construction workers. Needless to say, that went down like a lead balloon, I couldn't speak Greek, never mind Albanian.

As well as rent, there was an additional one-off non-refundable up-front payment of around two to three million drachmas, known as 'Air'. 'Air' however, was not only a con but was also illegal, which was probably why no-one could, or would, explain what exactly I would get by paying it;

which, I later found out was nothing. It was in effect a 'goodwill' payment; goodwill for who?

It soon became apparent that I was banging my head against a brick wall, because trying to negotiate a fair rent, fair in my eyes at least, was out of the question and all one way; the owner's way. There were properties in Argostoli that had been empty for years because the owners chose to keep them that way rather than reducing the rent; crazy but true.

After the unsuccessful attempts of meeting owners face to face I tried another strategy and approached the local Estate Agent, at that time the only one in the town. However, it was always pot luck whether his office was open when I called, and even if he was there, he was never particularly interested.

It felt as though for every step forward, I was taking five back, and getting nowhere. The Gallery was still very much a distant dream.

Routine

After moving into Piniatorou I went on a shopping spree and bought basic essentials for the apartment; the usual exciting stuff for any new home; sweeping brushes, dusters, washing up liquid etc. etc. There was a good selection of shops in Argostoli especially along the waterfront road which was lined with open-air fruit and vegetable markets, mini supermarkets and bakeries. To begin with, shopping was quite difficult and altogether different to anything I'd experienced in the UK, presenting a whole new challenge for me. Yet despite the pushing, shoving and general free-for-all normally associated with the London Tube at rush hour, like the tube, I got used to it. In those early days however, it did seem as though politeness and orderly queuing was out of the question, everywhere.

Getting my tongue round some of the Greek shop names was a bit of a struggle so for convenience sake I renamed some of them. The fruit and vegetable market I used most became known as 'Cardiff' (it's where the girl with the red hair working on the cash register came from). 'Mirrors and Fans', another market, sold an extremely strong sweet red wine, ranking in potency with dynamite. The mirrors were fixed to the walls and gave a feeling of spaciousness, whereas the ceiling fans offered movement of air, a welcome relief in the summer heat. The bakers directly opposite 'Cardiff' became 'Egg Cups'! After buying bread there one morning, Tony, a pal of mine who was holidaying for a few days noticed a well endowed Kefalonian beauty wearing a top with a rather revealing neckline. That was nothing new because most of the women, especially the younger ones, revealed as much as they dared.

Tony however, didn't miss a thing and turning to me with a beaming smile quipped, 'Peter, you'd never get those into a pair of eggcups.'

The small but well stocked delicatessen selling Marmite, Worcestershire sauce, Branston pickle and other British goodies moved into larger premises not far from the bridge to become known as 'Sliding Doors', for the obvious reason.

The nice thing about daily shopping was that as I became recognised it was sometimes possible, with a smile and a cheerful *'kalimera'* (good morning), to beat the Kefalonians at their own pushing and shoving game; it was really a polite form of queue jumping. As I perfected the art of argie-bargie shopping in Argostoli it remained a pleasure and never became a chore. Over the years the shopping routine rarely changed.

I never tired of walking through Napier's Garden, past the taxis (whose drivers sat like vultures, waiting for their prey) in the square, through the alley, past the Queen Vic. and out onto the quayside. The mountains across the water appeared so close as to be touchable, reflected on the glassy surface as they rose to touch the sky in their majestic and glorious splendour. There were days, when, like sleeping giants they bathed peacefully in the soft morning sunlight, and on others, mysteriously shrouded by angry storm clouds. Whatever the mood though, walking along the Argostoli waterfront was always a great way to start the day.

The waterfront, Argostoli

During the holiday season the quayside changed dramatically and became a totally different place as summer visitors idled their way along it, either to admire the visiting sea craft or just to pass the time of day. Spot The Turtle was a favourite pastime, as they waited, cameras poised in the hope of capturing snaps of them as they broke the surface of the murky waters near the Rock Café.

An Internet Virgin and the Mobile Phone

Despite my technophobia and lack of knowledge regarding computers I was emailing Pam regularly from the only internet café in town, Exelixis. Charis (pronounced

23

Harris) and his father, the aforementioned Costas were terrific, especially once they realised I was 'an internet virgin', and that, believe me, didn't take them long. Costas was the one who usually answered my cries for help from the computer suite upstairs, because there were times when even logging on was beyond my capabilities. However, I wasn't the only one affected by the slow dial up system in those pre-broadband days.

One morning a big bronzed Australian guy came and sat next to me and within seconds became dangerously incensed by the lack of response from his monitor. Then turning to me with huge sighs of frustration he asked,

'Here mate why is this bloody thing so slow?'

Not really sensing how delicate the situation was (and not as tactfully as I should have) I replied, 'It's a Greek computer, you know, it's a bit like the people, laid back, give it a bit of time, you'll have to be patient.'

But patience was something he was completely out of. I was only trying to bring a touch of banter into play, but it was as though I'd lit the blue touch paper and I was totally unprepared for what came next, because his outburst was a verbal attack on anything and anybody Kefalonian.

'Whad da ya mean mate 'laid back', I'm an Aussie, we're f**king laid back, these bastards are f**king lazy, that's a bit different to being laid back you know.'

Even as wound up as my Aussie 'mate' was, the ultra-patient Costas approached and calmed him down, it was amazing to watch; and then right on cue the computer burst into life. In those few moments of madness I had visions of it being smashed into a thousand pieces as a rather incensed Aussie hurled it to the shop floor below.

As well as paying for the internet in the UK and Greece, Pam and I were also spending a small fortune on phone calls, even though she had signed up for one of the so called money-saving deals on offer back home. I don't like mobile phones, but did a complete U-turn and bought one as a matter of necessity, so imagine my horror then as I unpacked it to find that the instruction manual was written in Greek only. OK, so I was living in Greece, but what I'd expected was one of those multi-lingual booklets containing about twenty different E.U. languages.

When I mentioned it to the sales guy he wasn't too concerned and replied with a smile, 'That's not a problem, I'll get English instructions for you,' but, full of empty promises he never did.

Once I'd mastered the basics, like making calls and topping up the credit I was in a comfort zone, but even then, something as basic as text messaging was a thing of the future and without the English instructions I really was lost. Given brushes and canvas I was fine, but when it came to the technical things in life such as mobile phones and computers, like Prue, I was living with the cave men.

A Holiday

At the beginning of May Pam and her daughter Deb arrived for a week's holiday and it was great to see them. Deb stayed in Lassi, in an apartment up the lane behind Ozzi's Bar, while Pam was my guest in Argostoli. That holiday was to have been the first of four for her, then, after the fourth we would return home together to resume a normal life in the UK.

The holiday passed quickly and while Pam and Deb were having a great time getting out and about round the island I got on with my work and became a slave to the easel. In the back of my mind however was the thought that as each day passed it brought their departure so much closer, which for me meant the return to the life of a monk and celibacy, but with one difference; I didn't live in a monastery.

Our parting was very emotional and left me low and empty as the plane taking her away from me became a dot, before completely disappearing into the heat haze of the Kefalonian sky. I did though have something positive to look forward to; Pam, like me, was fed up with us being apart, so when she got home she gave up her job and started packing.

An Outlet For My Work

It was in the Queen Vic. one evening that I struck up a conversation with a woman who showed an interest in my paintings, not so much to buy, but to sell, and the more we talked the more the idea appealed to me. She was a partner in a Lassi supermarket and proposed that I work there for the summer, painting, exhibiting and selling my artwork, yes, in the supermarket.

'Sounds good,' I thought, and then before I could give her any sort of answer she came up with another money spinner: printed tee shirts. Pam had already thought of this and had made prototypes using my artwork as the design. It was though a very laborious process involving the ironing of transfers onto each garment. That meant keeping the iron at a constant temperature which wasn't as easy as it sounds; too cold and the transfers wouldn't stick to the material, too hot and they melted, causing an awful stink and a messy iron. But despite those minor headaches the finished products of her cottage industry looked great.

The supermarket-studio-gallery plan sounded great too, so I went for it, and if that was successful we could talk about the tee shirts at a later date. I was just being cautious, although on the surface everything seemed to be under control; but little did I know…

With regard to painting in the supermarket there was a

tiny seed of doubt in my mind, and the more I thought about it, the more one word kept nagging at me. That word was 'disaster'.

During the summer evenings Lassi's main street was packed with tourists, dressed smartly casual in their new and spotlessly clean holiday clothes, and who, after browsing the many gift shops and supermarkets that lined both sides of the 'Lassi strip', would then settle down for their evening meal in one of the many roadside tavernas. My greatest concern was that as they browsed the supermarket while I was painting, there would be a risk of paint being transferred, not from brush to canvas, but from canvas to new, spotlessly clean summer clothes. This really was a recipe for a disaster that didn't bear thinking about, so I quickly went off the idea and carried on working at home as normal.

As a final touch to the supermarket project, two 'A' boards were made. One for advertising on the pavement, and the other, a much larger one, was positioned inside the supermarket on which the paintings would be displayed. Everything was ready and the scene was set.

Unwanted Visitors

The season was only a few days old, and in the excitement accompanying the expectations of another approaching summer, nobody had thought about, or even mentioned the dreaded Tax Police who often appeared not only unannounced, but also unwanted. The Tax Police wielded great power, enough to close a business in the blinking of an eye, and were not to be taken lightly.

The morning after my paintings went public I received a telephone call from a friend who had been to see them, the paintings, not the Tax Police. It was my American friend

Viva (the wife of Christos, the man with a van) and in an instant I sensed the alarm in her wavering voice.

'Hi Peter, I went to Lassi last night to see your paintings but they weren't there.'

'Weren't there, what do you mean Viva "weren't there", they've got to be there, are you sure you went to the right supermarket?'

In that moment of uncertainty I found it hard to think straight as my brain whirred into overdrive, but she'd definitely been to the right place and what she had said was true, there hadn't been a painting or an 'A' board in sight. Earlier that evening the Tax Police had been patrolling and in a moment of panic, the paintings, as well as the outlet for my work had disappeared into thin air. Worse still, and unknown to me the supermarket didn't have a licence to sell artwork and at that time I was still waiting for mine, which made the whole set up totally illegal. Huge fines would have been imposed (which I already knew about), not only on the supermarket but on me too if the Tax Police had discovered a business without the appropriate paperwork. It was rough justice, but that's the way the system worked and ignorance of it was no excuse.

The wool had been well and truly pulled over my eyes, and I wondered if it had been intentional and I'd been a naïve and trusting pawn in someone's cynical and greedy scheme? I'll never know, but like a lot of other things before and since, it had been an absolute nightmare, which fortunately, and like most nightmares didn't last forever. Thankfully the paintings turned up a few days later.

For the moment I changed my mind about looking for 'outlets' and worked flat out painting at home, while at the same time working on another plan.

Together Again

Pam arrived towards the end of June and we looked forward to enjoying the rest of the summer together. It was great, but even in the short time that we'd been apart our lives had changed, mine especially, so we slowly adjusted, just as we had done several years before, because once again we were stepping into the unknown to explore the uncharted waters of uncertainty. As well as the personal changes, there was a totally different culture and climate to come to terms with, and although most of the Kefalonians I'd met were warm and welcoming there was always going to be the rare exception, so we knew we had to tread carefully. Argostoli was a small town where almost everyone seemed to be related one way or the other, or if not related, very close, which in turn meant everybody knowing everybody else's business, including ours.

Pam was getting to know some of the people I'd already met, but what excited me most was sharing with her the places I'd already discovered. It was like falling in love all over again; complete with all the emotions that that involves. There was so much of the island to see, which is not always possible when you're on holiday and we were determined to make the most of it in the short time we'd be there. Not having a car wasn't a problem because there were buses, and walking was as natural to us as driving was to the majority; but she did draw the line at thumbing lifts.

Fiskardo

Not long after arriving on the island I had done the first of a series of hitch hiking journeys and headed north to Fiskardo. Fiskardo's main attraction, without a doubt, is the harbour, but a short walk around the corner from it is an unusual beach on which olive trees grow.

As I relaxed on it in the warmth of the spring sun a woman strolled past and slipped effortlessly into the sea, then after swimming for a while she casually walked back up the beach, water droplets glistening on her tanned skin. But what really caught my eye was the white bikini she was wearing, very similar to the one Ursula Andress wore in 'that scene' from the first Bond movie.

The best beach chat up line in the world must be, 'Was the water nice?' so I tried it and didn't get a wet slap for my audacity. It transpired she lived and worked in London, but was about to enjoy a summer sabbatical working as a representative for one of the up-market holiday companies based in the village. A few summers later Pam and 'Ursula', better known as Jane, became colleagues, but I never met her again.

Only days after Pam's arrival for her long summer holiday we caught the bus to Fiskardo, and, just as in the previous summer, we were transfixed by the stunning views along the west coast road on the journey north. The purpose of that visit was to try and interest some of the shop keepers in my paintings, but it didn't take long to discover they weren't interested in me or my artwork, which on reflection was just as well. At the time I was only painting 'small' canvases, so what I was offering would have been totally lost between the already packed shelves of summer goodies.

'Pam, do you remember that bloke Christian, the one I met in the accountant's office that time? He lives near Fiskardo. While we're here let's look him up.'

'OK,' she said, so we did.

His wife Carol worked in an office on the harbour front, and we met her there before driving the short distance to their home at Anti Pata. They had been living on the island for about five years after buying a couple of run-down stone cottages which they'd completely refurbished, using, wherever possible original local materials; they lived in one, the other was rented to summer visitors. Those natural materials were aesthetically more pleasing to the eye than the earthquake proof, pastel painted concrete buildings that were being thrown up all over the island.

The following week Pam and I returned to Fiskardo with a selection of paintings for Carol's boss to look at. He'd shown an interest on the previous visit and wanted to hang some in the reception area of the business as replacements for the faded prints that looked as if they'd been there forever, but alas, his interest was short lived and in the end the proposed deal came to nothing. The journey however wasn't a complete waste of time, because the ever helpful Christian introduced us to Stacey at the Environmental and Nautical Museum where I held two one-day exhibitions later in the summer.

On 8th August, 1953, the first rumblings of an earthquake were felt on Kefalonia and the neighbouring islands. As the tremors continued for several days, most of the population moved to live out of doors in relative safety, fearing the collapse of their homes. Finally, shortly before midday on 12th August a massive earthquake, measuring 7.4 on the Richter Scale and lasting 50 seconds, wreaked havoc on Kefalonia, Ithaca, Zakynthos and Levkas. Kefalonia suffered 90% destruction to its buildings with between 800 and 1000 Kefalonians losing their lives. One of the results of the earthquake was that many thousands of local people moved abroad, mainly to Australia, Canada, South Africa and the United States of America.

Fiskardo, unlike the rest of Kefalonia had virtually escaped the devastation of 1953, and retained a special charm of its own where original Venetian buildings, relatively untouched by the force of the earthquake, still stood alongside modern day concrete. That special charm though was lost for a few dizzy weeks of the high season as hordes of sun seekers poured off coaches, and, attracted like moths round light, descended into the harbour. However, the cool and quiet of the pines opposite, close to the old lighthouse, was the ideal refuge to escape the claustrophobia and madness of the crowded waterfront.

As well as coach parties and day trippers, the rich and famous were frequent visitors, but kept well away from dry land until the crowds had re-boarded their coaches and returned to base. It was then, under the cover of darkness that the celebrities appeared and could often be seen dining in the discreet lighting of one of the many waterside tavernas.

In total contrast to the buzz of summer, off-season Fiskardo and the rest of the north of the island became a delight to visit, when, like everywhere else in Kefalonia it was totally free of holiday makers.

Assos

Since our first visit to Assos it has had a special place in my heart. During our first holiday in May we were lucky in that our tour coach had been skilfully driven round the tight hairpin bends to the tiny village; I say 'lucky' because some of the other excursions didn't go that far. Assos was where I did my first Kefalonian artwork; a small pencil sketch that changed hands with Stelios, a waiter at the Ionio taverna in Lassi, for two large brandies. Although the tour itinerary allowed us only a short stop of less than an hour it was there on that day when my love affair with Kefalonia began.

Just a few days after the Bond encounter in Fiskardo I once again hitched a ride and headed north for Assos, getting a lift from close to the British Cemetery after walking across the narrow and dangerous Dhrapano Bridge, sometimes referred to as The Causeway, or just the Bridge.

The driver, whose name was Thomas, not only spoke good English, but like some other Kefalonians I'd met was curious and full of 'direct' questions as to what I was doing on 'his' island and why. After the non-stop inquisition he dropped me at the Assos turn from where I made the familiar journey down the narrow twisting road. The weather had gradually closed in since passing the Lixouri turn, but patches of blue sky appeared through the occasional gap in the damp swirling mist, and Assos itself was clear and the sun shone brightly, reflecting in the clear turquoise waters of the harbour like sparkling dancing diamonds.

I wandered around the deserted village streets before sitting on the end of the small pier to be captivated and mesmerised by the stillness of the water, which was only occasionally broken by the softest ripple caused by the slightest whisper of a breeze; as seductive as a lover's touch. In front of the pastel painted apartments on the opposite side of the harbour, perched precariously above the glassy surface, the white yacht, aptly named Assos, was moored. A cluster of small brightly painted fishing boats, tied up for the winter, gently bobbed in the shelter of the harbour wall directly in front of the taverna with the blue awning, so popular in summer; but, like everywhere else in Assos it too was closed.

The walk back to the main road was tiring, but not even that, nor the mist, or the ever threatening rain spoilt my day. I was in paradise, so it didn't really matter.

Clare

'Dad, why are you going to live in Kefalonia? You know you don't like the heat.'

That was my daughter Clare's response when I told her about my 'summer holiday', and she was right to a point, but I didn't go there for the heat. She did though, along with her friend Sarah.

They arrived for a week's holiday at the end of June and were determined to enjoy themselves, because, as she'd put it, 'I'm going to be a real tourist, just chilling out and having a good time.'

And she did, spending a week in nearby Lassi. Like most summer visitors they ate out, enjoying that special warm and welcoming Kefalonian hospitality. Lampros, one of the waiters at the Ionio taverna took a fancy to Clare, and although she'd made it clear she wasn't interested he was persistent, and even tried to sweet talk her on to the back of his motorbike.

Motorbike or not she was having none of it and told him so in no uncertain terms, 'I'm not getting on the back of that thing, and anyway you haven't got a helmet.'

And that really did confuse him. 'Helmet, what's that?' he must have thought.

Helmets are virtually non-existent on the island, and even though the law states they must be worn at all times, hardly anyone bothered, at least not until the police had one of their rare purges, then everybody wore them. The purges were inconveniences that people tolerated because they had no choice, but they only lasted a few days and then it was back to 'helmets off' until the next one.

Lampros was a nice enough bloke, but he was as crazy as the rest behind the handlebars of his big powerful bike, breaking every speed limit in sight.

It was good to see Clare, and even though she'd had a good time, I had a strange feeling that all was not well with her health. She seemed so fragile and there wasn't the usual sparkle in her eyes. Instinctively I knew there was a problem but it would be some years before the doctors got round to diagnosing and, more importantly, treating it.

'Hi Dad, it's Tom'

My teenage son Thomas and I were communicating quite often, although in truth it was mainly one way... from Kefalonia. He'd promised more than once to visit, but I wasn't quite sure when or how because he was always pleading poverty.

But I did give him some advice should he ever turn up:

'Don't come in high summer because that's the most expensive time, it's also very hot, and whatever you do, bring plenty of sun cream, oh, and one other thing; book your holiday in Lassi.'

He phoned one evening.

'Hi Dad, it's Tom, I'm coming to see you.'

'That's great,' I said, hardly able to contain my joy, 'when?'

He came with his close friend Guy at the beginning of August, which in anybody's language is high summer and when the sun was at its hottest. They were booked to stay in the idyllic harbour village of Agia Efimia, tucked away in the corner of Sami Bay, not exactly close to Argostoli, and certainly not the ideal hot spot for two testosterone fuelled teenagers with no car, and in Tom's case, no money.

I was furious, because I suspected it had been a blatant example of holiday mis-selling by a travel agent. In the event I tried to change the booking but soon realised I was hitting a blank, while at the same time Tom's mother was trying to do the same through the agent in the UK with the same result.

As a last resort I visited the holiday company's Argostoli office only to be told, 'Sorry, there are no beds in Lassi.'

No, I'm sure there weren't (in August, beds were like gold dust), and as things stood, the chances of Tom and I seeing much of each other looked slim. He may as well have been going to the moon. But all was not lost! With stress levels high and the bit between my teeth I began a frantic search for alternative accommodation in Argostoli, where, within a couple of days I'd found them a room at the Fokas Hotel close to the main square.

I was whingeing to Prue about it one day, but she just laughed and suggested sleeping them out on our patio, adding with a smile, 'Pete, think of the money you'd save.'

'Never mind the money Prue, what about the ants and mosquitoes, those boys will get bitten to death.'

She offered no sympathy and rambled on, 'Oh, but a few bites won't hurt them, and anyway it's all good character building stuff.'

In the end the lads had a great time, but because the fair skinned Thomas forgot to take his sun cream to the beach he got badly burnt, especially his legs, so much so that he was lucky not to have been hospitalised. Consequently he spent the rest of the holiday wearing long trousers… yes, in August.

But even with his burns and the fact he completely ran out of money, there was nothing fragile about him when he went home, just a pair of blistered legs.

The Vikings Are Coming

Deb was doing a great job building and maintaining the website, and judging by the incoming e-mails the power of the internet was evident, as news of the English painter in Argostoli was reaching all corners of the globe.

Ingrid from Stavanger was a regular visitor to Kefalonia and mailed to say she would be holidaying in Argostoli again in the summer. Having seen my on-line gallery she was interested in looking at some originals once she arrived, so we arranged to meet. It was only after the arrangements were made that it suddenly dawned that I didn't have a clue what Ingrid looked like, but Pam calmed me.

'Peter your photo is all over the website, so don't worry about recognising her, she'll recognise you.'

The rendezvous took place near the statue in the square. We hadn't been waiting long when a woman came and sat on the bench next to us, and although she wasn't fair or very Norwegian looking I whispered to Pam, 'Do you think that's her?'

'There's only one way to find out, ask her.'

So I did, and just my luck. She didn't speak a word of English, in fact she didn't speak anything, because in response to my question all I got in return was a grunt and a blank stare. It wasn't long though before the real Ingrid appeared. Heads turned, and waiters, preparing their tables for the evening looked up and stared, wide eyed and weak kneed, as a long legged, short blonde haired Viking goddess strode past them and across the square towards us. Her smile was hypnotic and warm, like the rising sun, casting aside any doubt that it could have been anyone else. We exchanged formal introductions, and for the first and last time shook hands. Forever after, our greetings were with kisses and hugs.

Ingrid and Peter

In the absence of proper exhibition space at the apartment we'd arranged an impromptu 'showing' by hanging a selection of paintings on the patio fence that divided the properties, it was the ideal home exhibition.

That evening Ingrid became my first patron… I'd gone international.

After the Heat of High Summer

At the end of July and for the whole of August the island was taken over first by the Italians with their infuriating convoys of camper vans, who in turn were followed a few days later by the Greeks, but not necessarily in convoy. Many were Kefalonians travelling from elsewhere in Greece, mainly Athens, but there were those who came from further afield.

Kefalonia has a strong maritime tradition, the Merchant Navy Academy is in Argostoli, and over the years large numbers of former sailors have settled abroad permanently in countries as far afield as South Africa, USA and Australia, to name a few. There were visitors who had survived the earthquake; families that had fled the island and who now returned on a regular basis to spend the summer with relatives who had stayed behind. The island wasn't exclusive to visiting Kefalonians though. Greeks from other parts of the country enjoyed the special warmth and hospitality their compatriots offered them.

During those short crowded weeks of high summer, as the main resorts burst at the seams, driving became fraught with frustration, stress and kamikaze madness; if possible it really was best to avoid driving altogether. The approach roads to many of the popular beaches such as Myrtos and Petani were no more than narrow lanes in places, where pandemonium often broke out as those heading for them had only one thing in mind, to get as close to the beach as possible, and if they could, drive onto it.

Caught up in that mixture of mayhem and madness were the more sedate northern Europeans, including the British, who found it hard to understand why the normally 'laid back' Mediterranean folk were always in such a hurry and so intent on risking life and limb in the process. Their overtaking skills (not the British), or lack of them, often proved fatal, because there were those who believed they could see round corners and over blind summits, with the all too common tragic consequences.

Argostoli, as well as becoming noisy and dusty became horrendously claustrophobic as the extra traffic gridlocked, turning the town overnight into the double parking capital of Greece and the horn blowing centre of Kefalonia. During those few manic weeks the frequent whistle blowing and arm waving of the Port Police proved to be totally ineffective as they tried, but without much success, to keep traffic moving along the waterfront road, and although it was a nightmare to get caught up in, it was hilarious to watch.

Despite the confusion it was difficult to escape the carnival atmosphere, and the added distraction that no red blooded male sitting behind the wheel of a car could ignore; it was a distraction that gave instant pleasure and light relief. The numbers of beautiful young (and not so young, or beautiful) women strolling along the streets scantily clad in only the briefest summer wear and flowing sarongs encouraged the predictable sideways glance. In that briefest lapse of concentration and sexual fantasy the inevitable shunt followed, but because the traffic moved so slowly any serious damage or injury was rare. What did follow though was a few raised voices and a lot of finger wagging, and of course, more delays.

After the exhausting heat of high summer and as the temperatures slowly dropped, so too did the number of visitors. It was then that life in Argostoli gradually returned to something resembling normality.

A CELTA Qualification

The Cambridge CELTA qualification to teach English as a foreign language is recognised in almost every country of the world. Greece however was one of the few exceptions and only recognised a university degree (in any subject) as a passport to teach, therefore making the much respected CELTA redundant. For a native Greek however, the rules were different. The Cambridge Proficiency Certificate in English was deemed by the Greek education authority to be adequate, which meant a school leaver with a proficiency pass could start, subject to a suitable vacancy, teaching immediately, with no experience or the necessary teaching practice.

Pam doesn't have a degree, but like most other things (for example, my licence) there was a way round her predicament, so she leapfrogged the degree hurdle to become employed at one of Argostoli's many local Frontisteria (Language Schools), as a Teaching 'Assistant'. Yes, a native English speaker with a CELTA qualification, being employed as an Assistant. Her employment was subject to a routine medical examination, as well as the official stamping and signing of paperwork that went with it. A straightforward process we thought, but because of the way the system worked, it sometimes wasn't.

Here's the procedure: Two public servants were responsible for each task; one stamped, the other signed, the same person couldn't do both, and although it was normal for the stamping and signing clerks to work in the same office it wasn't guaranteed, they could even be located on different floors, and even more incredibly, in different buildings. Those factors alone caused the inevitable delays associated with any bureaucracy, and even more so in a Greek one. The most common was if one or other of the clerks (or both) was out of the office for whatever reason, the signing and/or stamping had to wait, which could be a few minutes, a few hours, or even a few days.

An important part of the medical was a chest x-ray which was a routine check for tuberculosis. As far as Pam was concerned there had never been a problem in the past, but we were in the present, in Kefalonia, and in the doctor's custody. For reasons unexplained they weren't happy with the first x-ray, so they took a second, then they alleged she'd moved so they took two more; yes two. She went back a week later for the results but they'd been 'mislaid', which for Pam meant more photographs!

Eventually she got the results from a radiologist, who, sitting in a fog of her own cigarette smoke and not giving a damn about Pam, or the dangers of passive smoking said there was a slight problem and that she'd have to have a CT scan.

'We are just taking precautions you understand,' she said. What! Her first precaution should have been to put the cigarette out.

The scan revealed what the doctors called 'bubbles' in her lungs, but when asked what had caused them they couldn't say. Whatever the cause they weren't that concerned, and because it wasn't T.B. she was given the all clear to teach, or to be precise, to assist; which she started in October.

On our winter trip to the UK Pam took her x-rays (which in Greece the patient keeps and is responsible for) to show a lung specialist who confirmed there were bubbles in her lungs which he diagnosed as Emphysema. He went on to say the worst possible scenario was that one, or possibly both lungs could collapse, and if that happened she'd have to get hospital treatment as quickly as possible.

'And furthermore,' he added, 'although the condition is common it isn't life threatening.'

'Great,' I thought.

It was all said in such a calm and re-assuring manner that a collapsed lung, or both, seemed unlikely, and then came the final re-assurance.

'Under normal circumstances a collapsed lung will re-inflate itself.'

I loved that bit, 'Under normal circumstances'.

'There are however, some very definite don'ts,' he warned. 'Don't play rugby, don't bungee jump, and whatever you do, don't go deep sea diving, other than that life should go on as normal.' And for a while it did.

Saint Gerassimos

Contrary to popular belief the Greeks do celebrate birthdays, but the big date on their personal celebration calendar is the Name Day. The most common name in Kefalonia is Gerassimos (which is commonly abbreviated to Makis, although most American Greeks prefer to be called Gerry), the Patron Saint of the island, but who is never referred to as Saint Makis or Saint Gerry. Saint Gerassimos is famed for healing those with mental disorders and although the actual name day is on October 20th, there are, oddly enough two different celebrations held in his honour; confused yet? Read on.

August 16th commemorates the date of his death even though he died on the 15th. Still confused? That date was changed to avoid a clash with the Greek Orthodox feast day of the Assumption of the Blessed Virgin Mary which is on the 15th.

The second and more relevant date, the October one, was when, in the sixteenth century his corpse was exhumed and showed no trace of decomposition. It was instantly hailed a miracle, and what's more, miracles were performed wherever and whenever Gerassimos was around. In recognition of his special powers he was elevated from being a humble monk, who cured and blessed the sick, to become the venerated Saint.

Both celebrations are held in the Omala valley at the Monastery which bears his name, and on the evening before each, his body is taken from its resting place in the small neighbouring chapel to the monastery, where an all night vigil is held during which thousands of worshippers file past to pay homage.

The following morning the Saint's body is placed in a silver and glass casket, which is then hoisted to shoulder height and paraded between the crowds lining each side of the road leading from the monastery to the huge plane tree which Saint Gerassimos himself is said to have planted. A brass band leads the procession followed by the island's most important religious and political hierarchy who in turn are followed by a large number of lesser dignitaries and devout pilgrims.

Both ceremonies are very special, made even more so by the appearance of some of the island's sick who are brought forward from the crowd to lie in the road. It's the ultimate act of faith, because, in their desperation, the hope is that as the saint's body passes over them it'll be their turn for the miracle cure.

Without a doubt, it certainly is a very moving and unique experience, but I couldn't help feeling the significance and profoundness of the religious aspect is blighted by the presence of a tacky outdoor market, selling everything from plastic icons to corn on the cob.

Name Days

As far as name days were concerned Pam and I were fairly naive and hadn't been prepared for the island's big one, certainly not on our own doorstep.

It was October 27th and we'd been invited upstairs for dinner, or at least that's what we thought, because at the time we were unaware that Makis and Soula didn't do 'dinner', and even as we arrived the penny still hadn't dropped as to what was really happening. Makis greeted us, looking very dapper in a suit and tie (he obviously wasn't looking for a business premises to rent) and Soula was the elegant hostess, immaculate, in a lightweight flowing patterned skirt and matching top.

There was enough food and drink to feed a small army, with more in the kitchen as back up, so with all that laid on our dinner theory was immediately scuppered; but it didn't take long to work out that something else, something very special was about to happen and we were going to find out exactly what it was.

Having been the first to arrive we sat nervously twiddling our thumbs and wishing we could speak Greek, then within minutes a steady flow of people entered the apartment to join us. Family and friends were welcomed with kisses and handshakes, whereas Makis received the traditional name day blessing...*Chronia Polla* (pronounced kronn ya, 'pol' – as in Polly, 'a' – as in cat, and meaning 'many years') from everybody. Although the party was a few days late it was evident the name day celebrations of our landlord Makis, sometimes known as Gerassimos, were about to begin.

It turned out that most of the men were members of the Argostoli Male Voice Choir, and what a coincidence; so too was Makis. Accompanying the choir on guitar was a long white-haired minstrel named Christos, a familiar performer on the circuit of local tavernas during the summer, but who, as the evening progressed and the wine flowed, was out sung by the voices of the choir in what was an amazing exhibition of eating and drinking in true Kefalonian style.

A chance meeting

As well as being the first of many name days that we were invited to, there and elsewhere, it was memorable for one very significant chance meeting. In the early hours of the morning as everyone headed for the door a very strong and pronounced voice just behind my left ear said, 'You're English, welcome. I'm Stathis and this is my wife Irini,' and contrary to what I've said about the Kefalonians, we exchanged formal introductions and politely shook hands. It was a warm and sincere gesture, but after so much food and wine we thought no more of it until a few hours later.

Stathis and Irini

It's fair to say that most Kefalonians enjoy a good celebration, especially when a parade and a brass band are part of it, and during the course of a year there were plenty of them, parades that is. The day after Makis's musical evening was *Oxi* (pronounced ockee, och as in loch and key as in key for the door and meaning 'no') Day. *Oxi* Day commemorates the fateful chapter in Greek history when in 1940 the Prime Minister, Ioannis (pronounced Yannis) Metaxas defied Mussolini's ultimatum to Greece, relating to alleged incidents along the Greek/Albanian border. In a nutshell, he told Mussolini to bugger off, resulting in a disastrous wartime occupation of Kefalonia by Italian and German forces.

As Pam and I strolled through the square in Argostoli enjoying the spectacle of '*Oxi*' Day and the warmth of the autumn sun, a familiar voice, one I'd heard only a few hours before, said, 'Good morning, it's nice to see you again.' It was Stathis and Irini, who I recognised instantly.

There are, it's true to say, different nationalities from around the world who are recognisable, to a certain degree, by their stock characteristics, and the Kefalonians are one of them. Once I'd identified what those characteristics were it was easy to tell them apart from other Greeks, well, some of them at least.

Generally speaking Kefalonian men follow one or more of the following traits, they tend to be short(ish), and powerfully built with rugged facial features and short wiry black hair, that is until it turns grey, or in Christos the minstrel's case, white. As well as having a subtle sense of humour they can, and often are, outspoken and stubborn with a touch of eccentricity thrown in for good measure, and virtually all of them are proud and fiercely nationalistic, some to the point of xenophobia.

Of course there are exceptions to every rule, and Stathis was one of those exceptions. Although he was rugged, short, stocky, eccentric, outspoken, and had a wicked sense of humour, it was when it came to the hair that he completely broke the mould, because his wasn't short, black or wiry. It was streaked with various shades of grey (although it had been black once) and long, which stood him apart from almost anyone else, anywhere. It was even more noticeable as it flowed behind him in the wind when he was riding his red Vespa; like a Mediterranean Hell's Angel on a scooter.

There was only one Stathis and there weren't many red Vespas, so he was easy to spot around the town and along the Fanari coast road.

Irini was originally from Athens, and although outspoken too, she was, in total contrast to Stathis, very refined and elegant. Like most Greek women she was fastidious about her appearance and in particular her hair, which is probably why there were so many hairdressers in Argostoli. There was however one thing that set them apart from their peers; they were multi-lingual and spoke good English, French and Italian as well as perfect Greek.

Stathis and Irini

We'd been idly chatting in the square for a few minutes when Stathis asked, 'Would you like a coffee?'

Under normal circumstances when a Kefalonian offers an invitation to drink coffee it usually means sitting in the nearest café to chat and watch the world go by, and from where we were standing there were plenty to choose from, because the air was full of clinking coffee cups and the buzz of Greek chatter.

'Yes please,' I said, because the thought of sitting in the square that morning appealed to me, but Stathis had something else in mind.

Within minutes Pam and I were in the back of his Fiat, heading out of town along the coast road to their home at Fanari. 'Getting to know you' was the general topic and made for an interesting two-way conversation, but not only that, Irini's coffee was better than any I'd drank in any of the local coffee shops, indeed, it was some of the best I've ever tasted.

Intrigued, I asked her what the secret was, then, with a knowing smile she summed it up in five words, 'Peter, never use boiling water.'

Well, I never knew that, and like 'hard onions' I've never forgotten it.

That first get together was interesting, and I couldn't wait for more. As we left they loaded us up with bananas and pomegranates which were freshly picked there and then from their well stocked garden. Stathis offered us a lift home, but because it was such a nice day we declined, preferring to walk instead.

His parting shot was, 'You English walk everywhere, so the next time you're walking this way please call in, I mean it, it's not just a shallow invitation.' And it wasn't.

Their home was steeped in history, or at least the original pre-earthquake Venetian mansion was. During the wartime occupation it had been used by the Germans as a courthouse for the trials of their former allies, the Italians. The officers of the Acqui division were 'tried' and sentenced there before being taken up the road and executed. The sunken mass grave is opposite the turning for the monument on the road to Lassi and is marked by a commemorative plaque.

Fanari was easy walking distance from home, by a series of different tracks and trails as well as the main coast road, so it was no big deal for us to walk there, and a few days after that first visit we took Stathis at his word and 'called in'. I leant on the bell but it was a few minutes before he appeared, looking rather dishevelled and bleary eyed.

'Hi Stathi*. (*When talking about a Greek male with a first name ending in 's' that letter is pronounced, i.e. Spyros, Dimitris, Andreas. But when you are actually talking to that person, the 's' is dropped and becomes Spyro, Dimitri, Andrea and so on.) Did we wake you?' I asked with a smile, and because he was still rubbing the sleep from his eyes I knew we had.

'Yes you did, but now you're here you'd better come in and have a coffee,' which we did.

When he'd originally invited us to call in, there was one important time of the day he forgot to mention avoiding. It was the afternoon siesta when all visitors were actively discouraged or even totally banned. Siesta, or quiet time as it's sometimes referred to is normally taken between three and six in the afternoon, which was when Stathis (and most other Kefalonians) slept, but of course we didn't know that then. He forgave us for the intrusion that time, but warned us not to call in the afternoon again, unless we'd been invited for something special.

Stathis and Irini became close friends, two very special people who were there to help us during our darkest time.

The Special Place

On that Oxi Day and with our fruit in carrier bags we left Fanari and walked along the coast road in the Lassi direction. Shortly after passing the house behind high walls and through the 'pine tree tunnel' at the tiny hamlet of Piniatorou, we turned left onto a track leading up through what became affectionately known to us as 'The Special Place'. It's an amazingly beautiful olive grove, but as well as the familiar gnarled olive trees there are also fig, almond and fir trees growing in harmony. And also there is an array of bushes, shrubs, grasses as well as an abundance of wild flowers, all part of the Kefalonian landscape which comes alive with colour at different times of the year.

Towards the top of the track were two small chapels. The first was directly above 'Oskars' taverna, while a few steps further on was the Piniatorou family chapel which had its own grave yard.

At the top, the track branched off in opposite directions. By turning right an amazing panoramic roofscape of Argostoli opened up that offered a backdrop stretching south as far as the eye could see, whereas by going left the track led to the black marble monument, dedicated to the memory of the massacred Italian soldiers.

Living with Stretchers

As well as exploring and walking, I was also working hard to put a collection of paintings together. But buying materials, whether it was a tube of paint, a container of white spirit or stretched canvas often turned out to be a nightmare experience, and to make things worse there was only one artists' supplier in the town. A couple of stationery shops sold crayons, sketch pads and a few odds and sods, but that was about it. The other option was to take the mainland ferry to Patras, but that was out of the question due to the time and cost involved.

The main business of the 'art suppliers' was as a retail outlet to the decorating trade, and somehow I got the feeling, rightly or wrongly, that selling artists' materials was an irritating but lucrative sideline, especially when I walked in. The owner, Yiorgos (also known as Mr. George) was a decent enough bloke, and once he cottoned on I was a regular customer he greeted me with smiles, a handshake and a '*Yiassou* Peter'. Unfortunately he didn't speak any other English than that...'Peter'. But I did think he was another of those islanders who understood more than they let on, and although my phrase book was a constant companion it didn't make a lot of difference when I went there. More than once I was tempted, more out of devilment than anything, to swear at him in English to see what his reaction would have been, but I never did. After all, he was the only supplier in town and the repercussions of my prank could have backfired, resulting in a regular ferry ride to Patras and a possible black eye.

One morning late in May I happened to be in the shop and by sheer coincidence so did the salesman from the stretched canvas company, who, unlike Mr. George spoke excellent English, so I asked him if it was possible to make panoramic stretchers to order. Panoramic stretchers are wide and narrow, and ideal for painting some of the broad Kefalonian images I had in mind, but unfortunately they weren't sold in standard sizes.

'Yes of course, we can make any size you want, when you want, it's not a problem,' he said. Great, his words were music to my ears. It was though, a typical salesman's response, say yes and to hell with the consequences.

I should have known better, because when I asked, 'How much will they cost?' the reply was predictable.

'Oh don't worry about the cost, we can sort that out when you collect them.'

'Collect them, hang on a minute,' I said, slightly agitated. 'Excuse me, but I'm not collecting anything until I know exactly how much it'll cost, is that really too much to ask?'

'OK. I'll let Mister George know soon then you'll have to deal with him,' he said.

Soon to me means not long, usually a few days, or hours even, but to a Greek salesman time didn't really enter into the scheme of things. I was on a steep learning curve and was beginning to realise that most things on the island took longer to happen than I'd been used to, that's how it was; to the locals it was an accepted way of life.

As anticipated the prices took longer, a few weeks longer in fact. Eventually there was an answer from Mr. George, but it wasn't the one I was looking forward to. What I wanted was three sizes, which the sales guy had said was not a problem, but there was - three big ones. I would have to order a minimum of five hundred of each size. Fifteen hundred stretchers, that's a lot of canvas, a lot of space, and more importantly a lot of money, but I was still in the dark as to how much. Mr. George phoned the sales guy while I patiently waited. After finishing the call he turned to me, and through his interpreter explained that I'd have to place the order, then he would find out exactly how much it would be. It was there and then the deal fell through.

I was still determined to paint 'panoramic' and bought loose canvas, a staple gun, and had wooden frames made locally so that I could stretch my own. Buying the canvas and staple gun was the easy bit, but finding a good carpenter to make the stretchers was a different matter altogether.

Eventually, with the help of Kosmas, an artist I knew, and after a couple of false starts I, or rather he, finally found someone willing to do the work, but quality control was ultimately down to me. After each delivery I had to inspect every piece, sanding each one to round off sharp corners and rough edges. Overnight I became an expert at stretching canvas until it was difficult to tell the difference between mine and bought ones.

After a couple of years making my frames the guy suddenly and without warning stopped; yes; he downed tools and gave up carpentry. I don't know what he did after that, but no matter, stretcher production stopped with immediate effect, and despite the claustrophobia and stress of Mister George's store I had no alternative but to bite the bullet and buy ready stretched canvas off the shelf.

Make or Break Time

I'd worked hard through the summer to build up a stock of paintings, enough to hold my first exhibition in late September at The Bell Tower in the Cabana square, which is situated at the southern end of the pedestrianised stretch of The Lithostroto. The Bell Tower is a famous landmark dominating that part of the town and is a near replica of the original that was destroyed in 1953.

'The Bells' kafeneion on the ground floor was an initiative set up by the municipality of Argostoli to give people with social and learning difficulties a purpose in life, and although some, but not all, worked there on a casual basis there were two permanent full time supervisors; Eric on days, and Yiorgos who worked the evening shift. The exhibition space was on the first two floors, accessible only by a spiral staircase that continued to the top of the tower from where there were stunning views across the rooftops of Argostoli.

For the technically minded the clock mechanism was clearly visible inside, as was the clock face from the street below, but neither had worked for years. The original bell had miraculously survived the earthquake and was intact in its former position above the roof, and although also clearly visible, it, like the clock didn't work either.

The opening evening of the exhibition was informal and although invitations had been handed out (printed in Greek and English), everyone was welcome, whether they'd been invited or not. Wine and light refreshments were served, and while everyone socialised on the roof terrace, Yiorgos made sure their glasses were topped up, whilst I concentrated on the business of selling paintings.

Success was crucial because as far as I was concerned it was make or break time, and by the end of the week I was delighted with the number of paintings sold. The exhibition was a turning point and paved the way for my future life as an artist in Kefalonia. The remarkable thing is that every time I sell a painting I still get a buzz. For some, buying original art may be seen as a luxury or an investment, but for me it's a great way to decorate the home. Instead of hanging wallpaper, hang a painting.

The grand finalé of the exhibition came on the Saturday evening as Pam and I were about to pack up; it really was the icing on the cake. A couple came in, said hello, looked at the paintings then climbed the spiral to the next floor. They were up there some time before re-appearing with big smiles.

'Peter, we'd like to buy the painting of Fanari, it's the big one with the pink sky, number 19.'

As I packaged it up we talked, just small talk, and by sheer coincidence they lived near Swindon, then they asked if I knew a good framer there.

'Yes, go and see Mike Davies (known as Mike the Frame, and who'd been framing my work for years) in Old Town,' I said, which they did. Thankfully the painting arrived home safely! Due to the 9/11 attacks security at Kefalonia airport had been tightened up, severely restricting what passengers could and couldn't take into the cabin; fortunately, painting number 19 was given the all clear.

After finally leaving The Bell Tower on that Saturday evening Pam and I celebrated my success by splashing out at

Patsouras taverna. The exhibition breakthrough convinced me that I could earn a living painting on the island. So, over Patsouras famous cheese pie and a couple of jugs of red wine we decided to give it a go for five years (backdated to April) and when the five years were up we'd decide what to do next; whether to stay or go.

Patsouras Taverna

Kefalonia is a stunningly beautiful island, and as much as we loved it, deep in our hearts we knew even then that we would never settle there forever.

Captain Corelli's Mandolin

In the same week that I struck gold at the Bell Tower, Argostoli premièred the film 'Captain Corelli's Mandolin' which was adapted from the book of the same name; that, in my opinion was where the similarity ended. The original is an emotional story of love and death set in Kefalonia during the Italian and German occupation of the second world war, followed by events leading to, and beyond, the tragedy of the 1953 earthquake.

Thanks to some subtle camera work and a beautiful soundtrack, the film captured the beauty of the island, but unfortunately the originality of the book was lost somewhere in Hollywood. John Hurt's portrayal of the wonderfully eccentric Doctor Yiannis was one of the few highlights, so good in fact that he could have easily (except for his accent) passed for a Kefalonian. Rumour has it that when he wasn't in front of the cameras he was 'researching' with the locals, usually in tavernas and kafeneions, which is why he was able to play the part so well.

Part of the film set in Sami

I'd first read the book in 1999 and was moved by its tender love scenes that were interwoven with the futility of war. It was though a particular passage in the early pages, describing in vivid detail the special quality of the Kefalonian light that fascinated and stirred me, so much so, I have often wondered since, if I hadn't read the book whether I'd have ever gone there at all.

A Sting in the Tail

Immediately after the exhibition we made the travel arrangements for our Christmas visit to the UK. The proceeds (despite Yiorgos's wine bill - no wonder he kept the glasses topped up) from the sales more than covered the cost, and we were even able to afford the exorbitant return flights to Athens which, it has to be said, was a lot easier than the ferry/road journey that took around seven hours.

There was however a sting in the tail! Having booked the flights nothing could have prepared us for the shock when we collected the tickets from the airline office a few days later, because in those few days there had been an increase in airport taxes resulting in a hefty surcharge.

Naturally I objected to the price hike, but I was wasting my time and was told in no uncertain terms, 'If you don't pay, you don't go on the plane.' We'd been truly shafted by the national airline. In contrast, the onward and return flights from Athens to Luton had been booked online with a popular 'cheap flight, no frills' airline, it was easy, and there were no extra taxes to pay with them.

The End of October

At the end of October the holiday season came to an abrupt end. It was as if someone had flicked a switch, and as charter flights stopped, the transformation of nearby Lassi was dramatic. For six months it had been a bustling holiday village, but for the next six it would become virtually deserted. Although Argostoli isn't a package destination and there were a handful of hotels that catered for the independent visitor, those too were empty. The town became a lot quieter due to the reduced population, but the wonderful Eggcups, Sliding Doors and Cardiff, all an essential part of our daily life carried on as normal, just as though the hustle and bustle of summer had never really happened.

Although it was the end of the season that didn't necessarily mean it was the end of summer. The island was still bathed in sunshine and warmth, and despite the occasional early winter rain shower it was still paradise. Walking was always a pleasure, and despite our limited means of transport we explored as much as possible during the weeks leading up to Christmas.

On our winter trip we visited friends and family in the UK, spent Christmas with Pam's daughter Sarah, and her fiancé Bradley in Glasgow, whereas New Year was celebrated partying in a converted chapel in the small Wiltshire village of Minety. And the weather? Compared to what we'd been used to over the past nine months it was a shock to the system.

It had been nice to get away, but it was so much nicer to get home again, and because Kefalonia was our home we couldn't get back soon enough.

Fiskardo
Painting, oil on canvas by Peter Hemming

2002 – The Dream Becomes A Reality

The Unpredictability Of Winter

As luck would have it we flew out of Athens only hours before the city was blanketed in snow resulting in the airport being closed for almost three days. What a relief; the thought of camping in an airport terminal for that length of time didn't really appeal to us. Although Kefalonia had escaped the snow, high winds and torrential rain had caused havoc across the island while we were away. In Lassi a mini tornado had uprooted pine trees near Platis and Makris Yialos beaches, while bushes and other debris were seen flying around the Turk's Foot, the local name for the huge rock that sits at the end of the White Rocks Hotel beach.

The Turk's Foot
Painting, watercolour by Peter Hemming

Fortunately there had been no serious damage to property, and more importantly, no one had been hurt, but the unusually high tides had shifted sand, and where there had once been beach was now exposed rock. However, thanks to the miracle of nature the sand returned in time for the summer. Cleaning gangs appeared a couple of days before the arrival of the first holiday flights to make sure the beaches were in pristine condition for the forthcoming visitors.

Kefalonia is famous for its natural beauty and stunning scenery. The relaxed atmosphere of the island is unique, so too is the charm and friendship offered by the warm and welcoming Kefalonians. It's no wonder then that people return year after year, because it really is the perfect holiday destination, but not in those first few weeks of the year when the weather is so unpredictable. Out of season, though, the independent traveller can, with forward planning and some waterproof clothing, enjoy the magic qualities of the island, which includes sunshine. Contradictory but true.

The weather in early January had given us a taste of what was to come during the following few weeks, but because it was our first Kefalonian winter we weren't quite sure what to expect. Torrential rain lasting for hours at a time, and electrical storms were frequent and spectacular, especially at night when the mountains, illuminated by lightning, appeared like ghosts in the strange blue light that accompanied explosions of thunder, rumbling around the sky like angry Greek gods.

Mount Aenos often disappeared completely under dark layers of cloud, and when they eventually parted, like young lovers at dawn, the steep slopes were cloaked in blankets of snow that dazzled brightly in the winter sun. It wasn't unusual for the snow cover to last for days, or weeks even, with some of the more exposed mountain passes, especially the one between Sami and Poros becoming completely blocked. The Argostoli to Sami road is the busiest and most direct route to the mainland ferry, so any serious obstacles along it were cleared quickly to allow access, but it wasn't just snow that caused blockages. As it thawed and the winter rains continued, landslips and flooding became an additional hazard. It really was a far cry from the heat of summer.

Caught Out In The Shower

Immediately and bizarrely after heavy rain it was commonplace to lose the running water in our apartment, but we weren't the only ones to suffer, it affected everybody. The pumping stations serving the town were unable to cope with the increased volumes of rainwater that poured into the natural underground mountain reservoirs, and as a consequence the majority of homes in Argostoli ran dry.

There were times, even without the storms, when the sudden loss of water became a frequent and annoying part of our lives. When it happened we were never quite sure how long it would last, half an hour, half a day, we never knew, but we did know when it was being turned on again. The signal was a tell-tale gurgling in the pipes, which meant that turning the taps on had to be done with extreme caution as the initial flow of mud coloured water splattered everything as it exploded from them.

It was then that the telephone line to the mayor's office was red hot with angry callers, whereas others, so typically tolerant, muttered under their breaths, *'Ti tha kanoume?'* (What can we do?).

There was one particular time when Panagis next door encountered the problem head on. He was soaped up in the shower and got caught completely unaware as he turned the tap to rinse off, there were a couple of trickles and that was it. In those few vital seconds his shower had come to an abrupt end. When he appeared on the patio wearing nothing but a towel for decency, covered in soap and cursing the devil, his reaction and mood could be described as anything but tolerant. He, just like the Aussie in Exelixis was furious. It was hilarious, and to keep a straight face was my biggest concern, because from his tone Panagis was about to burn the mayor's ears in his fury, that was, once he'd rinsed the soap off his hands so that he could hold the phone.

It was also during the heavy rain that Piniatorou Street became a reddish brown torrent! Kefalonian soil, the colour of burnt sienna, was washed down from the woods above us, bringing an assortment of debris with it; but it wasn't just our road that became waterlogged.

Over the years many of the town's drains had become blocked with builders' rubble, mainly cement, plaster and concrete. At the end of each working day any leftover materials were washed down the roadside gutters, and into the surface water drainage system. The idea was good, in that everything would be diluted sufficiently and washed away, but in practice of course it didn't, and the reality was that the cement and plaster eventually turned to a solid mass, even under water. Subsequently, during the continuous heavy rain the drains overflowed and the steeper streets of the town, of which there were many, became fast flowing waterways that were impossible to walk along without wearing the appropriate waterproof footwear.

Despite the hazards and frustrations I enjoyed the varying moods of winter, and although there were never sub zero temperatures, at least not in Argostoli, it sometimes felt colder than it actually was due to the wind chill factor, when strong winds blew in off the sea, which without warning often turned into howling gales. Then after the rain there was a light of unbelievable clarity, so clear in fact that distances appeared almost close enough to touch.

Kion And Arabis

When the electrical storms were at their worst, Kion (pronounced key-on) became petrified. Kion was a big collie dog belonging to Minas and he lived in a huge kennel on the patio next door, and because Minas was, like his father a builder, or to be more precise, a roofer, it meant Kion had the best roof on the best built kennel in the neighbourhood, and compared to most Kefalonian dogs, lived in luxury. But having a five star home meant nothing to him as the storms raged. He cowered, whimpered and was generally in a state of panic. Furthermore, whatever Pam or I did to try and calm him never worked, which I suppose was understandable. After all he was a Greek dog and couldn't understand English.

In sheer desperation he often escaped, but that was only for a couple of hours or so, after which he'd return as if nothing had happened, but there were times when he was away for days. Because Kion wasn't street wise like most Argostoli strays, when on the loose he became a danger, not only to himself, but also to any unsuspecting motorists who just might happen to be on the same road at the same time. Many of the town's road's surfaces were smooth and unpredictable, even when dry, but when wet they became not only smoother, but dangerously so. Drivers often lost control of their vehicles at the slightest touch of the brakes, and a huge demented collie dog running in blind panic amongst them didn't help matters.

After one of his longer breakouts, I spotted Kion in the Lithostroto near the Post Office, and what a state he was in, bedraggled, bewildered and lost. As I called him over he wagged his tail and smiled (the way dogs do), then together we sat on the Post Office steps and waited for Minas to turn up in his van. Hooray for the mobile phone.

Freedom was always short lived for Kion, but not so for Arabis (pronounced arabeece, eece as in Greece), 'The Black Arab'. He was a stray, strong and fearless with real character and instantly recognisable by his jet black coat and upright tail; he was a great dog and I loved him dearly. Despite being a loner and free to roam the town at will, Piniatorou Street was his territory which he guarded with a passion.

I was working in the apartment when the sound of growling and snarling from the street below shattered the peace of the morning. Looking out I saw Arabis and a huge black Great Dane squaring up to each other.

'Arabis,' I thought, 'don't even bother, just walk away, because if you don't that big brute will kill you,' and then as quick as the blinking of an eye the two were locked together in deadly combat. As the contorted black shapes rolled around the road a cloud of dust rose, traffic stopped, and drivers were briefly entertained as the battle raged, but it was soon over and afterwards the victor sat nonchalantly on our door step watching carefully as the defeated Great Dane limped away with his tail between his legs.

Arabis, as well as seeing off all male rivals (especially when the bitches were on heat), also wound Kion up by strutting back and forth past the patio gate, giving off an air of arrogant independence. Although streetwise, Arabis often tempted fate, risking life and limb by chasing and snapping at passing cars.

A Television, A Choir And A Big Black Knocker

Although we had lived on the island for almost a year we still hadn't got round to buying a television, and although we'd talked about it that was all, it just wasn't on our list of priorities and never seemed to be that important.

But what was important was that we got to know as much about the Kefalonian way of life as possible, and to become part of it, if only in a small way. As our friendship with Stathis and Irini grew, they became a valuable source of information and we continually quizzed them about Greece, and in particular Kefalonia. Stathis, having been born and bred in Argostoli was knowledgeable about most things, so much so that we referred to him as 'The Oracle', because what he didn't know he could always find out.

We were with them one evening when 'watching television' became part the conversation. They, like many other Kefalonians enjoyed watching 'soaps', and just as the siesta ban had been imposed, we were warned never to call on them, and definitely not to phone while they were 'soaping'.

We joked about their addiction and said 'soaps' were popular in the UK too, at which Stathis asked, 'So, which programmes do you like best then?'

'Well Stathi, it's like this, because we haven't got a television we don't have any favourite programmes, not having a television has never really bothered us.'

'Would you like one?' His question threw me.

'If there's one on offer, OK,' I replied casually, and thought that was the last of it; but I should have known better.

The following morning our big black door knocker echoed up the stairs, and when I opened it Stathis was standing holding a television under his arm.

'There Peter, it's yours on a long term loan, but I might need it from time to time, when I do I'll let you know.'

'Thank you.'

I was lost for words and didn't really know what to say, but he did, and turning to leave added with a big smile, 'You know, watching television is a way in which you could improve your Greek.' I didn't answer, but just returned the smile.

When we lived in the UK, Pam and I had always been selective about what we watched on television, and nothing had changed just because we were living in Kefalonia. Stathis's TV was never in danger of overheating or blowing up due to over-use, but being so discerning probably hindered my journey down the road towards the rich world of the Greek language; or maybe I was just plain lazy.

There was no doubt about it, watching television was popular on the island and because most tavernas, kafeneions and bars had one or more, they were best avoided when anything popular, especially Greek football, was being televised. When a big match was on those places became packed, but worse than that, packed with cigarette smokers. I've never considered watching television a health hazard, but in the dense fog of an Argostoli kafeneion it was deadly.

As well as enjoying good conversation, Stathis and I had the love of music in common, and whereas he was a performer, I was a listener, enjoying it from the comfort of an armchair in my own home or in the atmosphere of the concert hall. For some time he'd been trying to get me to join the choir, so to pacify him I half heartedly went along with it, but not really knowing whether he was serious or not; then realising he was I did my best to wriggle out of it.

'Stathi you know I can hardly speak the language, how on earth do you expect me to sing it?' But he persisted.

'Peter, it will be OK. I will write the words phonetically for you, come along to one of our practice evenings and see what you think.'

So with nothing to lose I did. Sitting at the back of the rehearsal room was, if nothing else interesting, as well as entertaining. I wasn't sure what Stathis's Choir mates thought about me being there, but they didn't seem too bothered, and carried on cajoling and winding each other up with the friendliest Kefalonian banter, but when they did eventually put their minds to singing, it sounded good. However, I think maestro Vassillis is the only person I've ever seen conducting a choir with his hands in his pockets!

My Kefalonian singing career didn't progress any further than that evening, but I enjoyed their performances all the same, even if it was only as part of the audience.

And the big black door knocker? It was a 'landmark' for anyone visiting the apartment for the first time.

'Don't look for a number on the door because there isn't one,' we'd say, 'it's the door with the big black knocker.'

It was one of three, to three separate apartments all within the same building, of which none of the doors had a number, and yet they were all listed as the same address: number 9. Not 9A, B or C, just nine. Fortunately, Makis, our regular postman knew who lived behind each one, and because we didn't have a postbox he slipped ordinary letters under the door. Anything bulkier warranted a bang of the black knocker, and if there was no one at home he'd leave a note for us to collect whatever it was from the Post Office. That really was bad news, because queuing there as haphazard as it was at the markets and Banks.

To, Too And Two

Pam worked at the *frontisterio* through the winter, and because she was teaching local children, thought it a good idea to learn Greek, even though her pupils were supposed to be studying English. She took tuition on a one-to-one basis with her boss, the talented multi-linguist Marilena, but even with her diligence, determination and self motivation Pam could never get her head round the language completely, yet she was streets ahead of me.

Panagis, at the El Greco taverna found it funny that I should be finding Greek so difficult to learn, while at the same time honestly believing English was easy, which of course it isn't, and I told him so.

'Panagis, when English is spoken correctly, it is one of the most difficult languages in the world to learn, to speak, and what's more, to understand.'

However, unavoidably and boringly the language comparison became an ever recurring bone of contention with him as well as others, and when it did I used the word TO in the following short sentence to prove my point with English: 'The TWO of us are going TO the beach TOmorrow, will you come TOO?' That really made their minds boggle. English easy? Why do you think it took me so long to write this book?

Café Mystique

In my continued search for The Gallery I looked at what seemed to be ideal premises close to Antico, one of the most popular cafés in the Lithostroto. The television hadn't worked its linguistic magic, and because the owner of the property didn't speak English, Stathis agreed to be my interpreter for the meeting. But it proved to be a pointless exercise, and the owner turned out to be no different to the others I'd met with Dimitris, because as well as asking for a huge rent he expected me to commit myself there and then. As before, negotiations were one way, but that's how it was, all or nothing, with the owners expecting me to make important decisions on impulse.

It was only January, so moving in and paying a high rent, and air, the prospect of selling little, or nothing, didn't appeal to me. I'm not a hard nosed businessman, but knew the majority of my sales would be to summer visitors, and they wouldn't be arriving until May.

By now Pub Old House had become my local, so one evening I asked Lefteris about Café Mystique.

'Lefteri, who owns the property next door, the café, it's been empty since I've been living on the island and I wondered if it was available to rent?'

He peered over his glasses in that old fashioned way of his, and said, 'Peter, if you want Mystique I can arrange it, but you would have to make a contract with the owner (who also owned most of the street, including The Pub), but pay the rent to me. It would be better if you saw it in the day, speak to Colin and arrange to meet him there.' Which I did.

It was sound advice, but the more I thought about the rent agreement the more Kefalonian it sounded: complicated, without too much logic. I'd only ever seen the building at night, whereas in daylight it looked totally different (which, I suppose is only natural). The exterior was painted in pastel shades of blue and peach that contrasted nicely with the dark brown window frames and wooden double doors forming the impressive front entrance, which was approached by semi-circular brick and tiled steps. The east facing front windows looked out onto a narrow concrete patio and the street known as Harbouri. On the other side of Harbouri Street was a small square adjoining a much larger open space that bordered the busy Rizospaston Street some fifty meters away. A huge single window in the south elevation looked across the narrow road to a residential apartment block. At the rear of the building was a small concrete yard, almost hidden by overgrown trees and bushes. It was also where the entrance to the adjoining rear apartment was, which the owner used periodically, but mainly in the summer as a holiday retreat.

After looking round the outside we went indoors, and what a mess! Lefteris's two teenage sons Nicolas and Alexander, along with their mates, had hung out there and amassed all kinds of junk and rubbish, the majority of which was oily bike parts. In amongst the bike bits were remnants of the former café days; empty bottles, glasses and ashtrays. The internal walls were painted a deep blue and the ceiling was a rather smoke stained shade of mustard yellow.

Below the shelving that covered the back wall were handy sized storage cupboards, and in one was a small but useful water heater. But without a doubt the most outstanding feature of the whole place was the bar.

Sometimes my mind works in mysterious ways, because as I followed Colin up the steps and through the door, my first thoughts were, 'That bar will have to go.'

Then as my senses and sanity gradually returned I realised it was the centrepiece, and my irrational thinking could be best described as a sudden rush of blood to the head. The bar had a highly varnished wooden top along its full length and behind it was a stainless steel double drainer sink, a freezer that didn't work and a clapped out fridge with a six inch nail that held the door shut. Tucked away behind a blue door in the far corner was the toilet and wash-room, which, like the rest of the Café had a tiled floor. That was The Gallery.

Despite the mess it was ideal, so Lefteris agreed that I could move in on May 1st. That suited me fine as it coincided with the start of the season. It suited him too, because he'd been approached by other 'entrepreneurs' wanting to turn it into all sorts of money making ventures that included a music bar, a gay bar, and of all things, a late night drinking bar. Direct competition was the last thing Lefteris wanted, and the last thing the local residents needed was another late bar of any description on their doorsteps; one was enough.

Pub Old House was the ultimate late bar and closed only when the last customers left, which could be any time, even as the dawn was breaking.

As that big warm smile lit his face, Lefteris said, 'Peter, at least The Gallery will be peaceful, and you won't be causing any disturbances at night.'

No, I wouldn't be disturbing anything or anybody. There was no intention of changing anything structurally to Café Mystique either, indoors or out. The bar would definitely stay, and along with my artwork it would become the focal point of The Gallery. Colin (who, conveniently was a general handyman) was more than willing to help with any work and ended up doing most of it; it was more a case of me helping him than him helping me. But despite any work that Colin and I did, there would also be the mind boggling task of cutting through the miles of Greek red tape involved in the setting up of any new business.

Treating My Feet

Suddenly, without warning Spring arrived, and with it came the re-birth of Kefalonian colour that overnight became a dazzling tapestry across the landscape. By the end of February the storms were less frequent and there was real warmth in the air. Winter, if there really had been one, slipped by almost unnoticed, and unless the weather was particularly bad Pam and I walked every day.

One of my favourite walks was across the Lassi beaches, starting at the Mediterranee Hotel, crossing to the adjoining Antonio Beach and ending up at Makris Yialos where I walked back and forth along the water line to treat my feet. It was a way of giving them the full benefit of natural treatment, a miracle mix of salt and sand which had been recommended by Mike, a chiropodist friend in the UK; and it worked.

As well as loving the Special Place, Pam and I had a couple of other favourite walks. One was the track along the 'ridgeway' to the monument that continued, winding its way down through the pines to the Katavothres water holes. The other was a goat trail skirting the water's edge between Fanari and Lassi. At the end of that trail was a hideaway, a natural sun trap hidden from view where we often sat relaxing in the sun. It became affectionately known to us as the pulpit rock because of the shape of the large rock that dominated it. It was fascinating to watch sea life ebbing and flowing with the gentle tide in and out of a small rock pool there.

The pulpit rock was in fact one of a number of ruined Italian anti-aircraft gun posts, several of which had been built (and subsequently destroyed) along that stretch of water. They were built in 1943 to repel German aircraft as they attacked Argostoli and its coastline from their base in Lixouri.

As I've already established we loved walking, but the locals looked upon us as 'that odd English couple', which didn't concern us in the least, because being odd meant we were just 'fitting in' with everybody else.

When asked how often and how far we walked, people frowned in disbelief when we told them, prompting the following question, 'Why do you walk when you could drive?'

To which there was only one answer, 'We don't drive because we haven't got a car.'

Pure Caffeine Bombs

Curiosities were certainly aroused, especially amongst our close neighbours, those who saw us most. Mrs. Flowers (she got that name after giving Pam a bunch once) lived up the road on the way to the Special Place, and as we passed one afternoon she was standing on the doorstep, it was almost as if she was expecting us. Then right on cue she started talking, in Greek of course, repeating the word café several times. We were baffled, looking blankly at each other and in turn at Mrs. Flowers, then the penny dropped. The Greek word for coffee is café; and she was inviting us in for one. It was another example of the Kefalonian warmth that was being heaped on us, something we were gradually getting used to.

The Kefalonians are very family conscious and Mrs. Flowers being no exception took great delight in showing off the family photo album, especially the snaps of her grandchildren. After the photo session, the coffee, made Greek style arrived, and can only be described as pure caffeine bombs. It was served traditionally in small white cups consisting of one to one, that is one inch coffee, one inch sediment and an instant hit. Unfortunately, because we didn't drink coffee Greek style we hadn't been prepared for the sediment content until it was too late. Imagine drinking coffee flavoured sand, because that's what it was like. Needless to say, traditional Greek coffee didn't ever become our favourite tipple!

A little further up the road from Mrs. Flowers perched on the brow of the hill was a small one storey house with breathtaking views of the mountains to the north, east and south, and the Paliki with the open sea to the west. We had coffee there too. Dimitris, Eleni, and their grown up sons Makis and Dionysis (Denis; but pronounced thee-o-neesis) were one of the friendliest families we met; and they were always smiling... yes, always. But then I would have smiled too living in a house with those views.

They, like Mrs Flowers spoke excellent Greek, but any linguistic difficulties were ignored, and over a period of time communication skills developed with a combination of smiles and sign language.

Further on still, where the concrete road ended to become a track was the rather ramshackle home of Mrs Knickers, nicknamed so because she always hung her 'smalls' (which in fact were quite large) from the thorny branches of the bushes opposite the house. There were always waves and gummy smiles to greet us when we passed, and although coffee was offered we never got round to accepting her hospitality.

The Jumble Sale

Much had been crammed into that first full spring. We explored the Paliki; Pam bought a digital camera; we met Michael (and his dog Woody), a marine biologist who worked on the Glass Bottom Boat; drank Metaxas Brandy with Takis and Eleni as they prepared the Ionio taverna for the season; met Lampros at the Simatos apartments, he was preparing for the season too; received a regular supply of lemons from our neighbour, Theo; drank champagne with Kiki and Kosmas to celebrate my first year on the island; had an informal tour of the Gentilini winery with Gabrielle, the English wine maker; saw kites flying at Gradakia beach on 'Clean Monday'; had a short break in the north, courtesy of Christian and Carol ; were invited to two parties; and went to a Jumble Sale. But even with all that activity we kept mainly to ourselves and slowly adapted to the Kefalonian way of life.

The Jumble Sale was an annual charity fund raiser for UNICEF, organised by Francesca and friends. It took place in one of the waterside tavernas in Argostoli and was held in February. I hadn't realised there were so many ex-pats living on the island until that Sunday morning. As word spread, the so-called ethnic minorities, and let's not forget the British were one of them, turned out in large numbers to make it a highly successful and truly international affair.

It was inevitable Prue would be there, who, in her own words was 'full of beans' because she'd bought a pair of summer sandals. I enjoy browsing at jumble sales and, like her, was always looking for a bargain, but did draw the line at wearing other people's shoes never knowing what I might catch; especially with my feet.

On mentioning it to Prue the response was typical, she casually shrugged her shoulders and gave a totally unconcerned reply, 'Pete, once I've given them a scrub they'll come up as good as new.'

She was just living up to her 'cheapskate' image of which she was very proud.

Carnival

A couple of weeks after the Jumble Sale, Pam and I went to Lixouri for the carnival. While there we joined Prue for lunch and met the new addition to her dog family, Dolly, a sane companion for the ever manic Lizzie.

When we asked if she was going to watch the parade, the reply was once again classic Prue, 'When you've seen one, you've seen them all, but don't tell the Lixourians that.'

According to them their event is the best on the island, and as if to prove a point, by the middle of the afternoon the town was heaving with spectators. The celebrations were certainly lively and lived up to all expectations, and in keeping with local tradition were colourful and loud; very loud. I felt a bit like Prue though, as I'd been to a few carnivals over the years (but not Greek ones) and found them generally boring. However, I was living in Kefalonia, and being there was to experience the island's heritage and tradition at first hand; so I grinned and bore it and went totally with the flow.

Striding out at the head of the procession was the Lixouri brass band, looking very impressive in their smart uniforms, marching in step and not playing a note out of tune, or at least that's how it sounded.

Carnival Fun in Lixouri

The carnival floats of all shapes and sizes followed them, disappearing at the far end of the harbour, only to re-appear minutes later, coming from the opposite direction near the ferry boat terminal to start another circuit of the town, much to the enjoyment of the crowds lining the route. I did at one point feel as though it was never going to end, and lost count of the number of times they came past us.

Sailing To Lixouri

John and Kate, along with a cocker spaniel dog named Bosun were moored up in Argostoli on their yacht 'Spirit of Glenelg' for a few days. Pam and I had met them one evening as we strolled along the quayside, then having made introductions we were invited on board.

After a glass of wine and generally chatting for a while, John said, 'We're sailing to Lixouri on Saturday, would you like to join us for the afternoon?'

We met as arranged, and whereas I thought we'd be getting away to a flyer, that wasn't in the script, and was never likely to be. Boat people, I've since learnt, are a laid back breed and a law unto themselves, because instead of starting pronto, we relaxed in the sun and were persuaded into enjoying a couple of ouzos before gently slipping away from the quayside, past the Katavothres and the lighthouse to the open sea, that is if the gulf of Argostoli can be considered to be the open sea.

Now at this point in my story I need to explain one thing: water and I don't mix, at least not in a comfortable sense. It's a long story, but I have a natural fear, brought on as a result of almost drowning in swimming pools… twice, but, paradoxically I do love the sea. Being near it, on it, and to a certain degree, in it, but only as long as I'm comfortably within my depth, which means being able to keep my head above the surface and my feet on the bottom.

After living on the North coast of Cornwall for a number of years the sea has been a great inspiration for my work. There though the breakers of the Atlantic are wild, which, under normal circumstances is in total contrast to the calm of the Ionian Sea. Because we were sailing to Lixouri it meant all hands were required on deck, at least to begin with, but once we were in open water Pam, under John's expert supervision couldn't wait to take the wheel. There was something very special about being on the water and under sail that day. The wind whispered through the rigging, accompanied by the rolling silver waves in their rhythmic motion as the boat cut gracefully through them to make it all very hypnotic and magical.

Pam loved sailing in the Gulf and really couldn't get enough of it, but it was over far too soon for both of us, and on the approach to Lixouri John resumed his role as captain, guiding us slowly and safely into the marina. After tying up and making sure everything was 'ship shape' we thanked them for a great afternoon and got ready to leave, but they weren't interested. Kate had already uncorked the wine and the glasses were full, but that wasn't all. Lunch, albeit a late one had been simmering and was almost ready. It was a tough decision, but we couldn't turn it down, because after the rigours of sailing we were not only starving, but thirsty as well.

On the same day as the Lixouri voyage we were supposed to be having lunch with Prue, and in the evening there was a dinner date in Argostoli. Oh, what a mess.

When I explained our predicament to John he took it very calmly and said, 'Peter, that's OK. Don't worry, phone Prue and tell her to come and eat with us.'

She was once again 'full of beans', and thankfully left the normally ever-present Lizzie behind, to join us for what was a wonderful lunch and an equally enjoyable gargle. It was one of those memorable afternoons spent in the warmth of the Kefalonian sun and warm company.

Eventually it was time to leave so we thanked our hosts and, through a blissful alcoholic haze staggered the short distance to the ferry port, knowing that if we'd stayed on 'Glenelg' for much longer, especially the way the wine was going down, we would never have made it onto the ferry, not to mention climbing the steps to the passenger decks. After getting home we showered, hoping in some way it would freshen us up enough to keep awake and survive the evening - it helped a little. On our way to the dinner date (and already late) we met one of Pam's friends who insisted on bringing us up to date with the latest island gossip, there was always something going on somewhere; then my phone rang.

It was Dimitris with panic in his voice, 'Peter where are you? The food will be ruined if you don't get here soon.'

'We're on our way Dimitri don't worry, we'll be there in a couple of minutes, if you lean over your balcony you'll see us standing by the pharmacy on the corner near the theatre, we'll give you a wave, have a look.' He didn't bother.

He's Greek and should have known that arriving late was par for the course, even though it had never been our intention, but looking at it from a digestive point of view, the later we got there the better. Although we were still quite full from lunch the dinner was superb and wasn't ruined at all, we also managed to stay awake for the whole evening; it was though, touch and go at times.

Meanwhile

Meanwhile, what with jumble sales, sailing, and goodness knows what else, time was moving swiftly on towards May and a new summer season. Anticipating (m)any problems with the opening of The Gallery I collected the keys from Lefteris and started cleaning it up. What looked like a nightmare job to begin with turned out to be relatively easy as much of the dirt and grime was superficial and came off with elbow grease, will power and hot soapy water.

With the cleaning finished, Colin, with my help began the main task of lining the walls and boarding over the pigeon hole type shelving with chipboard; that was designed to give me maximum hanging space behind the bar. The next job was painting it, but what I hadn't realised was that chipboard soaks up paint the way a sponge soaks up water, and it was drying faster than I could brush it on; but Colin was at hand and came to the rescue again. He was working at the pub that morning and seeing I was having difficulties answered my cries for help.

'Leave it to me,' he said. Then, with all the skills of a true painter he watered down the paint and applied it with a big roller and within a couple of hours it was finished, whereas it would have taken me a couple of days, possibly more. Café Mystique was quickly transformed from a dark blue to a light white.

In the meantime, at the accountant's office Eleni was having her work cut out sifting through the mountain of paperwork necessary to transfer Café Mystique into my name. I had a gut feeling that she would never make that 1st of May deadline because it was Greek bureaucracy at its worst, and the main cause of the delays was the contract.

On the helter skelter journey to official approval, it travelled between Lefteris, the owner of the building, me, our friend Kiki (who was translating), Eleni, respective solicitors and accountants, not to mention the various departments of the aforementioned bureaucratic fortress, the tax office. It was faxed, re-faxed, copied, re-worded, and then in the middle of June, six weeks after opening (albeit unofficially) it was signed, counter signed, and finally stamped.

The Gallery, Argostoli

The good news was that Café Mystique no longer existed, and on May 1st 'THE GALLERY', complete with hand painted signs, opened its doors to the public.

Poster Power

Although The Gallery was some distance from the Lithostroto and the town's other hive of activity, The Square, I was happy where I was. The website was looking good and attracting lots of hits, and more importantly, favourable feedback. Locally though I was relying on my own advertising in the shape of the all important 'Poster Power' to catch the eye and spread the word.

Argostoli was awash with posters of all shapes and sizes advertising everything from live music to the Catholic mass. They were fixed to notice boards, in shop windows and doorways, tavernas and kafeneions, stapled to wooden poles, taped to concrete poles, and worst of all, ecologically speaking, stapled or taped to trees.

The most common poster size was A3, printed in full colour, as if to make the point that 'big is best', which of course isn't always the case. They also cost a fortune to produce.

Whereas one poster strategically placed was enough to catch the eye, it wasn't unusual to see multiple quantities of the same poster, horizontally, vertically, or both, positioned in such a way as to resemble a giant poster mural that covered a whole notice board, thus, completely obliterating any others that happened to be there first. The Catholic church in Argostoli was in on the act as well, when during the summer, papal posters advertised Sunday mass times. They were unceremoniously covered over too, in poster warfare nothing was sacred.

The Gallery posters however were slightly different. They weren't big and cost a fraction of the coloured ones to make. Black lettering was printed on eye-catching yellow A4 paper and unless vandalised or covered over (which, in July and August was often), stood out a mile and were easy to see. As a way of keeping one step ahead of the vandals I was vigilant and did a weekly 'poster run' in and around Argostoli and Lassi, which (other than Skala) was where the majority of tourists would be staying. It wasn't really a run, but a weekly walk to replace any posters that had been damaged or vandalised.

Local elections were held in September and huge campaign posters, glowing with the smiling faces of the various candidates, appeared everywhere in Argostoli, which sparked off a major political poster battle. Fortunately for me they stayed away from Lassi, and anyway, summer visitors weren't interested in local politics and neither were the business people that catered for them, unless of course, by voting for a particular candidate there was something in it for them.

As well as the standard yellow poster, Pam designed and printed full colour ones which were laminated and displayed in windows and wherever they could be seen by the public, but more importantly, where the vandals couldn't get to them. Having become friendly with some of the taverna owners, they were happy to help my poster cause by inserting them into the pages of their menus, all except Rosa. She didn't have the usual pocket type menu pages so she went one step further and printed my advertising directly on to the menu page itself.

Everybody's co-operation was reciprocated in the only way I knew how: by gladly handing out business cards, giving personal recommendations and where possible, linking to websites.

Every poster had an easy to follow map which the majority of people understood and were able to follow, but it was inevitable there would be the odd one or two who didn't, or couldn't, and ended up getting hopelessly lost; blaming the map of course. As a rule, tourists weren't poster vandals, at least not intentionally, but there's always a first time for everything! A couple walked into The Gallery one morning looking extremely pleased with themselves, while at the same time waving a piece of familiar looking yellow paper in the air.

'Ah Peter, we've found you at last, it's a good job we had this poster.'

'Oh great, where did you get it?' I asked in disbelief.

'It was close to the Mediterranee hotel in Lassi and we weren't sure if we'd remember the way without it, oh by the way it 's a great map.'

Fair comment I suppose. They weren't to know a poster was stapled to almost every telegraph pole from Lassi to Argostoli, which, had they known, they could have followed to The Gallery door; a bit like playing paper chase.

Having worked in a sales job some years ago I've always remembered what Frank, my boss told me, 'Peter, if you don't tell, you won't sell.' And similarly, like hard onions and never use boiling water, I've never forgotten his words. I was relying on selling my paintings to make a living, and at every opportunity I told everybody what I was doing. It didn't matter who, or how, the important thing was that everyone knew. Ultimately, Poster Power became a hugely successful part of my communication network.

The Cash Register

The first thing the accountant said when I told him about The Gallery was, 'You will need a cash register.'

But when I told Lefteris, he said, 'B****cks, of course you won't.' On the strength of his words of wisdom I thought I'd better check with Dimitris again.

'Dimitri are you certain I'll need a cash register?'

He looked confused and scratched his head. 'Certain, what is this word?' Because he wasn't sure I re-phrased it.

'Sorry Dimitri, are you sure I will need a cash register?' which that time he understood.

The misunderstanding of a single word then could prove to be costly later, and because the tax office would be involved at some stage, the slightest mistake would mean there would be hell to pay.

After a few more moments of head scratching he looked up from his desk and smiled (which was something he didn't do very often), 'No, you won't need one.' Even then I had my doubts, and sure enough a couple of weeks later my suspicions were proved right when he said I'd have to have one after all.

I couldn't afford a new one, so I talked to Lefteris about getting a used model. His fingers were in so many pies and if anyone could help me to find one cheap he could, because whereas Stathis was the Oracle, Lefteris was Mr Do-It-All.

He told me to go and see a guy in Vergotis Street, saying confidently, 'Peter, you'll get a cheap one there, but be sure to tell him I sent you.'

Which I did, but the name dropping didn't make any difference. He looked down his nose at me as though I'd just crawled out from under a stone, so there and then I decided he'd be the last person in the world I'd do business with, even if he had the cheapest machine in Argostoli.

All was not lost though, and shortly after I bought one from a shop at the top of Vyronos Street. Lefteris wasn't too happy when I told him, pouring forth the usual stream of expletives, including the already mentioned parts of the male anatomy.

Buying a cash register would, I thought, be a straightforward transaction in that it was simply a case of walking into the shop, paying the money, taking it away, plugging it in, reading the instructions and using it. That however, was pure wishful thinking on my part, because until then nothing had been that easy, so why did I think it would be any different that time?

Unfortunately there were more mind numbing visits to the tax office, and like the eternal guardian angel, Eleni was on hand to help. As well as having to register the machine in my name, the previous owner's details, all stored on a memory chip, had to be deleted first. That was where the super technical guy from Vyronos came in, and once the Tax Office had given their approval with the usual signing and stamping, he delivered it to The Gallery.

What then followed was a crash course on how to use it, after which he handed me the instruction book (which was printed in Italian), as if to say, 'You're on your own now chum,' and left, never to be seen again. Eventually I got the hang of using it, although there was one fiddly, but important task I could never master; that was changing the paper receipt rolls. Once again though Lefteris was there to help.

When I look back he really was a star, and I do have a lot to thank him for. Throughout my life anything to do with machines or technology has generally sent my stress levels soaring, because the harder I tried, the worse things got, and the cash register was no different. Within weeks of taking delivery the receipt feed spool stopped working which caused the paper to jam. After trying a couple of times to phone the guy at Vyronos, but unsuccessfully, I went there only to find the shop locked up and completely empty; as I said, never to be seen again.

'Oh no, now I really have got to be technical,' I thought, and I was. It didn't take long to perfect my own spool feeding technique: as I gently pulled the paper from the machine it stopped jamming, and more importantly the print was legible, which was vital, because the receipts were scrupulously checked every month at the Tax Office.

The cash register served its purpose for the amount of times it was used, but what completely puzzled me was why I had to have one at all. I was a painter, a one man band, all I was trying to do was make a living selling a few pictures.

My wise and philosophical Greek friends shrugged their shoulders and smiled as I poured forth my tales of woe.

'Peter, this is Greece, what do you expect?' they would say.

But they knew the system, and more importantly they knew how to work it.

Total Strangers

The website, and in particular The Diary, was attracting interest from visitors around the world and emails from total strangers were hitting the in-box on a daily basis. The very first one opened with the words, 'Hi Peter, it's Andrea from Liverpool…'

She and her boyfriend Ian were holidaying and promised to visit The Gallery, which they did. The moment they walked through the door it was as though I already knew them, like a sixth sense, or maybe their scouse accents made it obvious who they were.

Regular diary readers Spiro and Connie, Greek Australians from Sydney were visiting his family in the mountain village of Demoutsandata and made their entrance one morning with big smiles and a carrier bag! Once again the sixth sense kicked in, although it could have been their accent giving them away as well. He definitely looked Kefalonian, but as soon as he opened his mouth there was only one place in the world he could've been from.

'Hi Pete, I'm Spiro and this is my wife Connie, and here's a little something from Australia.'

'Thanks, it's great to meet you both at last, and after so many emails it's like we've known each other for years.'

He handed me the carrier bag which had two bottles of Penfolds wine in it, then I told them about the sixth sense. Spiro and Connie became close friends and at the time I didn't realise just how close, because when I was on my knees and in need of friends they were there.

Peter at work in the Gallery

With the internet, and in particular a friendly website I was catching up with long lost acquaintances from the distant past, which included an Evesham couple, Alan and Jane. He and I, in our teens, had worked together as apprentices for the same building company. By a sheer coincidence they were holidaying in Lassi and took time out to visit The Gallery. After so many years there was a lot of catching up to do.

Because we were receiving so many emails it was difficult to answer them all and to remember individually who they were all from, which could sometimes be a bit embarrassing, even more so when they turned up at The Gallery. Introductions would go something like this:

'Hi Peter, I emailed some time ago, did you get it?'
Followed by my, 'Welcome, thanks for the mail, are you

enjoying your holiday?' Unfortunately the sixth sense didn't kick in every time.

The French Connection

I was enjoying my usual morning walk to The Gallery along the quayside when I recognised the couple strolling arm in arm towards me, monsieur with his beard, and mademoiselle with her distinctive short black hair, so I greeted them in their native tongue, French. It was a very surprised Pascale and Patrice, our friends from Paris, who had come to see us and take a holiday at the same time. During their stay we saw a lot of them, especially in the evenings when, if we weren't eating out, we'd be treated to Pascale's superb cooking, which we enjoyed relaxing on their balcony overlooking the harbour.

Our times together weren't always spent eating though and one Sunday I took them, or should I say they took me, on a guided tour of the island. Kefalonian roads are completely different to the boulevards of Paris, but the majority of Kefalonian and Parisian drivers have one thing in common; they're mad. So Patrice didn't seem to notice the difference, and throwing caution to the wind he drove the little Fiat hire car around the tightest hairpins and along some of the roughest tracks on the island. Perhaps deep inside he was a wannabe rally driver, whereas deep inside me were the unmistakeable symptoms of car sickness.

On a completely separate occasion, and in no way linked to them was another French connection. A family of sailors had been to The Gallery early one evening and invited Pam and me aboard their boat for a drink, which we politely accepted, and because Pam's French language skills were a little rusty, we thought it would be good practice for her. Their catamaran was moored near the Port Authority office close to the quayside steps, but not close enough, and to make matters worse there was no gang plank. An inflatable dinghy bridged the gap between the boat and the quay wall and stepping in and out of it was the only way of getting on board, balancing precariously on what proved to be a very unstable floating 'stepping stone'.

Our French hosts didn't have a problem and demonstrated more than once the boarding technique to show us how easy it was. But it wasn't, especially after drinking large quantities of their brandy. Attempting to get back on dry land was even more hazardous than the earlier boarding fiasco had been.

More Chance Meetings

Kefalonia is such a beautiful island which is why so many people return there year after year. Some of them, over the years were destined to become welcome visitors to The Gallery, as friendships were forged through the occasional chance meeting.

I usually closed in the evening at around nine o'clock, and if Pam and I were eating out, which during the summer was often, it was safe to say we'd meet in one of our favourite tavernas, and on one of those particular 'eating out' evenings we were meeting at Portside.

As I walked through the front entrance a familiar voice close by said, 'Hello again.'

Earlier that evening a couple from Nottingham had been to The Gallery, and as well as looking for paintings they were also looking for somewhere to eat, so Portside was where I sent them. As we chatted, Pam, from a distant table could see us, but didn't have a clue what was going on and sat patiently waiting for me to join her. After a quick explanation she made her way back with me to make up the four, but because she was starting work early the next morning didn't stay late, I hadn't intended to either.

However, the three of us were in full flow and it wasn't until the early hours when Richard, Deborah and I left, well wined and dined.

Through another coincidence a friendship developed with another couple, but not particularly because of The Gallery (well, I suppose in a roundabout sort of way it was). Ian and Ann loved the island and visited as often as possible, which in some cases was twice a year. Having just closed for the evening I called in next door for an aperitif and was enjoying the pleasure of my own company when Lefteris strolled over.

'Peter, I know you told me before but I've forgotten, where in England did you live before coming to Argostoli?'

'Swindon,' I said, 'why?'

'Yes, now you say it I remember. You see that couple sitting at the bar,' pointing in their direction, 'they live there too, go over and say hello.'

So I did, and once again the seeds of another lasting friendship were sown.

Monkeys On Bikes

It's fair to say that living in Kefalonia had its moments, many of which were enjoyable, but occasionally there was the unwelcome and unexpected. I arrived at work one evening, about three weeks after first opening, to find a children's play park in the early stages of construction on the tarmac area between The Gallery and Rizospaston. The rides included elephants on wheels, bouncing castles, a huge inflatable red dragon, and Sarah's favourite, monkeys on bikes.

She and Bradley were visiting and thought the playground was great fun, but it took me a little longer to appreciate the funny side. Although noisy, thankfully it was only there for the summer and opened in the evenings only, then in September as the schools started back it was packed up until the following summer. Then once again that area became an impromptu football pitch for the youngsters living locally.

To coincide with the surprise of the fairground, Lefteris, with that wonderful big smile of his presented me with a little job, or rather a big chore.

'Peter, watering the roses is your responsibility, they come with the building and belong to you.'

'But I don't want them...' My words of protest fell on deaf ears and before I could finish he'd turned and walked away.

The roses grew in four big concrete tubs on the small square in front of The Gallery and although watering them was no big deal (I used Lefteris' hose, and his water), I hated it, like I hate all gardening, always have, always will. It was though only a summer job because, during the winter, rain did my work for me and the plants looked after themselves. Eventually though, thanks to the strangling effect of bindweed and the acidity of cat's pee, my gardening duties came to an end. Unlike some jobs in Greece, watering the roses wasn't for life!

Double Decker Pam

When we'd visited Kefalonia as tourists, instead of hiring a car Pam and I went on two island coach tours, one to the north, the other to the south, which together gave us an overview of what I often referred to as paradise. They were great fun and on both we sat on the upper deck of a green double decker air conditioned coach, which incidentally, should not to be confused with an English double decker bus.

Pam worked through the winter at the frontisterio which closed as the summer season began and re-opened in

October as it was winding down. With that in mind she looked for a summer job and quite fancied the idea of working as a transfer rep, which involved escorting holidaymakers between the airport and their accommodation, on arrival and departure to and from the island.

Jumble Sale Fran was a director of a company in Lassi who were involved in everything from car hire to coach tours; the company also employed transfer reps. Word was out that she was recruiting summer staff, so Pam met her to discuss what was on offer. There was no formal application procedure as such, just a casual chat over coffee, but when they did eventually get round to discussing work Fran asked her what she had in mind and promptly threw her hands up in response to the reply.

'No, no, Pam, you don't want to be a transfer rep. It's boring. I've got just the thing for you; you'll love it.' And then made her an offer she couldn't refuse, working as a tour guide with some admin work thrown in.

Fran's enthusiasm was infectious and Pam left the office buzzing with anticipation. She was also given a pile of reference books to browse through; a sort of beginners' guide to tour guiding Kefalonia.

Most summer jobs involved working long hours, usually over seven days a week through six gruelling hot months of the season, but Pam didn't fancy that and negotiated guiding for three and working in the office for another two. Fran knew a good deal when she saw one, and once again there was the handshake to seal it. It was a great job and she became known as 'Double Decker Pam', and loved the work, just as Fran said she would.

A Homage To Kefalonia

Makis (yes, yet another one) came into The Gallery one morning full of intent and purpose. I'd known him since the days before we bought our washing machine, because he owned Argostoli's only launderette which was conveniently situated a short walk from our apartment, on the Lassi road. It was his first visit to The Gallery, and because he gave the paintings only a cursory glance I immediately got the impression there was something else he wanted other than a piece of my artwork, and I was right. Being Kefalonian he quickly came to the point.

'Peter, would you do me a favour please?'

'Yes Maki, of course, what is it? By the way, if it involves me giving you money, forget it, I'm not interested.'

He smiled.

'I'm making a DVD called Homage to Kefalonia. The filming is complete and now we're recording the narratives. The Greek, German and Italian versions are finished which leaves just the English to record, and that's where you come in. You have a good voice, just perfect for what we want, will you do it?'

Makis paused, smiled again, and before I could reply added, 'Oh, and by the way, you won't get paid, but it won't cost you anything either, just a few minutes of your time.'

I wasn't concerned about a few minutes of my time, knowing it would be nearer to a few hours, and not getting paid didn't matter either. I could already see euro signs flashing in front of my eyes, and besides, becoming a film narrator was another Kefalonian challenge.

'Maki, I don't care about not being paid and yes I'll do it, but on one condition; I want The Gallery to be included in the film credits and on the DVD packaging, oh, and just one other thing, would you please let me have a copy of the script I'll be reading from.'

'OK Peter, thank you.' We then shook hands to seal the deal. A couple of days later he brought the script to The Gallery, where between visitors I learnt my lines, or at least I thought I had.

It was some weeks before I saw him again and then one steaming hot July evening he rushed into The Gallery out of the summer heat, and because Kefalonians don't normally rush anywhere I guessed there was something in the air.

'Peter, we're all ready for you to start.'

'Great Maki, just let me know when.'

'Tonight, we're doing it tonight.'

'Tonight!'

My reply must have sounded like an echo.

Then as suddenly as he'd appeared he was gone again, driving off in his beat-up Renault only to return a few minutes later with a bag containing refreshments, Bacardi, coke and other liquid delights. I'd wondered why he'd asked me what I drank, before dashing out.

When Makis, with all the chaos of a hurricane, blew into The Gallery that evening he'd startled some visitors by his sudden appearance and behaviour.

'It looks like you'll be closing early tonight then,' one of them said with an air of curiosity.

Kefalonians by their very nature aren't the best communicators in the world, especially when it involves planning more than a few days ahead, or in Makis's case a few hours. Once again it's an impulse thing.

The recording studio was in a building on the busy Vergotis Street, almost opposite the Metropolis Cathedral, and was also the office of 'Icon' audio systems, the business partnership of the sound brothers, Makis and Costas. Once sound checks and other preliminaries had been completed, and more importantly the mixing of Bacardi and Coke, I settled in my chair and waited for the signal to start. Makis (the sound) gave Makis (the laundrette) the nod, who then gave me the thumbs up.

I felt quite nervous at first, but having worked hard at perfecting the text, within seconds I was into my stride and away. Everything was going well until I reached the words 'Abies Cephalonica'.

They have haunted me ever since that evening, yes, even when I watch the DVD, because it was then that my train of speech was abruptly interrupted by Makis (the laundrette) as he loudly interjected, 'Cut, cut.'

'Bloody hell,' I thought, 'what have I done wrong?'

For a couple of moments, which felt more like a couple of hours, there was an unnerving silence and all eyes were fixed on me, homing in like eagles to their prey. Makis, with a voice as cold as stone said, 'Peter, the stress is in the wrong place,' which to a Kefalonian is totally unacceptable. Then what followed was a crash course in stress management, as we trawled over the finer points of where that particular stress went. I repeated it several times until he was completely satisfied it was right, then once he was, I waited for them to give each other the nod to re-start, and then more grief.

Makis (the sound), with a face as long as an English winter and in total stress (he obviously hadn't done the course) said, 'Maki there is a big problem. The microphones have picked up traffic noise from the street and it's on all the recording, we will have to start from the beginning and do it again.'

Great! That was all I needed. Obviously, all that was said in Greek (and kindly translated for my benefit), but I could tell from their voices and negative body language something was seriously wrong, and then, to add more confusion to the existing, the unbelievable happened, my phone rang; and once again all eyes were on me.

'Thank heaven for traffic noise,' I thought, great timing though. It was Nick Edwards. Needless to say, after the call I switched my phone off.

Once again and after adjustments to knobs, switches, slide controls and more slurps of Bacardi another attempt was made to re-start the recording. Makis the technical sound wizard gave the go ahead and we were ready to roll, all I had to do was focus, relax, and more importantly, stay awake.

Makis (the launderette) had obviously been influenced by the great maestros of the classical music podium, because on that second take he conducted me as if I was a one man symphony orchestra. On the approach to those dreaded words for the second time I twitched inside as the tension in the studio rose around me. But it was sheer perfection and we continued through to the final breath with no further stress fractures, as though nothing had ever happened.

As my final words melted into the silence of the studio, and Makis switched off his equipment, I felt the unforgettable feeling of total relief and satisfaction, then at that very moment there was spontaneous applause accompanied by the shaking of hands, slapping of backs and hearty congratulations all round. I felt great, it was as though electricity was running through my veins.

'Well done Peter, and thank you,' Makis said.

In spite of the minor interruptions and irritations the evening had gone amazingly well; but there was more to come. Arrangements had been made to meet Pam, Stathis, Irini, Patrice and Pascale at Portside at eleven, and with only a few minutes to spare I phoned to say I'd be a little late and there might be company.

Having told Makis about my plans, and knowing he

had something similar in mind, I suggested, 'Why don't we all go to Portside?' So we did.

There must have been over twenty people in total by the time we were all seated, which meant Rosa had to make some rapid adjustments to her table layout to accommodate everybody. Traditionally Kefalonians eat late, but as well as eating late there is another Kefalonian tradition involving pride and honour when it comes to paying the bill. It's usual (but not always the case) for the bill to be presented to the person who calls for it, and not just placed on the table, then that person normally pays. In that particular case it was Makis (the laundrette), and being truly Kefalonian he upheld the tradition. At one point though Stathis, who is also truly Kefalonian, wanted to pay, but Makis would hear of no such thing, because it was his honour and pride that was at stake.

Pam and I were prepared, and would have been happy to pay our share no matter how many ways it was split. That was normal procedure for us when eating out in company, and that included Kefalonian company (so much for tradition). We weren't Kefalonian and we didn't have to hold with tradition, so it was always a shared bill.

DVD Cover- Homage to Kefalonia © *NOKI 2002*

A few weeks after the recording session Makis invited me to watch the finished DVD which in every way is a very beautiful visual experience. He was the driving force behind the whole project and made frequent cameo appearances; he's the one with the rugged Kefalonian features, beard and cap.

My contribution was appreciated and he happily kept his word by including The Gallery on credits and packaging. The Gallery also became a lucrative outlet for a unique insight and an amazing 'Homage to Kefalonia'.

Nick Edwards

It was a stroke of pure luck that I ever met Nick Edwards at all. He worked for the Rough Guide travel books and was on the island updating the Kefalonia section of 'The Ionian Islands' edition. I'd been given his telephone number by another travel writer, Klaus, from the 'Marco Polo' travel guides who had called into The Gallery the evening before the recording session. When I'd phoned Nick's accommodation in Argostoli a young woman answered.

'Sorry, Nick is not here, please call again?'

Phoning again was always a bit hit and miss, so I told her, 'Please, you must tell Nick to call me as soon as he can, this is business and it's very important,' and with that I gave her my number. The rest as they say was in the lap of the gods, Greek gods. I don't know if 'important' is a Greek word, but that's where I put the stress.

The gods were smiling, because Nick came to The Gallery the morning after the recording session where we talked for about an hour. It's amazing how I'd built up a mental picture of him, because I imagined he would be a smartly dressed journalist with a middle England accent, but what actually appeared that morning was exactly the opposite. He was shortish and although balding, the full beard and moustache more than made up for any loss on top. His tie-dye tee shirt had seen better days and was stretched over a rotund stomach that hung over the waist band of a pair of faded shorts. His sun kissed feet sported a pair of well worn leather sandals and Nick's accent was more middle London than middle England, which proves, especially in that case, you can't judge a book by looking at the cover.

We got on famously, and he listened intently as I unravelled my story so far. During the few days he was around I introduced him to Lefteris who was totally knocked out, not only by Nick's hippy-like appearance, which in a way was similar to his own, but also by his fluent Greek; so fluent in fact, that at first Lefteris refused to believe he was English. In turn Nick thought the pub was great and couldn't thank me enough for taking him there. Subsequently, Pub Old House, along with The Gallery appeared in the next printing of the Rough Guide.

That Evening In July

At the end of July there were fierce and frequent electrical storms with torrential rain that lasted on and off for several days. The locals couldn't believe it, and many of Argostoli's senior citizens were adamant they'd never seen rain in July before. 'Well,' I thought, 'that's stretching it a bit,' and put it down to long term memory loss, while at the same time blaming the intense summers they'd endured over the years. The blazing summer heat really does affect the memory, even over a short period, and I write from experience. On the interior of the north wall of The Gallery, the Pub end, there were two grilles forming part of a ducting vent for a useless cooling/heating system that I'd only ever switched on once, and almost choked on the dust it had belched out.

One evening during the heavy rain I heard water trickling through the top grille onto the floor, and it wasn't long before the trickle became a steady flow.

'Oh b****cks,' I thought, and took the necessary action of removing all paintings from that wall before standing back in a state of mild shock and disbelief. Fortunately, thanks to the slight fall of the tiled floor the water found its way under the wash-room door and down the small circular drain under the wash basin. Due to the continual flow of water through the ducting, the chipboard wall covering was completely saturated and had to be replaced, so once again I turned to the ever reliable Colin for help. Once the rain had stopped he assessed the damage and, more importantly, found the cause, but that wasn't until we'd been up on the roof.

A low parapet wall had been built round the perimeter of the building's flat roof, with a rainwater outlet at each end of the back wall. But because the roof sloped upwards to the drain at the far corner (and because water doesn't flow uphill) it was useless and served no purpose, while the one at the other end had a brick wedged into it, rendering it useless too. As a consequence, when heavy rain fell and water levels rose to a critical depth there was only one place it could go, and that was through the ducting and into The Gallery, which it did.

I took the only action available to prevent any further flooding and removed the brick, whereupon the impact was instant. Once the outlet was clear the water flowed through it, and with nothing to hold it back, the water level on the roof dropped, while in the yard below it quickly rose to form a mini lake, which unfortunately was right in front of the door to the owner's apartment; oh dear.

After that, the days of a waterlogged Gallery were over. Colin re-built (and repainted) a new chipboard wall with a cavity behind it, and although rain still trickled through the ducting it was only after the severest storms, which, compared to that evening in July, were few and far between.

A Problem with the Boiler

When we had the phone connected in the apartment Pam drew the short straw and it sat on her bedside cupboard. There weren't many calls, especially late at night, but at about 2.45 on the morning of Sunday 29th September it rang.

'It'll be a wrong number,' I mumbled as she answered it, 'so whoever it is just tell them to get lost.'

'It's for you,' she said, 'you tell them.'

'Hello baby.' I recognised the caller's deep whiskey sodden voice straight away, because there were only three people on the island who called me baby.

'Lefteris don't you realise what the time is, I hope this call is important.'

'Yes it's very important, there's a flood in The Gallery, you'd better come quick.' I was wide awake and fully dressed in seconds, and got there at the double.

As Vangelis, a regular, was leaving the pub he'd noticed water running down The Gallery steps, so he alerted Lefteris, who in turn alerted me. Having used the spare key to let themselves in they traced the leak to the hot water boiler in the cupboard, and with water lapping round his feet Lefteris leapt into action, risking electrocution to switch it off, then he turned the mains supply off. By the time I arrived the leaking had stopped but the floor was still awash. I swore a bit, swept as much away as possible, swore a bit more, joined Vangelis and Lefteris for a nightcap, then went back home to bed.

The floor had completely dried overnight and the following morning Stathis came and disconnected the boiler from the main electricity supply. I never repaired or replaced it, and forever after cleaned my brushes with cold water.

'Hello baby.' That was the greeting from a little Albanian boy who lived up the road from us, he was about four years old, if that. We knew most of the kids in the neighbourhood and as they got to know us there was always a cheery 'Hello', or a friendly wave. That was, except for the young Yiorgos (pronounced yourgoss), who at that tender age didn't have a clue what 'hello' meant, let alone 'baby'. But all that changed over the years with extra tuition at the frontisterio, and as his English steadily improved it became a pleasure to talk with him. And of course, by that time he knew exactly what 'Hello Baby' actually meant.

Too Hot To Work

There were times when adverse weather, and not only rain, caused problems, well, not so much problems… minor irritations. Back in the dark evenings of winter when Lefteris and I were discussing 'Café Mystique' he'd said something that I really didn't take too much notice of at the time.

'Peter, you might want to erect shades above the windows to keep the sun out, especially the two front ones, because as it rises, it gets very hot in there, and even having the doors and windows open doesn't help much.'

Having survived the heat of one Kefalonian summer I knew how exhausting it was, but thought, 'Ah it won't be that bad, and anyway I'm not spending money to improve someone else's property,' and because I wasn't going to be there for ever it was pointless.

It wasn't long after moving into The Gallery that I was painting again, canvas, not chipboard, and although the weather was quite warm all went well, that was until about half way through June, which was when Lefteris's prophetic words rang true and the air temperature quickly rose. As the heat of the rising sun blasted through the east facing doors and windows it created The Gallery's own greenhouse effect. It was then that painting stopped for a few weeks, and in that time I read a lot, wrote a lot, perspired a lot and given the opportunity talked a lot. However the intense heat didn't last too long and, after all that reading, writing, talking and perspiring, in the relative cool of September I once again became a slave to the easel, continuing to paint almost non-stop until the following June when once again it became too hot to work.

A Wedding

Not only was The Theatre in Argostoli a Mecca for entertainment, it also doubled up as a venue for civil weddings, and one morning in October Dimitris and Julie were married there. After the short ceremony everyone disappeared, only to meet up again at the Phaedra for the evening reception.

It seemed odd to see Dimitris inside the taverna and not hovering at the entrance in his usual role as The Smooth Operator, even though he did glance over that way a couple of times, and wearing his big infectious smile was heard to say, 'Sometimes it's difficult to separate work from pleasure.'

Over the years, getting married in Kefalonia became a popular tourist attraction and could be arranged for a fee, as businesses specialised in organising matrimonial bliss - marriage on a package no less. The stunning locations of some of the island's churches made for wonderful memories for many newly weds, although there were no guarantees for the longevity of the contract.

A Night In The Gallery

There was never a dull moment at The Gallery, which is what made it so special. One evening in October, as heavy rain poured steadily and the wind howled like wolves in the wilderness, the door flew open and in rushed a very agitated and extremely wet Prue with Lizzie in tow.

'Oh Pete, guess what they've bloody well done now!'

So, full of sympathy and doing my best to keep a straight face I asked, 'Go on then Prue, tell me, what have they bloody well done now?'

'They've cancelled the ferry that's what, and I'm not paying for a taxi to go the long way round, it'll cost a fortune.' Then with a big smile she came out with the punch line, 'Pete, could I sleep in The Gallery tonight?'

'Of course you can Prue, but you know the floor's rock hard, so you'll need something soft to lie on.'

For a moment I'd forgotten she'd lived in caves, travelled with the circus and hardly switched the heating on in her house, so compared to some of her previous accommodation The Gallery was five star. After borrowing some makeshift bedding from Lefteris she was 'full of beans', but only until the following morning. The storms continued through the night and were still raging the next day, so the ferry still wasn't sailing. A rather disgruntled Prue had no other choice than to hire a taxi, which was never a problem in Argostoli, the town was full of them.

International Artist

In its first summer season The Gallery had been a great success, much more than I could have ever imagined. It was a great feeling; I was one of the happiest men on the planet. In the past I'd often been accused of being a dreamer, but because I was making a living from painting it was no longer a dream. Although most of my visitors were from the United Kingdom, they also came from other countries, near and far, which gave The Gallery a certain cosmopolitan feel, and because so many bought paintings, with tongue in cheek I wondered if that qualified me enough to really call myself an 'international artist'! It sounds a bit pretentious, I know, but there was another painter on the island who was using the self same description.

Ultimately though, I was happy doing what I loved doing best, and the 'international' thing was only a thought. Perhaps it was me dreaming again.

Walkabout: First stop Skala

At the end of October and coinciding exactly with the last day of the season I closed The Gallery and went on holiday, but it would be no ordinary holiday. No, it was a time to reflect, as well as a time to look ahead.

As the last charter flights departed I packed my rucksack and set off on a Kefalonian walkabout; a hitch-hiking trip round the island, where my accommodation would be a mixture of rented rooms and people's kindness. Skala was the first planned overnight stop, and en-route I stopped off in the delightful fishing village of Katelios for an early lunch. My first lift had dropped me off in Markopoulo, and as I walked towards the Katelios seafront I couldn't help noticing just how quiet everything was, and considering it was only the last day of the season there wasn't a sign to suggest any kind of activity, past or present, anywhere. There were no cleaners, no owners, even the swimming pools were bone dry, it was as though the place had been closed for months; it was deserted.

Luckily for me not everybody had closed their doors, because near the waterfront one of the tavernas was just about open so I went in and ordered a light bite before they too changed their minds and locked up.

'That's six euros and eighty cents please,' the guy with a serious growth of facial stubble said as I pushed my empty plate away.

'What, that's a lot of money for a salad and a small bottle of water!'

Then a lecture followed on the subtle difference between offering value for money and ripping people off. Having just spent most of my summer evenings eating in various Argostoli tavernas I was familiar with what cost what and wasn't about to be turned over because I was English and carrying a rucksack.

Then, after taking a few minutes of serious ear bashing a rather agitated Stubble said, 'OK. OK. You eat for free.'

'No, I don't want to eat for free, and I don't mind paying, but what you're asking is too much.'

And that really did baffle him, especially as I was still offering to pay. While I had been eating, I'd also been sketching. Through the window was a nice little view of a handful of small fishing boats tied up in the shelter of the breakwater.

'Do you like the picture?' I asked Stubble who was still in shock, to which he nodded.

'Then take it, it's yours as payment for the snack.' I didn't know if he was happy with the gesture but he took it all the same.

Leaving Katelios, and walking past the swaying eucalyptus trees and pampas grass which softly whispered in the light breeze, a builder's truck pulled up.

'Get in,' the driver (who was Polish, and one of a multitude of Europeans working on the island) said, so I squeezed in beside the assortment of tools that cluttered the cab, and it wasn't long before we arrived in Skala. He was an interesting bloke and the conversation flowed, but I kicked myself as he drove off, having completely forgotten to ask if he knew of anywhere I could stay that night.

Skala, like Katelios had all but closed for the 'winter', but eventually I found a room tucked away behind a bar in the main street, lovely people, but what a dump, and, for the time of the year it was cold. During the afternoon I wandered the huge deserted beach before lazing close to the rocks at the western end. Unknown to me then, another, and far more interesting Skala that not many visitors knew about lay hidden and deserted in the lower slopes of the mountains, and if I'd known about it then I'd have been up there like a shot. That time however, would come in the not too distant future.

The Walk To Poros

The walk from Skala to Poros is beautiful as it twists and turns to hug the coastline all the way to one of the island's main ferry ports. Travelling along that road was always an unforgettable experience, whether by foot or on wheels. The early morning sun was bright and reflected the millions of sparkling diamonds dancing softly on the gentle swell of the silver sea with the distant milky pink mountains of mainland Greece clearly visible. It was so inviting, and because there was much to see I gave up all thoughts of hitching; Poros wasn't so far to walk.

As arranged, I met our Dutch friend Ellen at the ferry port before settling in one of the towns cafés, where over coffee we brought each other up to date with our news. Having an afternoon to kill and knowing what a keen walker I was she suggested a mountain trek that would fill the hours. Until she mentioned it I'd never heard of Mount Atros, nor the monastery that commands spectacular views from its lofty perch high on the mountain's eastward side, so anticipating the discovery of another Kefalonian gem I set off in the warmth of the afternoon sun.

The monastery was still open to visitors when I got there, but only just, because it too was about to close for the winter. Apostoli, the guy who looked after all things holy, including the resident monk, looked after me too with an offering of Greek coffee, ouzo, Turkish delight and biscuits. After that much needed sustenance he gave me a guided tour of the monastery which is reputed to be the oldest, and, at 760 meters above sea level, the highest on the island. Despite the major refurbishment works that were in progress it still felt very sacred, and above all, peaceful.

Although they miss out on some of life's other pleasures because of their vows of celibacy, those monks don't have it all bad.

The Mountain Stage

After breakfast and thanking Ellen for her hospitality, I got off to another early start. It was a bright morning that greeted me on the walk up through the gorge out of Poros as I headed for Sami and the mountain stage of The Walkabout.

Within minutes of arriving at the Sami turn a small bright blue pick-up truck stopped, and as it did I noticed a passenger already in the cab and thought, 'That'll be a tight squeeze.' The driver, typically Kefalonian, sporting a flat cap and a huge moustache that covered most of his sun baked face pointed to the back of the truck and beckoned me to climb on, so I did, tucking in behind the cab so as to avoid any draught.

Those pick-up trucks are common on the island and were driven either by maniac builders, or the slower and more considerate farmers. Fortunately for me my driver was of farming stock which meant there was no danger of being bounced around the back all the way to Sami.

The sun was already high and the air as clear in the mountains as it had been at sea level, with views that stretched away for miles into the distance. It was, as it always is on that road, nothing short of spectacular. The considerate farmer negotiated every bend as carefully as he could, but found it difficult avoiding all the pot holes and bumps of which there were many, and my occasional discomfort highlighted just how bad the road surface was in places.

Modern concrete buildings and ruined stone shells stood side by side in the remote mountain villages we drove through as reminders of the past and present. There were other settlements, which, having been reduced to rubble by the force of the earthquake were now totally deserted, and had become partially obscured or even totally hidden from view by the contours of the wooded mountain slopes and valleys on either side of the road. Occasionally the distinct and distant music of goat bells drifted into ear shot on the wind, with glimpses of the odd one or two whose camouflage failed to hide them completely.

The olives were ready for harvesting and weighed heavily on the ancient boughs whose leaves shone green and silver as they danced in the soft morning breeze; the olives themselves glistened in the dazzling light like precious black stones.

Despite the natural air conditioning on the back of the truck, that mountain ride really was the ultimate trip.

My overnight accommodation in Sami was basic, as basic as it got; they should have been paying me to stay there! A central corridor, sandwiched between two spartan bedrooms on either side ran the length of the building, with a single bathroom and toilet at the end. Adjacent to it and tucked away in the corner was my room, and because I was the only 'guest', there was never any danger of being woken by banging doors, a flushing toilet or other sounds of the night; whether natural or passionate.

Having arrived in Sami by mid morning there was enough time to spend the rest of the day exploring, so I did, and headed in an upwards direction towards Agrilion Monastery, but didn't quite make it, stopping at the tiny hamlet of Dichala instead. There, a cluster of earthquake ruins are situated high above Sami Bay, just before the road drops steeply to Antisamos Beach. Along with Antisamos, Dichala was one of a number of locations in the Sami area which were used for the film 'Captain Corelli's Mandolin'.

To my delight the olive harvest was in progress when I arrived. The modern Kefalonian technique of harvesting the olives is by 'raking' or 'combing' them from the branches onto fine mesh netting that is laid out under the trees, but the elderly woman carrying out her task that morning was far from modern.

She was beating hell out of the tree with a big stick, and I asked the guy who was looking on, casually leaning against his car, 'Why is she doing it that way?'

Olive Harvest
Painting, oil on canvas
by Peter Hemming

111

'That is the traditional way to harvest the olives; it is my mother and she always does it that way.'

His mother was traditionally dressed too, in black from head to toe, which contrasted dramatically with her white shoulder length hair. That traditional scene made a great photo, and when I explained to him why I was taking it he translated to mum, whose face lit up with a big broad smile.

After stepping out of a brief time warp I sat amongst the ruins to take in the view before heading back to Sami, stopping momentarily to watch the mayhem and general chaos following the docking of the Patras ferry as it unloaded its assortment of mechanical and human cargo. Minutes later, and in complete contrast, an air of tranquillity greeted me on the approach to Karavomilos, a short walk along the shoreline from the town. The strong afternoon sun highlighted the blue church tower against the dark distant mountains. The branches of the giant eucalyptus trees creaked and groaned in protest, leaning like drunken men, against the sea breeze; and to complete that idyllic scene a handful of small fishing boats rolled gently in the lee side of the small jetty ahead. Soon I reached the pond where children excitedly fed the ducks who noisily flapped and quacked as they fought for every thrown morsel. The pond is fed by the overflow from the nearby underground Melissani lake, which then overflows into the sea, thereby completing an amazing journey!

The Melissani lake is continuously fed by sea water from the 'sink holes' at the Katavothres, near Argostoli, from where it flows through underground tunnels to its final destination... the sea. Research was carried out in 1963 when coloured dyes were dropped into the sink holes, the dyes then took fourteen days to appear, having travelled from one side of the island to the other. That is truly remarkable.

For me there was something special about Karavomilos that afternoon, with its picture book jetty scene, which along with the 'traditional' olive harvester became another of my best selling paintings.

Heading North

After the overnight stay in Sami I retraced my steps of the previous afternoon and walked through Karavomilos the following morning, heading north to Anti Pata. It was quiet along the road to Agia Efimia, even for a Sunday, except for the sound of rolling pebbles being washed by the ebb and flow of the gentle Ionian tide in and out of the small coves dotted along that coastline. Like so many of the island's coast roads it too is stunningly beautiful, so the walk to Agia Efimia, like the one to Poros was no big deal; but I was ready for breakfast when I got there; coffee and spinach pie never tasted better.

I was soon on my feet again and hadn't walked for more than a few minutes before getting a lift to Diverata, the village above Myrtos where three main roads meet, leading north, south and eastward. Continuing north, the village slowly disappeared behind me as I began the long steep climb to be rewarded with unrivalled views across Myrtos, which is reputed to be the most photographed beach in Europe. The views to begin with were just glimpses and snatches over roof tops and through the branches of trees, but by the time I'd reached the pull-in at the top of the climb it had become a spectacular panorama. The blinding strip of white beach hundreds of feet below was being pounded by a kaleidoscope of turquoise and bubbling white sea that was, as always, fantastically photogenic in the Kefalonian sun.

From a vehicle, even a slow moving one, the onlooker gets only the briefest of sightings from the road, but for me, 'walking it' was the ultimate Myrtos experience.

The village of Anti Pata is about five kilometres from Fiskardo and unusually boasts a fine Russian Orthodox church which is set back from the main road. Christian and Carol, my hosts, had been worried because I was running late (due only to a lack of traffic, after all it was Sunday) and were about to start lunch as I arrived, which was again, more great timing.

Despite the changeable weather, I made the most of my stay with them and spent a lot of time walking. Christian, who knew the area like the back of his hand gave me an insight into some of the hidden and overgrown pathways that he'd discovered. He would have made the perfect trekking guide. That northern tip of Kefalonia has a completely different atmosphere to the rest of the island in a strange but magical sort of way, almost like a feeling of total isolation.

A River Inlet

After my visit to the north it was time to head west, and as Christian and Carol were driving to Argostoli that morning, they gave me a lift to the Lixouri turn. It was only minutes later that a Mercedes skidded to a halt about fifty metres ahead of me, leaving fresh tyre marks on the road and the smell of burning rubber in the air. As he reversed I silently cursed my luck, got in and belted up.

'You won't need that, I'm a safe driver,' he said, then, when he told me he was going all the way to Lixouri I cursed my luck even more, but I was happy, in a perverse sort of way, knowing it wasn't a long journey and wouldn't take forever, but I also knew it would be a roller coaster white knuckle ride all the way.

That road to Lixouri starts twisting and turning just past the Zola junction, from where it drops dramatically to hug the gulf of Argostoli shoreline as far as the Atheras turn, on what is a flat, and on that day, fast stretch of road.

Approaching the ruined jail on our left, a car suddenly appeared on the small side road opposite, and instinctively, like all good Kefalonian drivers, without slowing he hit the horn hard, then turning to me with a hint of madness in his eyes, said, 'You can't trust these local drivers, they're crazy.'

'Oh really,' I replied and, unlike him, focused straight ahead, keeping my thoughts to myself not wishing to betray my emotions, but at the same time preparing for the next set of bends.

It was with a massive feeling of relief that I got out of that Mercedes in one piece; body intact, but nerves shredded. Walking the short distance to Prue's from the centre of Lixouri didn't take long, just long enough to gather my composure.

'Hi Pete baby, you're early,' she said as I walked through the open door. Then over a cup of much needed tea I explained why, and gave a detailed account of the white knuckle ride before bringing her up to date with the rest of the walkabout. Then after some general chatter and more tea I set off for Vatsa Bay.

I'd been told Vatsa was completely different to anywhere else on the island, and when I got there I saw why; there's a river. The narrow inlet is crossable by foot ferry, or for the more adventurous, by swimming. In this exquisite little-known hideaway, as well as a river inlet there is also a small chapel, a horticultural plantation, small intimate beaches, a pair of vicious geese and the legendary Spyros, owner of Spiaggia, the taverna I'd heard so much about.

On the day I dropped in he wasn't there, but one of his Asian workers was. My Greek language skills were still firmly fixed at zero on a scale of one to ten, which meant there was little chance of holding any sort of coherent conversation with him, at least that's what I thought. However, having travelled so far I was determined to give it a try and I'm glad I did because it turned out to be a worthwhile exercise in sign language for both of us. As we sat facing each other breaking new ground in language tuition he handed me a beer, possibly as payment for the pencil sketch I'd just done of him, or maybe just out of kindness.

After the much improvised course in communication skills I decided to return to Lixouri by the way of Xi (pronounced ksee by cutting the k short) and Megos Lakkos beaches, which, in fact is one long continuous narrow strip of red sand, broken only by a large rock jutting into the sea at the Xi end which I would have to paddle round, and because the water was shallow I saw no problem. After slipping my shoes and trousers off I was on my way with the water lapping gently just below my knees, until suddenly and without warning it was up to my waist!

I froze with the sudden shock, stopping momentarily to catch my breath and dry my eyes, but I was so close to the rock I could almost touch it. Turning back would mean a long walk to Lixouri, whereas going forward meant stepping into the unknown. So, I took that big step forward into the unknown and thankfully into shallow water again, from where I made a rapid beeline for the beach and the safety of dry land.

Later I spent more time recapping other walkabout stories over dinner with Prue, after which I caught the ferry home to the comfort and warmth of my own bed.

What a holiday!

Mariann

Mariann, was from Oslo and became a regular visitor to The Gallery, as well as becoming a friend and 'travelling companion'. If Ingrid was the typical Nordic beauty, blonde and fair, then Mariann was exactly the opposite; I don't mean she was ugly, she wasn't. Her dark complexion was matched by her flowing jet black hair. She was tall, slim and wore long flowing skirts to compliment the jackets, blouses and unusual waistcoats she often wore, but as well as being Norwegian there was one other thing Mariann had in common with Ingrid... she had the ability to turn heads.

She lived with her son and an eccentric shaggy dog named Pako in the mountain village of Dilinata, but her house, although in a fantastic setting, was architecturally a little odd. Odd in so much that the kitchen was detached from the main residence at the rear. In effect it was a chef's out-house, and although only a few steps from the back door I thought it a bit of an inconvenience, especially when it rained, but it didn't seem to bother Mariann in the least; and anyway, the views from the front of the house more than compensated for any construction quirks.

From a bench seat in the west facing front garden, the panorama stretched way beyond Argostoli to the vast horizon of the sea; with the sun in the sky, a good book, a glass of wine and some decent music drifting through the open window it was the ideal setting.

Mariann had artistic talent too and created some nice pieces, not traditional or conventional as such, but unusual interesting craftworks which included necklaces, bracelets, earrings and other accessories that she wore with her stylish clothes.

Pam and I enjoyed her company, especially driving round the island on winter excursions. The wild Pako (who would have been an ideal mate for Lizzie) sat in the back of the car with me as the women chatted away in the front. They were happy times when we enjoyed some great laughs; but sometimes in life the laughing and happiness don't last forever.

Three Sheets To The Wind

With summer over, not many boats, except for the local fishing fleet, tied up in Argostoli. It surprised me then to see a very sleek green trimaran moored up along the quayside. She was called 'Three Sheets to the Wind' and because she was green, I thought, 'Irish', but as the Canadian flag was flying, I thought again, 'No, she'll be Canadian.'

'Good morning', the guy up top said as I walked alongside.

'And good morning to you too,' I replied, 'nice boat, and being green I thought she might be Irish.'

'No, she's Canadian,' as if to clarify a point, and at that moment a woman's head appeared from below.

'Hello, I'm Kathleen, and I see you've already met my husband Mike, would you like to come aboard for a drink?'

Very tempting, but going on past experience I wasn't

quite sure what sort of drink she had in mind, so deciding it was too early in the day to find out, I played it safe and politely refused.

'No thank you, I'm going to work.' I told them about The Gallery and in turn invited them for a drink, only what I had in mind was tea or coffee. They arrived later that morning with a bottle of Baileys to spice up the coffee, it also brought work to an abrupt end for the day, because painting and Baileys don't mix too well.

Like most boat people they had a library full of interesting seafaring tales and were generally good company, but being nomads of the sea they were soon on their way, setting sail for the somewhat cooler and damper climes of Northern Ireland where it is known to rain a lot. Why do you think it's so green?

'Sherpa'

People came, and people went, and while some stayed forever, others, like the boat people just passed through, but every so often one stuck, like chewing gum to the bottom of a shoe! We met a woman who was currently researching for her company and had visions of setting Kefalonia alight with innovative ideas for future trekking holidays in the mountains. Her experience was extraordinary, because she had climbed every major mountain range in the world, from the Alps to the Himalayas; at least that's what she was telling everybody.

Pam, along with our friends Pete and Dee and other English speakers living on the island had been to a meeting where 'the Sherpa' outlined her programme, insisting that she must recruit English speakers to ensure its success. Pam had trekked in the Himalayas and wasn't convinced that 'Sherpa' was everything she claimed to be, so through contacts in the UK she made discreet enquiries about her and the company she was supposed to be working for. Unfortunately the information she got back didn't bode well, and although the company was real enough, they'd never heard of Sherpa or Kefalonian trekking holidays, which came as no surprise to me, because I'd doubted her credibility from our first meeting.

The first time I met her, her welcome hadn't been the usual polite, 'Hello, nice to meet you,' accompanied by a customary handshake. Instead it was a curt, 'We're going to the beach, there's a small boat half full of water, we'll bale it out and drag it to the shore.'

I wasn't quite sure who she meant by 'we', but because there was no-one else around I assumed the 'we' she was referring to must have meant 'us'. I knew the boat she was talking about because it had been grounded in one of the small coves near Gradakia beach for weeks, and was not only almost totally submerged but was also half full of sand. I don't have any knowledge of marine engineering, but I do know that a boat, even a small one, half full of water and sand is very heavy, and for three people, especially one as unwilling as me, dragging it on to the beach was impossible.

Armed with only a plastic washing up bowl between us we let 'Sherpa' go first, after all it was her idea and more importantly, her bowl. Watching her was like watching a slapstick film, because the faster she baled the water out, the more it poured back in.

With memories of history lessons and King Canute I turned to Pam and said, 'I'm not hanging around to watch anymore of this nonsense, come on let's go.'

That was the last we saw of 'Sherpa', because shortly after the great salvage failure she left the island; unceremoniously escorted by the Greek Police on to a waiting plane at Kefalonia airport.

Christmas Week

Argostoli, especially the Lithostroto was awash with colour as the recently hung decorations were a reminder to everybody that Christmas was coming. At the beginning of the week Soula gave us Seasons Greetings in the shape of traditional Kefalonian cakes and sweets, and at Francesca's annual Christmas gathering there was an assortment of festive goodies, including mince pies and a huge container of deliciously warming and spicey mulled wine.

Since we'd known Stathis, some of our Saturday evenings had been spent with him, other members of the choir (also known as the gang) and their wives, for a meal and a sing along in one of the local tavernas. The Mandolino taverna in Argostoli was a popular venue where guest musicians performed, but it was the gang's habit of not only joining in, but completely taking over the show to out-sing them.

On Christmas Eve we joined the gang at the Aqua Marina club in Lassi for a 'Christmas Special' where there was a full Christmas meal and live entertainment, which included music and dancing, but something not on the menu that evening was the unexpected 'gang show'.

As the evening wore on, and once their throats were lubricated, the gang completely out-sang Makis, the hired singer. For us it was fun to be part of and Makis knew what to expect, which was just as well, because on that occasion it wasn't just the gang that took over; everybody did.

On Christmas Day it rained, so Pam and I, like almost everybody else in Argostoli stayed indoors. We opened presents, ate slightly too much, and toasted Spiros and Connie with the Penfolds, so all in all it turned out to be a lazy day. Boxing Day was far more active, and with the sun on our backs we walked to Fanari.

After the Christmas holiday Irini was going to Athens for her 'city fix', and while there she would get some art materials for me, so our walk was twofold; to burn off excess calories, and to give her my shopping list. Our Boxing Day visit also gave us another chance to chat with Spyros, Stathis and Irini's son, and his wife, Maren. We'd met them on Christmas Eve, but because of the noisy celebrations there hadn't been much chance to talk, other than shouting across the table.

Time was getting on and we were conscious that Irini was preparing lunch, so we got up to leave.

'Where are you two going? You are staying to eat.'

It was said in such an assertive tone that I wasn't quite sure if it was a question or an order, but because the table was laid for six the decision had been made. After the meal, Stathis, as was his custom offered to drive us home, but because it was such a nice day and there were additional calories to walk off, we thanked him and said no.

The walk along the water's edge to the pulpit rock was exhilarating and we lay there for a while catching the last of the afternoon warmth. The sun was already low, and as we walked up through the Special Place the olive leaves, green and silver, filtered shafts of light that played tricks on our eyes, like open air strobe lighting. To round off the perfect day we sat at the Piniatorou chapel and watched while the sky turned from a vivid pink to orange as the sun sank slowly below the darkening horizon.

So Many Other Things ...

As the curtain came down on 2002 we looked back on some of the things that had touched our lives. Len and Carolyn closed the Queen Vic. and left the island; I registered with Spyros, (the dentist); we bought a new washing machine; the Ballet came to town; Clara's granddaughter, also named Clara, was christened; Pam was issued with her residents' permit; I fixed Prue up with a Swedish lodger named Tor and we were invited to more name day celebrations.

New Year's Eve

The Lithostroto on New Year's Eve came alive as crowds turned out to meet and greet each other with the customary hugs and kisses. Different groups of wandering minstrels, gang members included, did everything to outplay and out-sing each other, and amazingly, throughout it all there wasn't a drunk in sight.

Later that evening we went upstairs to celebrate the New Year with Makis and Soula. The usual mountains of food and copious quantities of wine filled the tables, and because most of the gang turned up it was inevitable there would be large helpings of singing to accompany the refreshments.

The party had been swinging all evening and on the stroke of midnight the choir gave an amusing Kefalonian rendition of 'Auld Lang Syne', and so as not to be out done, and to rapturous applause, I followed it with a solo version of the real thing.

The celebrations continued into the early hours to end what had been a truly memorable year, but twelve months on there would be no 'Auld Lang Syne' upstairs, at least not for us.

The Monastery at Atros, Kefalonia
Painting, oil on canvas by Peter Hemming

2003 – The Luxury Of Four Wheels

New Year and Spring

Although it rained on and off for New Year's Day, the Argostoli brass band were undeterred and still paraded the streets of the town for their annual tradition of music making, the strains of which floated up from the square to within earshot. In the middle of the month almond blossom appeared in the special place which, according to local folklore is the first sign of Spring. Yes, Spring arrived early in Kefalonia, and it felt like it too. But it was easy to get lulled into a false sense of security during the early warm spell, especially when more than once Pam and I had been caught out by sudden unexpected showers while out walking, often arriving back home with steam rising from our rapidly drying clothes.

The unexpected happened again as we strolled along Maistrato towards the recently refurbished headquarters of the Nautical and Sailing Club. As we got nearer, the bearded figure of Makis (the launderette) greeted us.

'Peter, Pam, Happy New Year, welcome, come and join us.'

We were ushered inside to join the rest of the party for the cutting (and eating) of the New Year cake which was washed down with some excellent Robola wine. It too was a Kefalonian tradition, and the fact that it was already the middle of the month didn't really matter to them. What mattered most was that everyone was enjoying themselves. Doctor Aleckos, who we would see more of later in the year delivered the New Year speech, and appropriately cut the cake!

Empty Handed

New Year wouldn't have been the same without celebrating it with Prue, so we went to see her early in the month, and because we'd arrived in Lixouri in good time, we walked to Lepada beach, and what a fascinating place that is. As the soft swell of the sea lapped round the unusual shapes of the red rocks, and with the main mass of the Kefalonian mountains towering in the distance to form an impressive and awe inspiring backdrop, it felt as though we were in the middle of a natural open air sculpture exhibition.

When we got to Prue's, she was on her hands and knees doing what she could to scrub our carpet clean; yes, our carpet. That first get together of the New Year was great fun and so was the customary gargle. The truth is, gargling with her was enjoyable at any time and there didn't have to be a special occasion for one. But as well as celebrating the New Year, there was another important reason for our visit. She was moving from Lixouri to live in an idyllic location overlooking the sea near the Lassi Hotel, and because the carpet was too big for the caravan she was moving to, it was gifted to us.

The plan was to roll it up and carry it to the ferry port, about a ten minute walk away. It wasn't all that heavy and under normal circumstances we'd have managed it easily, but by the time we'd finished celebrating, circumstances were far from normal. Needless to say we staggered away from Prue's empty handed.

Epiphany

The day after we didn't collect the carpet was the Orthodox Church festival of the Epiphany. Crowds lined the Dhrapano bridge and the adjacent quayside to watch the holy parade and the ceremony that followed. As well as the gathered crowds, a large number of boats varying in shape and size, from one-man skiffs to the heavyweight Glass Bottom Boat had arrived, adding more colour to the spectacle. They bobbed precariously close to each other in the choppy water, but no-one seemed overly concerned, or aware of the clamour, confusion, or danger around them. It was, nonetheless an amazing sight and tension mounted as the ceremonial climax approached. A temporary arch, heavily decorated with icons and flowers stood on the bridge from which the Archbishop would perform the cross throwing ritual; which, after all was what everybody was there to see. As he cast the cross into the water a number of young men dived off the bridge to retrieve it, and as they did there was tumultuous applause from the onlookers and a simultaneous 'salute' from the gathered flotilla whose sirens and horns blared continuously.

However, no Kefalonian celebration is complete without fireworks, and rockets headed skyward and fire crackers echoed across the water, leaving the coloured smoke drifting in the air like rising ghosts; I'd never seen anything like it.

The Epiphany is a very important religious celebration and the Archbishop carried out two significant blessings that morning. Firstly, he blessed the waters and all those who sailed upon them, hence the flotilla, then he bestowed his blessing upon the young man who had surfaced from the cold water triumphantly clutching the cross. That blessing lasts a year until the next Epiphany!

After the climax of the ceremony and as the excitement slowly died down, the holy procession made its way to waiting cars which drove them to the ferry port. The whole thing took place again in Lixouri, but on a less spectacular scale... the Lixourians don't have a bridge to dive off.

On the Move

A couple of weeks after Epiphany, and this time under normal circumstances, we successfully collected the carpet from Prue, and after laying it we carried on where she'd left off, trying to get rid of the mass of dog hairs. A high powered industrial vacuum cleaner would have been better than the stiff scrubbing brush we were using. After getting some good use out of it, but never being quite able to completely remove the dog hair, or the smell, the carpet was eventually donated to the jumble sale.

Prue moved into the caravan at the end of February. That same afternoon Pam and I collected wild flowers, calling in to give them to her as a 'welcome to your new home' offering. She'd been looking forward to the move for months, and the Pruism, 'I'm full of beans', was even more appropriate on that occasion. Although there was no mains power supply (yet) she wasn't too concerned, because she used bottled gas to make the all important tea, and anyway, power or not, the view was enough to send her into long-term spasms of euphoria.

Prue's intention was to turn the garden into a blaze of colour, so she built a low fence around it, not only to keep unwanted intruders out, but to keep her darlins (which was how she referred to her dogs) in. She also made sure the fence she had built was low enough so as not to spoil the view.

Prue's View
Painting, oil on canvas by Peter Hemming

On that first day, before we'd arrived, she'd been unfortunate enough to meet the local shepherd, a swarthy unkempt individual who without warning gave her a mouthful of abuse; in Greek of course. A rogue dog had been worrying his sheep and the sight of Lizzie fired him up into an instant rage. After the foul mouthed tongue lashing, of which Prue understood every word, she then, to his amazement and dismay answered him back... in Greek.

She wasn't the sort to be bullied, and eventually calmed the situation by cleverly convincing him that Lizzie was a good and obedient dog, which of course she wasn't; good maybe, but obedient, never, but Prue wasn't going to tell him that.

Bare Feet

As well as the daily morning shopping routine in Argostoli, I sometimes shopped out of town at the Lidl supermarket. There was always somebody going so it was easy enough to get a lift, and although I didn't care much for the place with it's narrow cluttered aisles, it was well known for being value for money shopping, and it gave Pam a break if I went because she didn't like going either.

I was there with Mariann one day, and as we pushed

and shoved, Greek style, to get past the parked trolleys and shelf stackers, she gave me a nudge and pointed, 'Peter look, that gypsy boy isn't wearing any shoes.'

'That's alright Mariann, he'll steal some, you watch.' Then right on cue as we approached the checkout there was an almighty commotion as 'Bare Feet' ran out of the store clutching a pair of shoes, with one of the security guards in hot pursuit, giving chase across the car park, where he quickly caught up. His breathing heavy, his face red and glistening with perspiration, he returned carrying the struggling boy under one arm and the rescued shoes in his free hand.

Mariann looked at me and asked, 'Peter how did you know?'

'It was just a hunch,' I replied with a smile, 'and anyway, with bare feet he wasn't going to be stealing cornflakes.'

Promises, Promises

After last year's walkabout I'd promised to take Pam to Vatsa. So one Sunday morning in the Spring we caught the ferry and enjoyed the walk through the undulating Paliki countryside. Most of it is rich, lush and fertile, whereas other parts of the same landscape contain strange shapes of sombre grey earth that rise out of the ground to resemble giant termite mounds.

Vardiani (pronounced Varthee-arnee) island lay low in the water, almost submerged from our viewpoint, like some mysterious creature about to be swallowed up by the shimmering silver sea, looking completely different to the view we got from the Argostoli side of the water.

We'd almost reached Vatsa when a car passed us with palm branches piled high on the roof, not on a roof rack, on the roof.

'What's that?' Pam asked.

'Oh that'll be Spyros with a new roof for the taverna.' That too was a hunch.

The car was parked in the 'Spiaggia' car park with the roof still piled high when we arrived a few minutes later. A group of men stood looking on as though it was some sort of holy shrine, and as we walked towards them I saw my friend from the walkabout, he still had that great smile. I did wonder if he still had the portrait, but didn't ask and instead gave him a wave which he coolly acknowledged with a silent nod of the head. Then turning my attention to the guy in the long flowery patterned shorts, I asked, 'Are you Spyros?'

Before answering he looked me up and down suspiciously, then in a deep throaty voice said, 'I might be, it depends on who's asking.'

After the introductions and handshakes, I recapped on last year's visit. He then invited us to join him for a drink in the shade of the existing roof which was definitely in need of repair, but with the special ambience of the place and the views out to sea it didn't matter and nobody really cared.

Although we were warmly welcomed, Spyros's reputation went before him. It was rumoured that if he didn't like the look of a person, a potential customer that is, it was possible they might sit and wait forever without a chance of being served. That was a classic example of the Kefalonian eccentricity, an image the locals seemed to be openly proud of and to a certain degree one they enjoyed living up to.

On approaching Spiaggia earlier I'd seen the two geese lurking in the distance close to the river, so I asked Spyros if they were vicious, because in my experience the ones I'd come across were.

'Peter they're fine,' he assured me.

131

As we bade him farewell to make our way along the riverbank the two geese spotted us and came in close, too close for comfort, with their heads high and hissing in obvious anger, with Spyros, a distant and smiling spectator confidently reassuring us that there was no danger. So taking his word for it we bravely walked on, and sure enough they backed off without any further incident.

Spyros had given us directions back to Lixouri by way of the scenic route, along tracks and trails, which we tried to follow but still ended up getting lost and only by sheer good luck managed to find our way back to the main road again. I was learning that not only were some Kefalonians slack when planning in advance, but their sense of direction also left a lot to be desired.

Later in the year I fulfilled another of my 'walkabout' promises, when in the relatively cool temperature of October we went to Atros, which, just as Vatsa had been, was still a mind-blowing experience second time round. That walk though was far more testing for Pam than it had been for me, especially on the steeper slopes where she suffered acute attacks of breathlessness, similar to the ones she got when we used to cycle in the UK; but back then we didn't know about the bubbles.

Arriving at the monastery I was once again welcomed by Apostoli, who, amazingly, recognised me, and not only were we given the guided tour, but also, as before, the much needed refreshments, which that time I handed over a donation for.

Employment Agency

As the season approached, emails flooded the website with an assortment of queries and comments, but one in particular from a guy named John caught my eye. He, as a regular diary reader was not only inspired by what I'd done, but furthermore by what I was doing, so he decided to give Kefalonia a try as well. Just as I had been, he too was at a loose end, needing to find space and a change of direction; so with help from us that's exactly what he did.

After arriving late in the evening (due to a delayed flight) by taxi from the airport to the square, the first thing Pam and I did was feed him. I then introduced John to Menos at Hotel Agamemnon (the name Menos is short for Agamemnon) where he stayed until finding somewhere more affordable.

It was bed and no breakfast there, so the morning after his arrival I gave him a quick introduction to essential Argostoli; Egg Cups, Cardiff, Sliding Doors etc. etc. and if he had noticed the plunging necklines and inviting cleavages the way Tony had, he was very discreet and said nothing.

Fran and Pam between them found John a job for the season as a holiday rep. at Trapezaki Bay. He and I became good mates and throughout the summer shared some great laughs over a beer or two. He was also involved in a very serious holiday romance that lasted way beyond the summer.

I was painting in The Gallery one morning and sensed someone standing behind me in the doorway. When I turned it was Christian with an attractive young blonde woman who he introduced as Kerry.

'Crikey,' I thought, as they stood there smiling, 'he hasn't left Carol surely?' No, it was nothing as earth shattering as that. He'd met Kerry earlier in Exelixis. She worked as cabin crew for one of the major airlines and was taking a sabbatical in which she hoped to work on the island, preferably locally, for the summer, and had asked Christian if he could help.

'I can't,' he'd told her, 'but I know someone who can.' Which was why they were standing on my doorstep.

Like John, I sent her to see Menos, again for the short term. Then I told her how to find work, the 'tried and tested' way. The season was only days old so she started looking in Lassi where there was as much chance of finding a job as anywhere, and it was conveniently close to Argostoli which was what she wanted.

John and Kerry hadn't been the only job hunters to walk through my doors, and I advised everybody to do the same thing, 'Walk down one side of the Lassi High Road as far as the White Rocks Hotel and knock on as many doors as possible, then go back up the other side and do it again, sooner or later you'll find something.'

Kerry though didn't have too much walking to do because she found a job almost immediately (courtesy of The Gallery Employment Agency), high above Lassi at the Olive Garden pool bar, and as luck would have it, she, like John had accommodation thrown in with the job.

Finding a Good Hairdresser

When I'd lived in the UK a traditional barber used to cut my hair, and because it had thinned in recent years what was left was never styled, coloured or cut to the latest fashion; all it needed was tidying up every so often by someone who knew what they were doing. Finding a good hairdresser was important, and equally so was finding one who not only spoke English but understood exactly what I wanted in the way of a haircut, or more specifically a trim. Although there were traditional barbers in Argostoli, all of them were Greek speakers and the last thing I wanted was to be scalped in the aftermath of a linguistic mix up.

Eventually I found someone who was as close to being a natural English speaker as I could, although she was far from being a traditional barber; her name was Maria. She was Australian/Greek and I'd met her not long after arriving on the island. During our chat she'd let on about her hairdressing skills, telling me how good she was.

'That's fine,' I thought, and went to the salon where she worked. The good thing was that her English was perfect - after all, she'd grown up in Australia.

Maria eventually left that salon to open her own in the middle of town. She called it Mia, a shortened version of her own name, and despite the number of hairdressers in Argostoli her reputation grew steadily and the business flourished, because like me many of her existing clients followed her there.

It wasn't long before I met her husband Tim, who, as well as being an Aussie/Greek was also a football fanatic. We became good mates and football buddies; strictly watching, not playing.

Maria's hairdressing success however came at a price, when a savage vendetta against her by 'persons unknown' turned into a bizarre and frightening experience for them both. Tim was attacked in the street amid continuing and constant threats of physical violence that culminated in the salon being virtually destroyed in an arson attack. Understandably they were devastated, but, undeterred, Maria was determined to rebuild the business, and after some rapid repairs and stylish interior design, Mia re-opened within a couple of weeks for Maria to carry on the good work.

English, Greek and Albanian

Despite the vandals and the occasional storm, Poster Power had been successful in 2002 so I planned to use them again (posters, not vandals) to advertise not only The Gallery, but also the Charity Jumble Sale. Pam had joined the Jumble Sale committee and was responsible for publicity, so it seemed only natural that I got involved as well. Fran was no fool, she got two heads for the price of one.

The posters were printed on the familiar yellow paper in three languages, English, Greek and Albanian and were displayed to give maximum exposure for the event round Argostoli, but with only days to go disaster struck. A combination of high winds and torrential rain ripped most of them off boards and poles which necessitated a quick visit to the printers for replacements.

As in previous years the Jumble Sale took place in one of the kafeneions along the waterfront road and was a great financial success, with total takings almost doubling that of the year before. Pam scored in the raffle by winning a coveted 'Mia' cut and blow dry and Poster Power had triumphed again.

The Iraq War

After much speculation the war in Iraq started, and as well as causing 'shock and awe', caused concern and uproar worldwide, including Kefalonia.

The Protest for Peace march in Argostoli coincided with similar marches that were taking place, not only country wide, but around the world. A rock band played 'peace anthems' in the square which was appropriate for the time and feeling.

The war was yet another stark reminder to the world that the killing of innocent people was starting again, even though there were still countries where genocide, or as it is often known, ethnic cleansing, has been going on for years, but unless those countries happen to be 'oil rich' then the powers of the western world don't give a damn.

While Pam and I were marching we chatted with a local man, Stelios. We'd often seen him walking along the coast road, so the peace march gave us a chance to get to know each other better; which we did. It wasn't too long before we met his wife Eleni, whose English was as limited as my Greek, but that didn't matter, because Stelios spoke English well, as did his sons Angelos and Yiorgos. They, like other intelligent young Kefalonians had not only improved their language skills in one of the local frontisterio, but had built on that basic foundation by living and studying in the UK.

It's fair to say our common denominator was walking, so one Sunday morning we all went for the testing trek to the summit of Mount Aenos, (but not all the way from Argostoli).

Eleni missed out that day because there was no room for her in the car, but that wasn't the only reason.

Stelios, when I asked him was quick to point out, 'She is a good Greek wife and mother and has to stay at home to do kitchen duties, so when me and the boys get back there is something ready to eat.'

It wasn't long before Pam and I were invited to dinner with them and found out for ourselves just how good a cook she was, which made it easy to understand the reasoning behind Stelios's statement.

The UK was playing a major part in that crazy war, which as a consequence made Pam and me easy targets for those who were against it (weren't we all?) to vent their anger on. Although it didn't happen often, when it did we were left with a bitter taste in our mouths, because sometimes the ridicule and foul mouthed abuse came from those who we thought were close to us.

When those situations arose I tried in our defence to be as diplomatic as possible by explaining that we didn't support what was happening any more than they did, after all it was the politicians' war not ours. If that softly, softly approach didn't work then I'd really go for the jugular by reminding them of the savage brutality of the Greek Civil

War, which had not only destroyed whole communities but had also ripped apart close loving families.

A Dog Kennel

To coincide with the start of the war but in no way connected with it, The Gallery fridge (the one with the nail) finally stopped working. It had been seriously icing up for some time so I asked one of the technicians from Stavros's kitchen equipment shop, which was next door to the pub, to check it over for me. The bad news was it had packed up, so I needed a new one. Luckily, Colin came to the rescue yet again.

He was working at the pub, and when I mentioned the fridge to him he said, 'Pete, don't worry, Jan's buying a new one, you can have our old one.'

So for fifty euros I got a fridge that was as good as new, and Lefteris took the old one which he said would make a good dog kennel; poor dog.

Another White Knuckle Ride

Last summer a couple from New York, Roubina and Alexis, came to The Gallery and wanted a painting of Avithos Beach, but because I didn't have one as stock they commissioned me to paint it, and would collect it this year when they were visiting the island again.

Towards the end of April, with sketch book and camera I hitched a ride to Avithos. After walking as far as the Montenero taverna in Lassi a rather battered red Golf GTI screeched to a halt alongside me.

'Oh no,' I thought, 'not another one,' as the familiar smell of burning rubber once again stung my nostrils.

Unlike the driver of the walkabout Mercedes, this guy didn't speak a word of English, but pointed ahead, obviously understanding the words, '*Avithos paralia* ('Avithos beach'),' then with a grin as wide as his face he pointed to the passenger seat so I got in, once again cursing my luck. I belted up and hoped for the best, and as the lock clicked into place there was a curious sideways glance at me, but at least there were no smart alec comments about being a safe driver, not that I'd have understood even if there had been.

To his credit he drove slowly through Lassi until the bends just past the Princess Hotel, at which point there must have been a severe explosion in his head, because it was then that his right foot pushed the accelerator hard to the floor, and as the G force pinned me back in my seat I realised once again it was going to be another white knuckle ride.

Not many minutes later we reached the small parking area above Avithos beach where I got out, and to my surprise and total amazement he switched the engine off and got out too. After finishing what I needed in the way of preparatory work, quick sketches and photos (having purposely taken my time, knowing what was coming next), I slowly made my way off the beach, only to be beckoned over to the car by my waiting 'chauffeur' and invited to get in.

'What have I done to deserve a double dose of manic driving?' I asked myself. Once back on the main road he turned left at the crossroads and followed the scenic route through Svoronata, past Crazy George's Bar, The Garden taverna and the beautiful Ammes Beach. At the tee junction he had a choice. Whereas most people take a right turn for Argostoli, and drive past the main entrance to the airport, he didn't. Instead, he took a left and followed the road that runs parallel with the perimeter fence along the back of the airport, and, where, against the odds he actually kept to a safe cruising speed. That, I felt, was a ploy, because once we'd reached the end of the runway he was into suicide mode again, showing off his rallying skills up through the narrow twists and turns of Minies village. There were more glances my way, as if to say, 'this is good fun', accompanied by the now familiar wide grin, and by the time we'd turned onto the main Argostoli road my nerves were once again in shreds.

There was only one way to escape this madness and that was to implement my own cunning plan, so I got him to stop and let me out at the bus stop above Platis Yialos beach. I'd had enough of Kefalonian style rally driving for one day.

As well as defying death in the red Golf, 'the grin' rode an all terrain motorbike and could often be seen with a huge black wolf-like dog as passenger, balancing precariously on the petrol tank, and if he ever spotted me walking there was always a cheerful wave and the offer of a lift, which, of course I always refused. There would never be another white knuckle ride, not with him anyway.

He was though, just another one of those friendly Kefalonian guys, who will, if he lives to grow old, be equally as warm and welcoming as the generations that have gone before him.

Graffiti

Graffiti, whether we like it or not is common the world over in many shapes and images, so much so that we often take it for granted. As an art form it is interesting and innovative, but, after the vandals have been at work, it can be totally mind numbing in the extreme.

A graffiti vandal had been at work in and around Argostoli during the spring when the same romantic message appeared on a number of buildings, but it was the lighthouse and the small isolated Piniatorou family chapel at the top of the special place that the love struck Romeo (or Juliet) targeted on a regular basis.

The words, sprayed fresh from Cupid's aerosol were in

eye-catching bright red or green, and whoever the 'artist of passion' was, they must have been suffering with a severe heart condition of the romantic kind. He, or it could easily have been a she, it was difficult to tell, had been hopelessly smitten, because every message read the same; *'Ntina sagapo'* (Dina I love you).

Looking Back at The Website

Just before the season got underway I reflected on The Website, as well as on some of the other things that had happened since the turn of the year. The film season started at the theatre with appropriately, 'My Big Fat Greek Wedding'; Julie gave birth to a baby daughter and christened her Faye; Pam and I were given the freedom of Peter and Dee's garden to pick oranges and lemons as we needed them; Prue took in another stray dog and called her *Meli* (the Greek word for honey), and we celebrated Easter in traditional style with Stathis and Irini.

I was never in any doubt that the website was responsible for so much of The Gallery's success, and although I wrote and edited the diary every week, it was Deb's skill and knowledge that made the rest of the site so informative and user friendly, and with Pam's help she maintained and updated it every week. As each painting was finished, it was, by the appliance of science in the shape of a digital camera and computer wizardry electronically forwarded to Deb, who then added it to the on-line gallery.

She created some amazing imagery too that made the whole site a pleasure to browse, but as well as her obvious design skills she created the established 'contact us' page which was an important lifeline for my business.

Through it we were receiving an increasing number of interesting emails, some complimenting the website and others saying how much they enjoyed reading The Diary which was attracting a huge readership to almost 'cult' proportions. So much so that if it went out late, for whatever reason, there were some regular readers who were onto us like a shot wanting to know why.

The White Pandas of Kefalonia

There were hundreds of White Pandas in Kefalonia and not one of them had ever seen a bamboo shoot, but lived on unleaded petrol instead. Not only were they extremely reliable, and cheap to run but also easy to work on, especially by a qualified mechanic; Pam bought one as the season got under way, a Panda, not a mechanic.

Because of its box shape the White Panda would never be classed as a breakthrough in aerodynamic design, and to say it was basic would be an understatement. There was one wing mirror, on the driver's side, and no radio. Other than that, it was a great little car which we came to love, regarding it as more of a friend than a box on four wheels. Pam took delivery of KEA 6628 on May 25th.

Our White Panda

Buying the Panda however was a complete u-turn for Pam because her original idea had been to buy a motorbike, not a power pack, just a small 50cc model.

'You can't be serious,' I told her, but she was. Then, after going along with her crazy plan for a few days I decided it was time she saw the light.

'Listen, do you mean to tell me that you're really going to bring the weekly shopping back from Lidl along that dangerous narrow main road, and in the rain, on a bike, and don't forget one other thing... you won't be the only one driving along there. And just remember this, some of those drivers are total nutters and the chances of you getting knocked off the first time you go out on it are very high.'

She thought about it for a few minutes, and then did the u-turn.

'OK,' she said, 'you're right.'

As well as being the principal town of the island, Argostoli was also the motorbike capital of Kefalonia, Greece even? Everybody in and around the town seemed to ride one and they came in all shapes and sizes; there were even family bikes. It was not uncommon to see dad up front, with two, sometimes three children squeezed in between him and mum who'd be sitting almost on the rear mudguard doing an amazing balancing act just to stay on the thing.

Nikos, who worked at Cardiff (and later opened his own market shop near the Bus Station) was a classic example of the 'family bikealong', because not only did he ride around the town with his two children holding on for dear life, but just to make steering that much more difficult, he always carried bags full of fruit and vegetables that hung precariously from the handle bars.

Showing Off His Medal

2003 was the 50th anniversary of what everybody referred to simply as 'The Earthquake', and during the summer a number of surviving crew members from the Royal Navy warship HMS Daring visited the island to commemorate it. It was in 1953, when news of the disaster reached the outside world, that Daring sped to the scene, and had in fact been the first relief ship to arrive in Argostoli with much needed food and medical supplies. Unfortunately, by the time she'd arrived the town had been completely reduced to rubble.

A colourful character named Cid (pronounced Sid) had been one of Daring's crew members, and as well as returning for the anniversary, he had, along with his wife Henrietta, holidayed on the island almost every year since (certainly since the advent of package holidays) and it was through Pam's guiding that we got to know them.

One of Cid's favourite party pieces was showing off the medal that he proudly hung round his neck, he wasn't slow at coming forward and showed it to everybody and anybody, anywhere. It had been presented to him some years before on behalf of the Kefalonian people as a token of their gratitude. Another gesture of gratitude was the free ride in an Argostoli taxi driven by our friend Costas, one of the taxi brothers.

He was driving Cid and Henrietta back to the Mouikis Hotel in Argostoli after the reunion dinner in Lassi, and was totally unaware of their Kefalonian connection until Cid pulled out the medal; he then gave the unsuspecting Costas the full and unabridged story of HMS Daring's rescue mission.

As he dropped them off, Costas smiled warmly and said, 'Thank you for what you did for us in 1953, there's no charge for the taxi ride.'

I introduced Cid and Henrietta to Stathis and Irini who entertained them at Fanari one evening. It was an emotional experience for them both, one having been a rescuer, the other a survivor. It also gave Cid another chance to show off his medal, but when it came to story-telling he met his match in Stathis.

Radicals and Eccentrics

It was the eccentric Costas (the taxi) who made a radical suggestion on how to stop theatre audiences from using mobile phones during performances. He was a regular patron there and got very upset when it happened, which unfortunately was often. Pam and I had been to a recent concert and our enjoyment had been spoilt by the continual phone conversations, although I was never sure which upset me most, the chatter, or the nauseating ring tones.

Costas was sympathetic when I told him about it and offered an instant solution, a way of stopping it once and for all.

'The first person,' he said, 'to use a phone would be taken onto the stage and shot, at which the rest of the audience would get the message; end of problem, end of story.'

There was of course a less radical solution. An announcement before each performance, 'Please switch off all mobile phones, because there is a taxi driver waiting in the wings who will shoot the first person who doesn't.'

'And what about the latecomers Costas, what will you do about them?' I asked.

'Peter, this is Greece, we do things one at a time.'

He was born and bred in Argostoli and knew his

suggestion could never be implemented, not even in Kefalonia; but it was a good idea all the same.

Gilles and The Sailor

I'd first met our friend Gilles (pronounced jeel, as in eel) in Swindon after work as we both waited for the same bus. During the conversation that followed it transpired that he was paying a small fortune for his rented accommodation, meals were extra; so I made him an offer he couldn't refuse. We had a spare room which he jumped at the chance of moving into, at a fraction of the price, and with à la carte menu thrown in. It turned out to be the ideal arrangement, and what's more, being French he knew how to handle himself in the kitchen; better still, he loved cooking, and even better, he left the kitchen clean and tidy. Most evenings when we got in from work together he prepared the dinner for when Pam got home. I, on the other hand, went upstairs and painted; *parfait,* (pronounced parfay, French for perfect).

As well as his culinary flair, living with us was an ideal opportunity for him to improve his English language skills, which was one of the reasons he was in the country, while at the same time giving Pam the chance to brush up on her French. And me? With Kefalonia in mind I brushed up on my painting skills as often as possible.

Eventually he returned to France, but we kept in touch and he visited us in Kefalonia in June; Gilles however wasn't the only visitor. Pam's friend Gill (pronounced Jill, who she had studied with on the CELTA course) and her husband Peter were having a sailing holiday in the Ionian and had moored up in Agia Efimia where they invited us to join them for a day on the water. Pam, with her previous sailing experience didn't need asking twice and jumped at the chance, taking Gilles with her, who, by coincidence was also an experienced deckhand. Fortunately, and by a stroke of good luck, I couldn't go.

They sailed to Antisamos bay on a sea that was as calm as a mill pond, dropped anchor, swam a bit and then relaxed in the sun to enjoy lunch. The return journey however wasn't quite so calm, or relaxing. A force 5 gale blew up out of nowhere and caught them totally unawares in the middle of it, but Peter, with his knowledge and sailing skills, and helped by an anxious crew, soon had a potentially dangerous situation under control; it was nonetheless, in Pam's own words, 'bloody frightening'.

Taking everything into consideration it was just as well I didn't go that day, but I did go on the next outing with Pam and Gilles, to Avithos beach, and with not a red Golf in sight. Lying on a beach bed under a sun umbrella is not really my idea of a day out, but I took a good book, 'grinned and bore it', and somehow still managed to get sun burnt. Costas (the taxi brother) was right! He'd warned me more than once about the strength of the sun, saying, 'Peter the Kefalonian sun has teeth,' and it did, which was why I was always so careful to smother myself with high factor cream if there was the slightest danger of being exposed to it. I honestly thought those shades were supposed to keep the sun off, but how wrong I was to be so presumptuous, because by the end of a boring few hours (even with the book) I'd turned a pale shade of pink.

Something else happened that day at Avithos which I hadn't expected and was totally unprepared for, but the longer I lived on the island the more often it happened.

As I settled into the comfort of my lounger the young Greek guy collecting the rent approached me with a big smile and in perfect English said, 'Hi Peter, how are you this morning?'

'Fine thanks,' I replied, wondering who he was and how he knew me.

Greetings on the beach were rare because I hardly ever went there (except to walk, and then my walks were off season), but I was known almost everywhere else, especially in the streets of Argostoli where the greeting was normally accompanied by a customary handshake, and either a *'Yiassas* (or *yiassou*), Peter,' (Hello Peter), *yiassas* being the more formal greeting of the two. There were also shouts from passing cars and motorbikes, but the most common greeting was the honking of the car horn, not to be misconstrued as Kefalonian road rage. And just as it was with the guy at Avithos beach that morning, I didn't have a clue who most of them were, but it was a nice feeling all the same.

Napier's Garden

Napier's Garden was built by the Kefalonians to honour Sir Charles Napier, the British Governor of the island from 1822 to 1830. He was responsible for greatly improving the basic infrastructure, which included the difficult task of major road construction, but no matter how hard his engineers tried, they could do nothing to straighten out the bends and level the natural contours of the land. Nevertheless he was a good bloke and achieved a lot during the time he was in charge, which is why the islanders thought so much of him, hence the gardens.

A huge blue sign had been erected next to the main entrance to the gardens indicating the imminent start of major renovation work, but what was more significant was that over a million euros worth of European Union money had been allocated to pay for it.

As the mechanical diggers and work force of muscular Albanian navvies moved into the neighbourhood we braced ourselves for the inevitable noise and disruption that would follow.

Work continued throughout the year, and although there was some noise, disruption was minimal and not as bad as people had feared, and what's more, it didn't stop my morning walk through the gardens on my way to the shops.

Visiting Musicians

When asked about their artistic culture, a Kefalonian's response would probably be, 'We are musicians, it's what we are famous for,' and most of the music I heard more often than not justified that proud claim.

What puzzled me though was why the theatre was always half empty for so many concerts, and why the majority of those half empty audiences happened to be friends and family of the performers. Rightly or wrongly, I got the distinct feeling that despite the rich musical heritage, there was a general apathy towards live music in Argostoli. But maybe the real reason for the low attendance figures was advertising, or to be more precise the lack of it.

It was frustrating to see a great many of the concerts so poorly supported, which also included the free shows that were often put on. Stathis would have been a good P.R. man because he was the one who always gave us the nod when anything worthwhile was happening. Without that inside information there was so much we'd have missed, which only goes to show how slowly the wheels of the publicity machine turned. Perhaps the theatre manager should have taken a leaf out of my book, after all, Poster Power worked well enough for me.

It was midsummer, and an ensemble of Serbian musicians were in town to perform. For once the theatre was more than half full, almost packed in fact. That evening we were treated to stunning performances of traditional Kefalonian and Serbian music, performed in the first half by the aged Argostolians, who, after the interval were followed by the exuberant and youthful Serbs. It was however, the grand finale that pumped the adrenaline, because when the curtains re-opened, age and youth had combined to bring the house down with a memorable encore that can only be described as breathtaking.

After the concert Pam and I walked the short distance to Rosa's for what turned out to be another Portside 'special'. 'Special', because shortly after we'd arrived, so too did the Serbs and Kefalonians. And what we thought was going to be a quiet end to a wonderful evening turned out to be an unexpected encore of spontaneous and remarkable musical feasting.

Earthquakes

'The Earthquake' changed so many lives forever. Since then tremors have been frequent and of varying magnitudes on the Richter scale, but they've never been as devastating as on that August day in 1953. The occasional 'jolts' we felt were a constant reminder of how fragile and vulnerable we are to the forces of nature.

Pam's ex boss Nick and his wife Daisy, along with their two daughters were holidaying on the neighbouring island of Zakynthos, and being so close, relatively speaking, they took a day out and came to see us. Pam met them off the ferry at Pessada (pronounced Pessartha) and courtesy of the White Panda Touring Service they enjoyed a short but professionally guided jaunt.

The highlight was a visit to the Venetian fortress at Kastro which wouldn't have been complete without light refreshments at the wonderful café, 'To Kastro', where they met the English slave to the kitchen, Nicki, and her charming Kefalonian husband, the ever smiling 'front man' Spyros.

Views from Kastro (St George's Castle)

After their mini tour we all met up at The Gallery and then strolled the short distance to Kiani Akti, the taverna on stilts. During the winter it was one of our favourite eating places, made homely and comfortable by the warmth of a wood burning stove. In the summer it is completely transformed into a unique outdoor eating experience when the dining furniture was moved onto the adjoining wooden platform that stood about a metre or so above the sea and was supported by huge timber props, 'the stilts'.

As we sat quietly enjoying our lunch the whole place suddenly, and without warning shook with a violent force that lasted for about three seconds, which, by the way, is a long time for a tremor. Thankfully, everything stayed on the table, although the bottles and glasses did wobble a bit, and we weren't thrown off our chairs, but Daisy was not impressed.

'Was that a tremor?' she asked.

'No, no,' we reassured her, tongue in cheek, 'the wooden floor vibrates when the waiters walk around.'

She quickly regained her composure, and despite the experience everybody enjoyed their meal. It was soon time to go, and as we got up to leave Pam introduced Nick to the owners of the Gentilini winery, Petros and Marianna who were sitting at a nearby table. Nick was a partner in a wine broking company in the UK and was promptly invited to visit the Gentilini site on the way back to the ferry; which meant the unenviable task of mixing business with pleasure.

Café Culture

A common start to the day for most Kefalonian men is to meet their mates and drink some coffee (not as an accompaniment to breakfast, that came later at mid morning, and breakfast was usually a portion of cheese or spinach pie and not a bowl of cereal). The guys usually met in one of the many cafés to discuss some business deal or whatever, and if there was no business to talk about, they were happy to chat about anything to pass the time. The coffee was usually of the Greek variety, served in small white cups (just as Mrs. Flowers would serve it), and while some were content with the occasional top up, there were those who drank it non-stop through the day; they were the caffeine bomb addicts.

Café culture is a way of life in Argostoli with the main meeting places being the cafés around the square, which would become packed, especially if there was a parade or something out of the ordinary going on.

Running a close second in popularity to the square was the pedestrianised Lithostroto, where tables were positioned along it in such a way as to give the casual coffee drinker, as well as the hardened caffeine addict a view of the world passing by.

One of the most popular cafés in the Lithostroto was Antico whose tables lined both sides of the street, and walking between them was what Pam and I often referred to as 'running the gauntlet'. Behind the obligatory dark glasses, unseen eyes tracked passing pedestrians, and in particular attractive females with their skin tight trousers, voluptuous curves and of course the plunging necklines.

It was fascinating to watch groups of young (and not so young) men drooling over their coffee and fantasising, as anything resembling the female species passed in front of them, who, if the truth be known, equally enjoyed their brief moments of titillating pleasure on the Lithostroto 'catwalk'.

The following few lines of poetical observation sums up that whole scenario and came in a flash of inspiration minutes after 'running the gauntlet' one day, and like many other things it was quickly recorded in the diary to capture the moment:

> *Provocatively close, yet a million miles away,*
> *They glide with a casual neglect,*
> *With the boys in the café, sipping their frappé,*
> *Their penises fully erect.*

Sooner or Later

Rizospaston is the long straight avenue that runs northwards from the square with huge palm trees lining either side. Closer to the square were small businesses, including an ouzeri, a newsagent, a gift shop, a taverna, a wine 'cava', and a sweet shop. There was also the dominating and impressive Philharmonic Hall, which, despite its grandeur, excellent acoustics, intimate and comfortable auditorium played second fiddle as a music venue to the larger but uncomfortable theatre, which proves once again that big is not always best.

Further along Rizospaston and close to The Gallery was one of the few remaining habitable buildings in Argostoli to have survived the earthquake. It was the single storey (the top floor had to be demolished for safety reasons) Venetian mansion of the Cosmetatos family.

Although The Gallery was set back from Rizospaston, there was a good view of that section of road where wannabee boy racers reached dangerously high speeds on powerful motorbikes and in 'go faster' cars. In the time I'd been at The Gallery there had never been an accident, but going by the law of averages sooner or later there had to be one, and one hot evening in the middle of summer there was. The irony was though that none of the 'wannabes' were involved, which in itself was a stroke of good fortune, because there would have been total carnage if they had.

Two cars were travelling side by side towards the square, which wasn't exactly the best place for an overtaking manoeuvre, especially as the car on the inside suddenly and without warning tried to turn left between the Blue Paradise apartments and the Panem office which faced each other from opposite corners. Realising, but too late what was about to happen the driver of the overtaking car braked and swerved to avoid the inevitable collision, then, in the blinking of an eye the sound of crunching metal signalled that both vehicles had not only come together, but together they had smashed into a parked car. A double whammy.

Inevitably, and especially on such a hot evening, tempers quickly exploded, and what followed was the usual shouting, finger pointing and fist shaking as drivers and passengers remonstrated with each other amongst broken glass and crumpled metal. They in turn were subjected to the gawping of the gathered onlookers who had congealed to form a mass of human uselessness, then twenty minutes later the police arrived to add their own brand of confusion.

Student Unrest

During the peak summer months of July and August the Blue Paradise studios catered for tourists, but off season they were home to some of Argostoli's student population, who, like most young people generally were no trouble, but there would always be the odd one who proved to be the exception to the rule. She was the one who played her music at full volume with the thump, thump of extra bass that reverberated across the square into The Gallery. It became such a distraction, especially when I was painting, that more than once I had to ask her to turn it down, albeit nicely and with a smile, and although she always obliged, the low decibels didn't last long and within days the volume was back to distraction levels, which meant more walks and more smiles. Then suddenly everything went quiet! I wondered if she got fed-up with my smiles, or maybe the other students in the building had got fed up and had asked her to leave. Whatever, it was good to have peace at last.

As a way of expressing themselves, the young (and I never forget that I was young once) let off steam. There's nothing wrong with that as long as it's all in good spirits, can be justified, and is peacefully within the law, which is exactly what happened on one particular morning at around 3am, but unfortunately it wasn't exactly within the law.

When it comes to noise the Greeks are naturally good at it, that's the way things are and they are capable of exercising high degrees of tolerance towards those extreme levels of noise. But in the early hours of that particular morning their tolerance levels were pushed beyond the limit so that even Lefteris complained, so it must have been loud.

The long arm of the law wasn't far away though, because in the neighbouring apartment block close to The Gallery and with an unobstructed view of the Blue Paradise apartments, lived a high ranking policeman named Grigori, (pronounced Grigoree). Like the rest of the neighbourhood he was not amused at being woken in the middle of the night, and although off duty and out of uniform he approached the partying students, some who were on the roof, in an attempt to quieten things down, but unfortunately they didn't know who he was, or more importantly, what his occupation was. Grigori's plea for sanity had no effect, so after receiving a torrent of verbal abuse and middle finger gestures for his troubles he casually walked back to his apartment; and still the noise continued... until minutes later when a noise of a different tone added to the general mayhem. Sirens, flashing blue lights, vans, dogs and Argostoli's night shift of police officers quickly rounded up the revellers and took them away to cool down behind bars for the rest of the night. It was a swift and peaceful end to the student unrest.

There is though a moral to that little chapter. Before calling a person in a dressing gown and pyjamas a *malaka* (Greek for w**ker), make sure you know who that person is.

Practical Joker

Pam was working later than usual on Stathis's name day, so I walked to Fanari while she drove direct from the office in Lassi.

Arriving on my own Stathis asked, 'Where's Pam then?'

'Oh we've had a row and she won't be coming.' His face dropped like a stone. We hadn't argued, and when she turned up a few minutes later I gave her a quick brief of my 'wind up' with Stathis, but she couldn't keep a straight face and once he cottoned on, his smile soon returned.

He was the king of the practical jokers and the smile turned to a laugh when I said, 'That's the one I owed you.'

Just before his name day a woman came into The Gallery. I couldn't understand a word she was saying as she rambled on in Greek before breaking into a stream of fluent English, with not a trace of a Greek accent, at which point I was totally confused; then the plot unfolded. In the doorway behind her appeared none other than the beaming Stathis who introduced me to the Greek speaking English woman, Lesley. He had well and truly set me up.

Some years earlier he'd employed her as a nanny to his two children, and while working for him she'd obviously learnt the language well (it was probably a condition of employment!). Unlike me she'd spent time in front of the television.

In the end we all had a good laugh, and as they left The Gallery I whispered in his ear, 'One day I'll get you back for that.'

'Yes,' he said, 'I know you will.'

Where's Arabis?

A large number of Kefalonia's strays, cats and dogs that is, live in Argostoli, and whereas the cats were content to get on with their lives, mainly scavenging in wheelie bins and giving birth, the dogs either roamed around the town in packs, or, like Arabis, were content to be loners.

Throughout the summer he'd been out and about being his usual self, and had even walked to Lassi with me on several poster runs. One day, Pam arrived home in the car and saw Arabis was lurking around. She opened the car door to get out and Arabis came over to the car, put his front paws on the sill, poked his head through the door and just stood with his head in Pam's lap so he could be stroked – then off he went. He didn't ask for much. As I've already mentioned he had an obsession with chasing cars and then one day the inevitable happened. He'd hopelessly mistimed his run and as a result ended up with a severely damaged hind leg which was so bad he was limping for several weeks. As a precautionary measure he kept a low profile, out of harm's way from his rivals, but only until the leg healed.

For no other reason than curiosity Pam and I suddenly realised we hadn't seen him for some weeks, which in itself was highly unusual because Piniatorou was after all, his territory. None of the neighbours had seen him either, but, we were only too aware what happened to stray dogs in the town and feared the worst.

Periodically, large numbers of them vanished without trace and no-one seemed to know why, or where to, but most people knew how. It was common knowledge that organised culls took place, but once again no-one could actually prove who was ultimately responsible, or who physically did the culling, because they always happened under the cover of darkness. But what people did know was how the dogs died. The unsuspecting animals (who ate anything) were baited with poisoned meat which led to a slow and agonising death. There were even rumours that some of them disappeared when the travelling circus came to town; after all, their animals had to be fed.

Nevertheless, Arabis disappeared at around the same time as one of the infamous culls and we never saw him again but always lived in hope that one day we'd find him in one of his favourite places, asleep on our step, just as though nothing had happened, but of course we never did.

Sad times, bad times.

The Visitors' Book

I introduced The Visitors' Book to The Gallery at the beginning of January and throughout the year it attracted some interesting comments. People were never forced to make an entry, but most were happy to when I made the suggestion, and by the end of October there were hundreds of comments complimenting the paintings and The Gallery, while others added what a nice bloke I was.

One of the last entries of the summer was very coincidental and read: 'Great to meet such a nice guy with a great name. Appreciated the great artwork as well as your help in offering suggestions for beautiful walks. Fantastic!' signed... Peter Hemming, Brisbane, Australia.

The season had been another successful one despite the drop in takings on 2002, but the ever increasing overheads for The Gallery were my biggest concern, especially when overall visitor numbers to the island were on the slide following a general year on year trend. Over the six months of the season I'd met a lot of interesting people, but for me it was great to welcome back 'old friends'.

I had always said, but never in a mercenary or big headed sort of way that people would come back to The Gallery for more, and I didn't mean more paintings. There was more tea, more coffee, more wine and more streams of conversation, as well as more of the warm welcome culture I was proud of. Maybe I was becoming Kefalonian after all. The Gallery was unique to the island, a one off, and my philosophy was to make people feel so welcome they would never forget me. The Visitor's book was written proof of that.

Corfu

Stathis and Irini were going to Corfu for a long weekend and invited Pam and me to join them, and because it was somewhere new to visit we jumped at the chance. They'd been planning the trip for some weeks (I did say Stathis was different), but due to recent heavy storms ferry services were being cancelled at short notice, so Stathis put the date back until the end of October, which, according to the official forecasters was when the weather would improve. Weather forecasting was something the Greeks were good at and got it right almost every time. What was more important, they got it right that time.

There's something very special about Greek ferries when the weather is good, and the two crossings from Sami to Astakos and Igoumenitsa to Corfu on the day we travelled were ideal. It was the very slow dreamlike approach into our first port of call, Vathi, on the neighbouring island of Ithaca that completely knocked me out. It was a truly sensational entrance as the tiny port finally came into view with the ferry slipping silently towards it. It was worth taking the boat ride for that experience alone. Then, just to add icing to the cake there was a spectacular Ionian 'postcard' sunset as we approached Corfu. The lights of the island lit up one by one like stars in an ever darkening sky, when day gives way to night.

Between the ferry crossings Stathis not only drove, but acted as official guide. He did though have a long way to go before matching Pam's professionalism, but it was an amusing commentary all the same.

We stayed at Stathis's 'other' family residence for the weekend, in the top two floors (the ground floor had been converted to offices) of a huge Venetian mansion overlooking The Tennis Club, not far from Corfu town centre. Exploring the 'Old Town', which included the market with its interesting characters and exotic aromas was fascinating, as was the labyrinth of narrow streets and alleyways, which in every way was reminiscent of Bath, in the west of England. Pam and Irini spent most of their time perusing the fashion shops and boutiques, whereas Stathis and I admired the architecture, which unlike Kefalonia's hadn't been ravaged over the centuries by seismic shifting.

Because Pam and I wanted to make the most of our weekend we didn't siesta (which in any case wasn't really necessary, after all it was Autumn) and visited the Municipal Art Gallery instead, where an interesting exhibition of paintings, 'Art in Corfu' was showing. Afterwards, we relaxed in the terrace garden of the gallery, admiring the distant views across the harbour to the rugged mountains of Albania that shone in the soft afternoon Autumn light.

After returning from our evening meal Stathis decided it was time for some musical fun! He removed the dust cover from the piano, handed me a pair of cymbals, thinly disguised as saucepan lids, and then burst into an alcohol fuelled rendition of god knows what. Whatever it was it was Greek.

A musical evening with Peter and Stathis

As he and I were providing the music, Irini not only found, but more importantly poured the brandy. There was a frequent chinking of glasses and many *yiammases* (Greek for cheers) all round as we toasted a good weekend and wished each other *chronia polla*. Then as the warmth of the brandy took effect, our performance broke up to laughter and general light hearted nonsense.

Corfu was celebrating the feast day of its patron Saint, Spyridon, so the following morning we went to spectate. Stathis knew the Kefalonian owner of the 'Café Olympia', and after introductions we were invited to join his family at their table, only feet away from the parade as it passed by. The Café Olympia is situated in the French architecturally designed terrace, The Liston, which overlooks the English designed cricket pitch with its all weather wicket. Imagine that - cricket in Greece!

That evening we were his guests again for dinner at a 'musical' taverna in the country. The people of Corfu enjoy their music every bit as much as the Kefalonians, and many of the diners, including Irini, joined in the singing and dancing in honour of the saint, but Stathis, because there was no gang in support was rather subdued, which meant there was never any danger of a musical takeover.

It had been a great weekend, but the time passed too quickly, as it often does when you're enjoying yourself, and because we were there just for a few days we'd only caught a glimpse of what appeared to be a very beautiful island.

An Ordnance Survey Map

While we were living in Kefalonia the intention was to see as much of it as possible, and now we had the car there lay ahead a winter of exploration and discovery. But it was difficult to find a detailed map, one that would be ideal for locating the hidden tracks and trails, hundreds of which criss-crossed the island. Having searched every stationery shop in town, not one sold anything remotely suitable for what we needed because, as well as exploring off the beaten track Pam intended to write a guide book of 'alternative' Kefalonian walks, and to get that right a large scale map was essential.

I'd asked a few people who I thought might know where the best place to get the elusive map might be, and oddly enough they all suggested the Army office in Athens; what, all that way for a map!

'So,' I thought, 'if they've got them in Athens, they're bound to have them in the Army office in Argostoli,' so with all good intentions I went there. It wasn't the most friendly welcome I've ever received, as I knocked, entered, introduced myself and explained the reason for my visit, or, as they saw it, judging by their suspicious glares, my intrusion.

The officer in charge (the one with more shiny bits on his uniform than anyone else) said that no maps were available to the public, and when I asked why, which in my eyes was a reasonable question, the whole office turned to look; it was all eyes on me again, but he insisted, 'It's secret, go away.'

'Secret,' I thought, 'had he not heard of Google Earth?' but it was pointless trying to reason so I left empty handed. I did actually think about going to Athens, but the thought of arriving there only to be told, 'Get lost' didn't really appeal. The outcome was that we weren't able to explore as much as we'd have liked, not without the danger of getting lost or wrecking the car, and as a consequence Pam's book was never written.

To The UK

The day before we were due to fly to Athens en-route for the UK, Olympic Airways phoned to tell us our flight had been cancelled because of a strike. The only option was to travel by the ferry/coach route, so we bought tickets at Argostoli Bus Station and started out early the following morning.

For some time Pam's brother Arthur had been looking after their elderly mum who was living with him and his wife Sue near Cambridge. They needed a break, so Pam looked after her mum while they took a well deserved holiday.

It was a very stressful couple of weeks for Pam and on the coach journey back from Athens she complained of an overwhelming tiredness, so much so she slept for most of it. I thought that after a good meal and a decent night's sleep she'd be over what I put down as 'travel fatigue', but she wasn't and the horror story was just about to begin.

A Greek Tragedy

Her first words on waking were, 'Peter, I can't breathe very well.'

'It's probably the weather,' which is my standard reply when something out of the ordinary happens, but it wasn't the weather, and her distress was obvious as she continued to struggle with her breathlessness. I asked if she wanted to go to the doctor, and when she said yes, but I'd have to drive her there, I knew something was seriously wrong.

Driving to the surgery at Keramies, my mind was flooded with all the terrible things connected with emphysema, and in particular what the Specialist in the UK had said a couple of years previously. 'The worst thing that can happen is that the lung could collapse.' He had also added, 'Although any treatment is very routine.'

Those words had haunted me ever since, but I thought, 'If the lung has collapsed at least it's no big deal.' However, I'd forgotten where we were living and didn't realise that our Kefalonian dream was about to turn into a Greek tragedy.

The doctor diagnosed a collapsed lung and gave Pam a note to take to Argostoli hospital immediately. It really wasn't what we wanted to hear or where we wanted to go, but she couldn't very well get on a plane and go back to the UK, but oh, if only…

On arrival at the hospital her pain was severe and she was deathly pale. Unfortunately we didn't know our way round the maze of corridors and wasted precious time searching for the right department, when what she really needed was rest. Eventually, a social worker who had sensed our desperation left her office and took us to where the doctors were, then the note was handed over which was when things happened fast.

The Doctors, totally ignoring me, disappeared with Pam through a door opposite where I sat in the corridor and waited, for what seemed like hours, with stress levels soaring and everything becoming a blur. All I wanted to know was what was happening to her and how she was, and because they'd been in there for so long I couldn't stand the tension any longer and tentatively opened the door, then immediately wished I hadn't. Not only was she attached to several tubes, but a pipe had been inserted into her chest, which was fastened to a draining device which we later christened, The Dog, because wherever Pam went it went too. It was made of heavy duty transparent plastic, rectangular in shape and slightly larger than the average size briefcase, but more importantly it was the machine she was relying on to re-inflate the damaged lung.

It was only a matter of seconds after my untimely appearance in the treatment room that I was unceremoniously ejected to continue my lonely wait in the oblivion of the busy corridor. Some hours later she was formally admitted to hospital and placed in the care of Doctor Aleckos, who, as well as singing in the choir, cutting the New Year cake and being a Pub Old House regular was also a highly respected surgeon. Stathis said his doctoring was better than his singing so we were assured that Pam was in the best possible care and would be well looked after.

After going home to get clothes and toiletries, I made phone calls to a handful of friends to let them know what was happening. As word spread, her hospital room quickly became a steady flow of well wishers, but it was obvious what she needed most was rest, not visitors.

As a result of the acute pain, she was losing strength and not even the most powerful painkillers (when she was allowed them) had any effect. Then, as a desperate last resort and with the bit between my teeth I took drastic action, hassling the doctors into doing the same. To their disbelief the pain was being caused by the incorrect positioning of the drain tube, which meant even more discomfort as it was re-positioned correctly.

In the meantime I just felt so totally inadequate, seeing the woman I loved as I'd never seen her before; helpless, in a hopeless situation.

Under normal circumstances, we'd been told, a collapsed lung took between seven and ten days to re-inflate, so with that in mind we began to count them down. It came then as a bit of a shock when one of the junior doctors hinted that she might have to go to the mainland, probably Athens, for surgery. I was hoping he was wrong, because since the drain tube had been re-positioned the pain had eased and colour had returned to her face.

A Slight Misunderstanding

Taking everything into account, the doctors in Argostoli coped well considering their limited resources, sub-standard working conditions, and compared to some doctors in other parts of Europe (for example, the British National Health Service), their lousy pay. That however, was no excuse for the abysmal standard of nursing and hygiene, which was far from acceptable, but what I hadn't realised then was that within a few days we'd be putting up with conditions that were far worse than we could ever have imagined. It was like stepping back into the dark ages.

On the morning of December 20th another of the junior doctors told Pam, 'The tube will come out today.' That was great news and we were obviously delighted, only to be brought down to earth with a big bang minutes later, because the tube wasn't being removed at all. What he'd meant to say was, 'The tube dressing will come off today'. I was devastated, but Pam, as philosophical as ever put it down to a 'slight misunderstanding'. Later that day Doctor Aleckos confirmed what the other young doctor had already told us.

'Pam, we are unable to re-inflate your lung here, which means you'll have to go to Athens for surgery.' It was like he was passing a death sentence. As it was, the lung had almost re-inflated, but not fully, so arrangements were made for the dreaded transfer.

Stathis and Stavros (another member of the gang who had contacts in the hospital) had, unknown to us, been keeping an eye on things, making sure the admin staff got it right with regard to the all important transfer paperwork. It was good to have allies on the 'inside' because I'd had visions of us arriving in Athens only to be told some important document or other was missing, or hadn't been signed; thank goodness for the choir. Yes indeed thank goodness, because when we got to Athens there were no guardian angels!

I made a check-list of essential items; passports, health book, clothes and money. The health book was proof that Greek National Insurance payments were up to date, passports for identification purposes; and money. It would prove to be an expensive trip and that was before we left the hospital.

Two Hundred and Eighty Four Euros

As well as the essentials and personal effects, the all important flight tickets had to be collected from the Olympic Airways office in Argostoli. I handed over the hospital's letter of authorisation and waited.

'That'll be two hundred and eighty four euros,' the guy in the wheelchair at the ticket office said.

'What?' It was difficult to hide my disbelief, because as well as the up front cost of the flight, which, incidentally was one way (perhaps they didn't think we'd be coming back), there was an additional payment for a bottle of oxygen and the mask that went with it. In the event, neither were used, but to add insult to injury there was no money back on the bottle. When I queried the payment the ticket guy was very sympathetic and said the money could be claimed back from IKA (The National Insurance Office for the Employed) on our return from Athens. Ultimately there was no other choice than to pay.

So, with everything in order, including somewhere for me to stay (Pam was already fixed up), Spyros and Connie were putting me up for what I thought would only be a few days, we were ready to go.

The Long Journey......Out

Christmas Eve. Of all the days to be going anywhere, but that's the day Pam was transferred to Evangelismos Hospital close to the centre of Athens. We waited around in Argostoli hospital for what seemed like an age before travelling by ambulance to Kefalonia Airport, we being Pam, me and 'the dog'. There was a surprise send-off by Fran who came to the airport to wish us *'Kalo taxidi'* (pronounced kalo taxeethee), safe journey. After the short flight we were greeted at Athens airport by a waiting ambulance on the tarmac.

'Top marks for efficiency,' I thought, 'and if the hospital is as on the ball as this we'll be home well in time for the new year.' But nothing could have been further from the truth. It was Christmas and routine surgery was off the agenda.

It was a long drive from the airport to the hospital, and once there the ambulance drove straight into the bowels of the huge monolithic building, dropped us off and was on its way again. While Pam went through the admittance procedure I dealt with the other administration formalities in a separate smoke filled office, it was then I started to have serious misgivings about the hospital's efficiency, or at least the competence of the admin staff.

After the woman behind the desk had completed the relevant forms, she asked, 'How will you pay?'

'Pay,' I asked, 'what do you mean pay, she pays IKA.'

'Ah, so she has insurance then?'

'Yes, didn't I just say that,' I stabbed back in frustration.

In her haste to complete the forms she had filled in the wrong ones, and had, which I thought was rather unusual, forgotten to ask for the all important health book first.

'I'll go and get it.' As I walked away she heaved a huge sigh, rolled her eyes heavenwards, gave me one of those familiar 'Anglika malakas' (English w**ker) looks, then lit another cigarette. Minutes later as I handed over the health book, she smiled, checked it, filled out the correct forms, signed and stamped them (yes, she did both), passed them back to me and lit yet another cigarette.

Pam was located in a four bed room, number 581, and shortly afterwards Spyros and Connie arrived. Once she was comfortable, the three of us, Spyros, Connie and I travelled by trolley bus, which stopped not only conveniently close to the hospital, but also terminated outside their apartment in Ano Patissia.

Spyros and Connie left for Kefalonia on Christmas Day while I got on with hospital duties.

The Big White Chief

Pam in the meantime had met 'the big white chief', the surgeon in charge of her case, who told her, 'I will operate on Monday and recovery time will be seven to ten days and there are no options.' No options, what on earth did he mean by no options? But it was pointless asking. I'd heard about settling in, but Monday was five days away and doing nothing, especially over Christmas, in a filthy hospital ward was no joke. But that wasn't all. I'd told Spyros and Connie that Pam would be in the hospital for a week at the most. So once again it was stress levels up, feel good factor down and good bye to celebrating New Year at home.

After spending Christmas Day at the hospital, I arrived back at my temporary home not only exhausted, but starving. The little taverna just along the road was closed, so I searched and found one open a few minutes walk round the corner. After a good meal and a couple of drinks I relaxed for what seemed like the first time in weeks, leaving as the festive revellers started to arrive.

Five Days of Waiting

In those five days of waiting Pam got used to the anaemic food, lousy conditions, and suffered the endless chatter of other patients' visitors, when what she needed most was peace and quiet. Whereas I'd thought conditions in Argostoli hospital were bad, they were like a three star hotel compared to her new surroundings. The nurses, with the exception of one or two, generally didn't give a damn, and getting information from the senior doctors was a joke. They constantly ignored us when we asked for updates, breezing

170

in and out of the ward with an entourage of junior doctors and nurses trailing in their slipstream.

The ward itself was a disgrace. Paint hung like giant snow flakes from the ceilings, while floor tiles cracked and curled, creating a haven for germs and bacteria.

Most of the curtains dividing the beds were missing, offering little or no privacy whatsoever, and Pam, who by that time had virtually mastered the Greek art of tolerance (whereas I was going backwards and still had a long way to go before catching her), said more than once, 'A person couldn't die in this place with dignity.' It was true.

Her operation took place on the Monday morning, albeit, and unknown to me, later than scheduled. It was a time of uncertainty, anxiety and stress, as I paced the corridor for what felt like an eternity, until suddenly a giant of a porter appeared pushing Pam on a trolley. 'What, just one, he's never going to lift her on his own surely, and what about her stitches?' I asked myself, then in the blinking of an eye she was off the trolley and on the bed where he discreetly covered her up and was gone.

Later that day Sarah and Bradley arrived, having flown from Scotland. Unfortunately, they'd arrived outside normal visiting hours which caused something of a stir at the reception desk, but once the Security Staff realised just how far Athens was from Glasgow, and how much Sarah wanted to see her mam, concessionary passes were issued for out of hours visiting for the rest of their stay.

The Tuck Shop

On New Year's Eve Pam was moved from the 'heart' ward to one for 'lung patients', number 562, where incredibly and unbelievably conditions were much worse than before, because as well as the peeling ceiling and curling tiles the only available bed, Pam's bed, was broken.

Despite my protests and pleas it was neither repaired nor replaced, but no worries, only a matter of hours later one became available. Sadly though the person in it had to die first.

In the meantime Bradley and Sarah were not only on a mercy visit, they became bona-fide tourists, taking in some of the many historical sights Athens has to offer, and from their city centre hotel room watched a spectacular firework display that heralded the new year; a year in which Greece would host the Olympic Games and surprisingly, to everyone except the Greeks, stun the football world.

I, on the other hand sat in Spyros and Connie's apartment contemplating the future, while also looking back on some of the things that had affected us in the last few days, and over the past six months.

Julie took Faye to the UK, on a one way ticket; Makis and Soula became grandparents for the first time; Greek mobile telephone numbers changed; teachers, taxi drivers and Olympic Airways staff went on strike... again.

And in Athens; I went to the Acropolis, which was closed; went up Lycabettus Hill (from where I could look down to Pam's ward); travelled on trolley bus number three, often; drank draught Guinness at the Beer Academy; introduced Spyros and Connie to Martini's taverna, and patronised the hospital 'tuck' shop on a daily basis.

And unlike one year before, there would be no Auld Lang Syne.

Lycabettus Hill, sketch by Peter Hemming

2004 – Over The Wall

New Year's Day

There were no celebrations for me on New Year's Day.
I arrived at the hospital as Sarah and Bradley were just leaving. It was farewell time and a very emotional one, as Pam and I watched them walk away, arm in arm along the corridor for the last time. It was reminiscent of the closing scene from the Chaplin film Modern Times.

There was one consolation that day though. A breakthrough, although a minor one, took place, because there was a welcome change to the hospital menu. Fresh fruit in the shape of a rather pale green apple and a portion of coleslaw with an olive on top, appeared on the tray. But that was where the gourmet's delight ended, because everything else was still the same tasteless anaemic shade of grey that had been dished up since she'd been admitted.

There was another breakthrough which was far more significant than the addition to the diet; one of the Dog's pipes was removed, so maybe it was celebration time after all.

Discharge

Noise, in the form of high volume chatter was a way of life in the ward, which at times became so loud that when a doctor needed to talk quietly and discreetly to a patient the room had to be emptied, and all visitors had to wait in the corridor.

One of those instances took place when the surgeon spoke to Pam about her discharge, which wasn't a question of if, but when, and even more importantly for us, how? Perhaps that's what he meant by, 'There are no options!'

Although she was recovering it was a slow process, and there was still an ugly open wound where she'd been butchered, which looked as though it was doing anything but healing and was constantly weeping. However, the doctors insisted it was time for her to go.

My biggest fear was how on earth do I get her home in one piece, because the only way to travel, whichever way we looked at it, was by public transport, and in Athens, as in most capital cities, that meant a lot of pushing and shoving.

'How will we get back to Kefalonia?' I asked the doctors repeatedly. That, they said was not their concern and dismissed my questions out of hand, saying we'd have to travel back the best way we could (but Pam wasn't allowed to fly for at least 4 weeks), and if it meant by public transport there really was nothing they could do about it. My god, not only had they done a first class job of carving her up, they wanted to stitch her up (again), me too.

It was by sheer good fortune that Stathis and Irini were in Athens, staying with their daughter and son-in-law for the New Year. They'd visited Pam several times, and although Stathis had returned to the island, Irini turned up as the discharge crisis was reaching its nerve racking climax. Once we'd explained to her what was happening she diffused the situation with a few calming words.

'Don't worry, there is always a solution, you will stay with me at Eleni and Lorenzo's, then we'll travel back to Kefalonia together at the weekend.' Which is exactly what we did.

Pam was discharged that evening, but the following morning Irini and I returned to the hospital and completed the necessary paperwork, which meant more signing and stamping, and even more waiting around. But once again it was good to have a Greek speaker there to help.

No matter what, Pam was thankful to be away from it

all; from the noise, the death, and most of all the incompetence.

The Long Journey......Back

Although Pam had been as comfortable as possible at Eleni's she was still in pain. The wound was not only inflamed, but angry, and to the layman, me that is, was showing no signs of healing. It was as though a child, and not a qualified doctor, had tried to stitch it up with a knitting needle.

We left a cold, wet Athens for Patras and the ferry, and by coincidence met Pam's doctor from Keramies on the boat, who, like us had been away for Christmas, but for totally different reasons, and was completely unaware of the chain of events that had overtaken us.

Patras

The crossing took a little over three hours and as the island slowly appeared in the distance I thought, 'Oh dear God, we're almost there, thank you, that's another long journey almost over.'

The rain had stopped and the clouds gave way to clear blue skies as the snow capped Mount Aenos shone in the distance. The last few weeks had been some of the worst of my life, and as the door with the black knocker closed behind us we climbed the stairs to the apartment, where standing together we held each other close, let all our emotions out and unashamedly wept.

Although that journey was over, for Pam a new one was about to begin; the long hard road of recovery. It was then I thought about the people, who in a short dark chapter of our lives had helped us through so much stress and trauma. The most valuable and genuine friends are the ones I never thought we had. They are real friends. The others were just people we knew.

Two days after getting home we exchanged our Christmas gifts.

Back to the Real World

Within hours of getting back home we were transported from the unreal world of hospital life to the real world of day to day living. The daily routine started again, but before it did Pam went to see the doctor, the appointment had been made on the ferry. Her reaction to Pam's wound was one of anger and disbelief, that's how bad it was.

As well as frequent trips to the surgery there were visits every other day to Argostoli hospital, and it was there that the wound was cleaned and re-dressed, which became such a routine that all formalities were dropped, because by that time she knew the doctors so well they were all on first name terms.

Pam slowly regained strength and friends began to visit the apartment, but in nowhere near the numbers of those first days at the hospital. Rosa came frequently, turning up more than once with huge bags of fruit and containers of home made soup. Asked why the soup wasn't on the Portside menu, she replied through that wonderful smile of hers, 'Peter, at that time of the year would you want hot soup?' Point taken Rosa. Dee and Marilyn were regulars too, and like Rosa arrived with a variety of mouth watering goodies.

As quirky as it sounds I'd missed the daily walk to the shops while we'd been away and was amazed by the number of locals who noticed we'd gone missing; they all thought we'd been to the UK for Christmas. It was only when I told them about Pam that their inquisitive looks turned to expressions of dismay, surprise, and in some cases, shock.

Their concern was deeply touching but they were quick to ask, almost in hushed tones, just as though some piece of secret information was being divulged: 'Peter, did you hand over the brown envelopes?'

'Peter, did you pay the doctors?'

'Peter, how much did you give them?'

At first I didn't understand what they were talking about. 'Brown envelopes, pay the doctors, what do you mean?' I needed to know, and it was only after making some discreet enquiries that I realised they were talking about corruption on a grand scale within the Greek National Health Service. I'd read about it in the papers, and heard about it through whispered gossip, but what I didn't realise was that the system was rotten to the core, where seemingly the only way to get proper medical treatment was to pay extra for it, over and above the normal contributions that Pam was already paying. I couldn't, and wouldn't believe it at first, but it was true, and the more people I asked, the more the answers were the same.

I'm Not a Holy Person

During those first few days after our return from Athens there were problems with the car. It was losing power, jumping like a kangaroo, and worst of all stopping on hills......while driving up them. Our regular mechanic diagnosed faulty spark plugs, so he fitted new ones; but that didn't work.

When I went back he scratched his head and with a look of total surrender mumbled, 'There's nothing wrong, I can't find a problem.'

So he referred me to a couple of his mates who, he claimed, were experts in the highly confused world of car mechanics, but like him they failed too, echoing his pathetic, 'There's no problem,' but I knew there was. At one point it felt as though I could be cracking up, which at the time was highly possible, so in desperation I turned to the oracle, who referred me to his mechanic and took me to see him at his workshop in Travliata.

He looked and listened as the engine ticked over, then without hesitation turned to Stathis and said, 'It's an electrical fault, which I can't do, but I know someone who can,' and told us where to find him.

His name was Makis and he was a specialist in vehicle electronics; he also owned a state of the art diagnostic computer. It was indeed an electrical problem, so he fitted a new coil and replaced the 'new' plugs (which weren't new at all), problem solved. I'd thought about confronting the other guy, but it would have been folly, and anyway I'd found a new mechanic so there was no point.

Now I'm not a holy person by any stretch of the imagination, but at the time it seemed as though the chips were stacked well and truly against us, so one afternoon in those dark days before meeting Makis, the electrical wizard, and as the waves of despondency washed over me, I drove to the monastery for solace.

If there was a god, or any other spiritual force capable of lifting me out of my depression now was the time, because there was no-one else to turn to. And if the car was really going to die, as it kept threatening to, then why not do it in the mountains which was as good a place as any; and just to put me out of my misery I might as well die with it.

Inside the small chapel beside the Monastery of St Gerassimos

I'd intended to sit in the tranquillity of the small chapel where the body of Saint Gerassimos lay, but just my luck; a mass was being said when I got there. Within minutes though it was over, and after the priest and small congregation left I sat in complete silence, isolation and semi-darkness, alone with my thoughts.

It felt as though I'd been there for hours, but it was in fact, only minutes. Minutes in which the warmth of calm filled me. Then stepping from the darkness of the chapel into the blinding afternoon sunlight I got into the car, whispered to my spirit, and for the journey back to Argostoli my prayer was answered - the car was fine.

Is it crazy to have faith and trust in something we can't see?

A Change

Although Pam loved her work 'on the buses' she decided it was time for a change. There was a vacancy for an administrator in an up-market British holiday company so she applied for it. Unlike the informal chat with Fran a couple of years previously, for the new job there was an application form and a formal(ish) interview, but because she was still very much under doctor's orders and confined to home, the interview took place in our kitchen with the country manager, Andrew, who she already knew well.

The job move was bizarre for a number of reasons, because Fran's business, as well as being involved in coach tours, car hire and airport transfers was also the agent for Andrew's company which meant that Pam would not only be working in the same building, but she'd be only the thickness of a wall away from the office she'd worked in for Fran.

She was appointed to the job, which in our eyes was a total blessing, insomuch that she wouldn't be climbing on and off tour coaches for the six months of summer, but instead, would enjoy the comfort of an air-conditioned office; there was of course, another plus. As a result of the agency link she already knew most of the existing staff, so now, instead of being people she knew, they became colleagues, one of whom was the Fiskardo Mermaid, 'Ursula'.

The season was still months away, which hopefully would give her enough time to fully recover. Andrew was hoping that too.

Those Dark Days

We were well into the year and Pam was still visiting her doctor on a regular basis, and as a way of relieving the constant discomfort she underwent a course of acupuncture which to some extent worked, but not completely. We were beginning to think the discomfort was something she would have to live with forever.

The wise men in white coats had imposed a flying and driving ban until the wound had completely healed. Flying, they said, may have been the cause of the collapsed lung in the first place, but we thought their theory was a long shot, at least based on what the specialist in the UK had told her.

'There are millions of emphysema sufferers who fly all over the world on a regular basis without problems.'

Shortfall

It was payback time, so we made a claim for the expenses incurred for the hospital trip. Unfortunately there was no payment for the return journey, on the grounds that she'd had the treatment and was going home; it was in effect a one way ticket. To this day I'm still trying to get my head round the logic of it all. OK, so we came back with Eleni and Irini, but it still cost money to travel on the ferry.

I went to the IKA office with the relevant documents, only to be told the transfer papers, along with the authorisation from Argostoli hospital was missing. Very convenient, I thought, so I called in 'the allies', Stathis and Stavros, who obtained duplicates. How, I don't know, but they did.

We eventually received payment of 125.00 euros which represented a huge shortfall compared to what we'd paid out. It was time to grin and bear it again. Some of our Greek friends discreetly queried the shortfall on our behalf and were told authorisation to travel should have been sanctioned by an IKA doctor. What difference did it make who authorised it? A doctor's a doctor, IKA or not. Stitched up again. But because I still had to fork out a lot of money the IKA officials said the balance could be claimed against tax. Fine, but I, like almost everybody else in Greece, wasn't paying any.

Road to Recovery

After acting as Doctor in the House for a few weeks I went back to work at the beginning of February, which was also the day Pam took to the streets again! Being cooped up in the apartment all day and every day wasn't her idea of fun and what she needed was fresh air, so on that first day out she came to The Gallery. Walking home together, slowly, with her arm slipped through mine and with the sun on our faces was such a lovely feeling, and although I told her it hadn't been the best idea in the world, that it was too early to be walking that sort of distance, she took no notice, saying it was part of her road to recovery.

Therapy

As a way of strengthening the muscles that had been weakened by the operation she started a course of physiotherapy at the hospital, that coincided with some real therapy; the visit of daughter, Deb the web.

Because Pam was siesta-ing, Deb and I got out and about as she slept, either on guided drive-abouts or by walking locally, and although it wasn't quite the same as having my usual companion with me, it was great having company to walk with again.

Deb had arrived on the island during a few days of wild but exciting winter weather, and on one particular afternoon, when, in a strong gale and after almost being blown into the sea along the water's edge we stopped at Prue's for afternoon tea.

Sitting in the shelter of the caravan, chatting and generally admiring the view I noticed a catapult on the table, and unable to contain my curiosity, asked, 'What's the catapult for Prue?'

'Oh that, it's for when the cats are on heat, I use it to keep the toms away, but it's not very effective.'

Their intrusion was a nuisance as they howled, and worse, sprayed everywhere. I was only too aware of howling cats, living close to the Piniatorou colony, but I was never quite sure how good Prue's aim was. Perhaps that's what she meant by not very effective.

Deb's stay passed quickly and she was due to fly back to the UK at the end of the week, there were though unforeseen problems and her journey didn't go quite as planned. The weather worsened and heavy snow (yes, snow!) closed Athens airport, and as a consequence all flights in and out were cancelled.

Closer to the weekend we checked with Kefalonia airport who assured us that all flights were 'as normal', but I had my doubts. The strong gusting winds we'd experienced showed no signs of easing, so we drove to the airport and checked for ourselves; things looked ominous. Every part of the airport including the runway, was in darkness, and because there were no taxis at the rank it could mean only one thing.....no taxis, no flights.

One of the main travel agents in Argostoli confirmed that Athens airport was still closed, but he did say the weather was improving and flights would be back to normal by the weekend. Just to be on the safe side, Deb implemented plan B. She re-arranged her onward flight from Athens, and booked a ticket on the early coach for the ferry trip from Kefalonia to the mainland.

And the weather? The Greek forecasters got it right again. Deb flew home only two days late, that was two days extra with her mum.

The General Election

For Greece 2004 was a big year, in the world of sport especially, because not only was Greece hosting the Olympic Games, but the national football team had qualified for the European championship finals in Portugal. Adding to all that excitement, but completely off the sporting calendar was the added thrill of a General Election which was anything but sporting... or exciting.

Pam and I weren't eligible to vote, but such was the fervour around Argostoli that we couldn't help but be interested, in a perverse sort of way, receiving regular updates from our Greek friends of the election's progress and the candidates' promises. There were of course, differing opinions depending on the political bias, and in the end we were probably as confused as they were. Politicians around the world seem to have that numbing and mesmerising effect on people.

As well as local updates, we followed national news and events through the pages of the Greek on-line newspaper *Kathimerini*. Opinion polls indicated that things weren't looking too good for the present government. It was so bad in fact that the outgoing Prime Minister and leader of the ruling Pasok party, Costas Simitis, visited the island, traditionally a Pasok stronghold, to whip up support.

It was time for new blood, everybody agreed, but most were sceptical, saying that no matter who got into power, nothing would really change. That rang a familiar bell in my ears as I thought about the state of British politics; old

Conservative or new Labour, what was the difference? In Greece the political rhetoric may have differed depending on who was spouting it, but the sentiment was the same - me, me, me.

The people however, were unanimous, 'Our country has been governed by the Pasok party for over twenty years and things haven't changed at all.' That was the general opinion echoing around the nation and not just the island.

Polling Headquarters

The main political parties were well represented in Argostoli, and New Democracy, the main opposition party had set up their polling headquarters in the ouzeri, To Steki, in Rizospaston, a stone's throw from the square. I'd always had a bee in my bonnet about the amount of TEBE contributions I was paying; 156.00 euros a month, a lot of social security contribution for a self-employed painter.

On the way home from work one lunchtime I called into To Steki to get the bee out of my bonnet. Walking in it was obvious an important meeting was taking place, because everybody was engaged in loud conversation, round a table in a smoke-filled corner of the taverna.

'Signomi parakalo, milate Anglika?' (Excuse me please, does anyone speak English?) I asked, at which the chatter stopped and everybody peered through the haze to see the intruder who was speaking Greek with an English drift to it.

There was an uneasy silence until a woman with a friendly smile stepped out of the smoke, appearing like the genie from the lamp, and answered, 'Yes, I speak English, what can I do for you?'

I asked her if the opposition party planned to reduce TEBE payments once they were in power.

She smiled again and thought for a moment before replying, 'I wish I could answer that, but I can't speak for the politicians.'

Then turning to the gathered meeting she threw my question at them to chew on, that time in her native tongue. The silence was deafening, but not as deafening as the laughter, once they'd digested what she'd said. I laughed too, because their reaction was probably the same as a politician's would be, once he or she was voted into power, of course.

She thanked me for taking the trouble to call in and was sorry no-one had taken me seriously. I assured her that calling in was no trouble and in turn thanked her, while at the same time promising to come back, but the next time it would be to eat.

It wasn't long after that first meeting (and once the election was over) that Pam and I went there with Costas (the taxi). It was good, basic, value for money Greek food, and Irena, the English speaker with the smile, remembered me and welcomed us as though we were royalty.

What had started off as a bit of a laugh a few weeks earlier became the start of a lasting friendship.

The Rolling Stones and Jimi Hendrix

On the run up to polling day, meetings and rallies by all the main political parties became more frequent with the intention of attracting as many votes as possible, for each and every political cause. Most took place in the square, where huts had been specially erected from which the party faithful handed out propaganda leaflets to passers by who had nothing better to read.

Before the speeches and inevitable stream of empty promises started, the unsuspecting public, if they chose to hang around long enough, were treated to a spectacle of patriotic musical anthems and general razzmatazz, accompanied by the thump, thump of ear splitting disco sounds, coloured lighting and gyrating Go-Go dancers hideously dressed in their party's colours. It was hoped they would whip the nonchalant audience into a voting frenzy, like sharks at the smell of blood.

The Communist party didn't bother with dancers though, instead, they had their own way-out brand of patriotism and played music by the Rolling Stones, Jimi Hendrix and other sounds of a bygone but much loved rock era.

As forecast, New Democracy won the election. And my TEBE contributions? Payments increased every year, just as they had with the previous government.

A Bag Full of Lemons

Pam and I were walking one afternoon when we met a young guy and his over-friendly brown dog at the pulpit rock. Greek dogs are much the same as their English counterparts, they either want to shake water all over innocent bystanders, or lick them to death; this one did both.

He had been diving for octopus, the bloke, not the dog, it was Nikiforos who lived nearby. Once he'd caught three or four, his next task was to tenderise the skin which was necessary if they were going to be eaten - and those were. That was done by beating them on the flat concrete slab of the pulpit rock.

The dog's name was Fok, a shortened version of the family surname, the 'a' and 's' had been dropped off the end. There was in fact more than one dog in the family, all of whom had the same name, which proved to be really confusing; call one and the lot came running.

As Pam was still recovering she didn't walk every day, but it didn't stop me getting out on my own. I was walking along the coast road heading for Fanari, and having just come out of the pine tree tunnel spotted a man working in his garden.

'*Hairete* (pronounced herry tay*)*,' I greeted him.

'Ah you are English then,' he replied in a heavy mix of accented English, having easily seen through my poorly disguised Greek, and because there was no way I could have been Kefalonian he was bound to get it right first time. 'I've seen you many times passing by, come in and have some coffee.'

He led the way, introducing himself as Spyros, I reciprocated the introduction. 'I will call you Petros,' he said, and it was Petros forever after, then before sitting down to enjoy his hospitality I was shown round the smallholding. As well as an abundance of chickens running scatter-brained around the place there were two beautiful peacocks, but thankfully no geese.

In the distance, partially hidden by a huge palm tree was the small family chapel, which over the years had been renovated using original materials. As he proudly proclaimed, 'Petros, it is natural, not concrete'. There was also a beautiful huge eucalyptus tree that he'd planted a year before the earthquake. The bark shone like silver in the bright sunlight as the leaves whispered and danced in the warmth of the soft afternoon breeze.

As well as his own smallholding Spyros shared a vegetable garden with his brother Nick (the father of Nikiforos), on the other side of the road almost opposite, and between them they also owned some of the finest olive trees I've ever seen; pruned to perfection. Needless to say his house hadn't escaped the earthquake or the ravages of war, because the ruins were a lasting reminder of those terrible times.

After the walkaround he took me indoors for the coffee, Greek coffee, made by his charming wife Dimitra (pronounced Theemeetra, the female version of Dimitris). She was a woman of no airs and graces, and like Spyros was warm and welcoming, with a kind smiling face that said, but without words, 'Welcome to our home.'

They didn't have a car, but rode around together on his pride and joy, a vintage BMW motorbike. He perpetually dragged on a cigarette, a smoke screen on two wheels, and she rode side-saddle behind him; it's true, she rode side-saddle. And as was the norm there wasn't a helmet in sight.

*Peter with
Spyros and Dimitra
(and the famous BMW)*

It was always difficult to judge the age of Kefalonians, men and women, and Spyros and Dimitra were no exception. He, like most of his peers was short and stocky and carried the slightest of stoops in his gait, brought on no doubt by years of toil and exposure to the harsh elements. The same harsh elements had also given him one of the most rugged faces I'd ever seen, anywhere. His dark sunken eyes were not only warm and humorous, but at the same time piercing and searching. A shock of grey hair trailed in the wind as he puffed along on the bike; like Stathis, Spyros also broke the mould.

Dimitra in no way resembled Spyros, in fact it would be fair to say they were complete opposites. Her skin, although sun kissed, was smooth and her face warmed by one of the most radiant smiles ever; it was a permanent smile.

I spent most of that afternoon with them and left feeling we'd known each other for years and not a couple of hours, such was their genuine welcome.

As other Kefalonians had done, they invited me to call in whenever I was passing, but then, remembering having heard those words before I reminded them about siesta. 'We don't,' he said, 'call any time, and Petros, the next time you come you bring your wife.'

I don't think he could quite get his head, or tongue, round Pam's name, referring to her as simply, 'your wife', either that or he'd got a poor memory for names. Heaven knows what he'd have done if I'd let on we weren't married, how would he have coped with the word 'partner', or more to the point how would I have explained it?

By the time I'd got home I was leaning slightly, with the distinct feeling that my right arm was longer than the left. As I was leaving I'd asked Spyros for a couple of lemons from one of his trees.

'Of course Petros, take as many as you want,' and not content to let me help myself to a handful, which I could have carried comfortably in both pockets, he, in keeping with Kefalonian generosity filled a Lidl carrier bag. I mention specifically the Lidl carrier, because they were the most common on the island, certainly in the Argostoli area, where everybody carried them whether they were Lidl shopping or not!

I didn't reach Fanari that afternoon, and the walk, which usually took about twenty minutes from Piniatorou hamlet to Piniatorou street took a lot longer because of the stopping and starting caused by the weight of the lemons.

Navigational Aid

When I first knew the taxi brothers their car stuck out from the others in the rank like a sore thumb, because not only was it a Nissan, but there were advertising logos on each of the doors. Then, like every other respectable cab driver in Argostoli they went upmarket and bought a Mercedes, but still kept the logos.

As I walked through the square one morning Costas called me over to show off the new taxi, and in particular the navigational gadgetry. Mercedes or not, in my eyes it was just another car, albeit a very sophisticated and luxurious one, but unlike Costas I could never get enthusiastic about it, but then he had to, he owned it, or at least half of it.

Later in the year Pam and I were due to travel to Edinburgh for Sarah and Brad's wedding, and because she was still grounded I asked Costas to do a route check with the navigational aid, which he did; then I asked him for a print out.

Laughing, he said, 'Peter, this car will do most things, but printing, no.'

I smiled knowingly, because it was all part of the good natured banter between us.

In his early thirties, Costas was not only the older of the two brothers, he was also the more serious, especially when it came to philosophising and radicalising. For a Kefalonian he was tall and athletically built, similar to that of a middle distance runner, and had once been an up and coming road cyclist, aspiring to compete at the highest level, but when asked why he hadn't, the reply came with a shrug of the shoulders and a down turned mouth.

'To compete at the top I would have had to have taken drugs, which I couldn't do, that's why I stopped riding.'

Costas and Makis with Peter

Makis on the other hand was the light hearted brother and was rarely seen without a smile. Like Costas he also had a serious side, but his philosophy and radical ideas were more on the lighter side. He was also a serious cyclist and thought nothing of riding round the island just for the fun of it.

Some years ago after having to give up running due to injury I took up cycling and did some time-trialling and mentioned it to Makis, never thinking for a moment that it would trigger off one of his crazier suggestions, 'Petros, we could ride together.'

Oh no, I was never going out on those roads riding a bike. Walking could be dangerous at times, but cycling, and up through those mountain passes, no thanks. So I politely refused his offer.

'Another time maybe Makis.' But being the perpetual

coward, I knew there would never be another time.

Makis and I got round to talking about the present birth-rate problem that was affecting Greece. And the problem? The population was shrinking, so I took the opportunity and suggested he should become a sperm donor, and being a single guy he agreed wholeheartedly, 'But not by artificial means Petros,' he said. 'I want to donate it the natural way, by direct injection.'

Makis reckoned the ratio of Kefalonian men to women was high, something like 5:1, and compared his life of celibacy to that of a monk in a monastery. So I made another suggestion and told him to go and join a monastic order, live the high life and enjoy being celibate along with the others.

'What,' he said smiling, 'I can't be a monk and increase the population at the same time.'

Like most siblings they were as different as chalk and cheese, but great to be with for different reasons. If I wanted a laugh I'd chat with Makis, whereas Costas was a man with whom to discuss the more serious side of life.

Without Fear and Armbands

Living on a small island and by the sea was frustrating insomuch that I still couldn't swim, at least not with confidence. For example, if I jumped into ten feet of water I wouldn't be very happy, nor, after a few minutes, very much alive.

Not only were some of my Greek friends still highly amused by my lack of linguistic know-how, but they also found it hard to believe when I told them about the swimming skills.

'You don't speak Greek, and now you tell us you can't swim,' they'd mock, and although it was all in good humour, for me it was true, and highly exasperating.

However, early in the year it seemed my days of no

confidence swimming were over. A Bulgarian guy had walked into The Gallery, introduced himself as Christos, and during the following conversation it transpired he was a qualified swimming coach working at the open air pool in Argostoli.

Whereas one of my unfulfilled ambitions in life was to swim well, without fear and arm bands, his ambition was to improve his English language skills, which he did with frequent visits to The Gallery. Not only was I able to help him with general conversation and correction, but when I'd finished with the Sunday papers they became an essential part of his reading practice.

One good turn deserved another so in return for the English tuition he offered me swimming lessons, but because of his many commitments, either at the pool, or travelling away with his squad for weekend competitions, it was always difficult to pin him down.

The postponing and re-arranging went on for weeks until we finally agreed to meet at Gradakia beach early one Sunday morning. On that morning I was fired up and determined to give it a real go, arriving a few minutes early and in time to do some stretching and warming up exercises; I would need to keep warm! He turned up about an hour later, by which time I was thoroughly cheesed off and very cold (Gradakia, that early in the morning is always in shade).

By that time, learning to swim was the last thing on my mind, and although I made a few token strokes and got my hair wet it was too late, my heart just wasn't in it. It had been a pointless exercise, so, bother going back for more? I didn't.

And Christos? Shortly after the aborted tuition he left the island, and just as the cash register guy had, he disappeared without a trace.

After the swimming lesson fiasco I perfected the art of 'floating'. Close to the pulpit rock was a sheltered cove where the water was always warm, and more importantly shallow enough so that I was always within my depth; it was a floater's paradise.

St. Patrick's Day

Easter to the Greeks is what Saint Patrick's day is to the Irish; the ultimate celebration. For forty days leading up to Easter the Kefalonians fasted, which meant not eating meat, especially lamb. Imagine then, a Guinness drinker going without a pint for the forty days of Lent!

Shortly after arriving on the island I'd been in the Argostoli square to see the Easter celebrations for myself, and somehow got the impression they weren't a true reflection of the religious festival I'd heard so much about. For most of the evening, fireworks, or to be precise, bangers and firecrackers were being continually thrown into the square by young and old bystanders alike.

Just before that Easter weekend I'd met a couple of English boat people, Nick and Patsy, who were sailing round the Ionian in their red yacht 'Panache', and had moored up in Argostoli. On the evening of Easter Saturday, after a couple of drinks in the Queen Vic, the three of us walked the short distance to the square. Nick wasn't impressed with the fireworks, and like me failed to see any link between the smell of gun powder and a religious ceremony; he was so disappointed that he left Patsy with me and went back to the pub.

We stayed long enough to see the procession of the priest and his young entourage as they filed through the crowd to mount a raised platform from which he gave the Easter blessing, at least I assumed that's what he was doing, it was difficult to tell, and although his lips were moving, I couldn't hear a word over the exploding bangers. As the holy group left the stage, Patsy and I did the same and left the square, rejoining Nick in the pub.

According to the locals, the square in Argostoli is the last place to go to experience the spiritual side of a Greek Orthodox Easter. Every church in Kefalonia would have been celebrating it in a more profound and reverent way, but I didn't know that then.

In total contrast to my first Greek Easter, this year's was set in a more relaxed atmosphere and without a firework in sight. We'd been invited to the family gathering with Stathis and Irini, and although there was nothing happening of religious significance, other than the roasting of the lamb, it promised to be a good feast. Stathis was in charge of cooking the meat which had been slowly turning on the electrically operated spit for a few hours, and even to me, a vegetarian, it smelt good.

Irini was in one of her more assertive moods that day and as we arrived she said, 'Welcome Peter, you will be eating lamb today!' And there were no options. I couldn't wriggle out of that one, so lamb it was.

After a wonderful afternoon we slowly walked the well trodden scenic route home, along the water's edge to the pulpit rock and up through the special place, and although the Greeks aren't known for their love of walking long distances, any distance really, Lorenzo (Stathis and Irini's son-in-law who was staying in the square) walked back to Argostoli with us. He was amazed at the network of tracks, and even more so when he realised how easy it was to walk from Fanari to the town.

Easter was a special time, and as long as Stathis and Irini were at home there was an open invitation for us to enjoy it with them.

Grace

There are two marinas in Argostoli. The one I referred to as the 'old' marina is in the area of Maistrato at the northern end of the town close to the outdoor swimming pool, and although much the smaller of the two, it's where most of the locals moored their boats, which is why it's so full of character.

The other marina is at Dhrapano, near the far end of the bridge, and in total contrast to Maistrato is a new, much larger concrete construction and completely devoid of any character. It hadn't long been completed and was generally thought of by the locals as a waste of money (E.U. money that is) because of its isolated location and lack of facilities. In contrast to the 'old' marina, fewer boats were moored there, half a dozen at the most maybe, one of which was the sailing yacht 'Grace'.

I'm not an expert on boats, but Grace, compared to some of the newer models that sailed in and out of Argostoli in the summer months, was beautiful and full of old charm. She was timber built, double masted and had been sailed single handed across the Atlantic by her skipper and owner, Malcolm, who Pam and I had met, along with his partner Marilyn not long after they'd moved to the island, and the friendship developed from there.

Grace had been out of the water for a few weeks undergoing routine maintenance work, mainly the cleaning of her bottom, which Malcolm, who, being a technical sort of bloke and an experienced sea dog, did himself. But now he'd finished and it was time to get Grace back afloat. It's common knowledge within the sailing fraternity that when a timber hulled boat is left out of the water for any length of time there is a danger of the wood shrinking, and therefore leaking once it's re-floated.

Pam and I had been invited to celebrate the grand re-launch and as we arrived a huge mobile crane was in position for the big lift. Slings had been positioned underneath Grace and she was slowly raised, before being gently lowered back into the water without so much as a splash. It was as straightforward as that, and although it wasn't Malcolm's first re-launching he'd certainly looked apprehensive from the moment Grace left the supporting blocks, and especially when she was momentarily suspended high above the ground as the crane swung her into position for the final lowering. It was a delicate operation and Malcolm was visibly stressed. We, however, couldn't wait to get on board to open the champagne.

Understandably, Malcolm wasn't interested in partying, his main priority was checking for leaks, and although there were some minor ones he wasn't concerned, knowing the hull would automatically expand and re-seal itself within a couple of hours, which it did. From our apartment window we had good views across to the new marina, and Grace was still afloat when we got home later that afternoon.

Striking it Lucky

Considering the high number of stray cats in Argostoli, and in particular those living in our neighbourhood, a handful were lucky enough to live the good life!

During the years before we met, Pam and I had both kept cats as pets, and as much as we'd loved them, vowed never to have any more, no matter where we lived. Cats were part of the scenery in Argostoli but unfortunately were abandoned by the score as they grew from being cuddly, kitten sized, affectionate play things to unwanted nuisances. Some of the more fortunate ones were rescued and taken into good homes, whereas most of the others, who were semi feral, looked after themselves, but there would always be those, who, through no fault of their own perished within days of being born.

Runts of the litter, those who had been abandoned by the mother cat, didn't have a chance of surviving those first few days, and if they didn't die through malnourishment they were usually killed as they strayed blindly across the roads. One such straggly mite that couldn't have been more than a few days old was staggering about oblivious to danger in the road outside our apartment, but luckily she was plucked from certain death by our neighbour opposite, Theo's mum.

She was the kittens' saviour, as it wasn't the first one she'd rescued, and because we didn't know her name, Pam and I called her Mrs Saint Theo; and the kitten who flourished in home care bliss, we christened Kitty Bad Eyes.

Pigi, (pronounced piggy) was another stray the saint had adopted, but she, like Arabis had come off worst in a hit and run incident with a passing car, ending up with a severely damaged front left paw, so much so that she learnt how to walk on three legs.

Pam and I were concerned that she would pick up an infection and die, so we suggested, but without much luck, to Theo, that Pigi should be taken to the vet. He was unable to grasp the seriousness of the situation however, and his mum, who spoke no English was completely out of it, so we contacted the cat loving Irini. She and Stathis had a house full of cats, so at least they were sympathetic to our cause.

Irini spoke to Mrs. Saint Theo about the vet idea. After some discussion the saint eventually got the message and agreed, the kitten should definitely see the vet, and it was kind of us to bring it to her attention. But somewhere along the intricate web of translation the saint had completely missed the point, because not only did she expect us to take Pigi to the vet, but, and here's the sting, she thought we would pay for the treatment.

After that slight misunderstanding Pigi never did get to see the vet, but over the following months her wounded paw healed completely, and it wasn't long before she was giving birth to offspring of her own.

Abandoned

I, too, was involved in a bizarre abandoned animal rescue mission one morning. Approaching The Gallery I noticed a small cardboard box on the top step with a crudely written note attached to it that read, 'You English love animals, look after this one', and inside was a tiny kitten. I was upset and furious at the same time, because how could someone be so cruel and stupid. Not only had it been left on my step, but if I hadn't turned up to work that day it would never have survived in the searing heat of the day. Now what do I do? But as with Colin and the painting of The Gallery, help was conveniently close. Lefteris's son Nick was in the pub garden, and when I explained about the kitten he was happy to take it.

Pub Old House was a haven for cats, where one more wouldn't make any difference, and besides, it would probably end up at Makis's place anyway. Makis was a pub regular whose mother lived in Lassi and owned the land where Prue had her caravan; it was a cats' paradise. After living at the pub for a short time the little one moved to the open countryside of Lassi and became a free range country cat. No doubt it was one of the many that hung around Prue's caravan enjoying the benefits of her free handouts.

Looking Back

Around the middle of April the holiday reps. started arriving for another season, and although most of them were regulars, returning year after year, there were those with less experience, and some with none at all. They were in for a shock as they quickly discovered there was more to rep. work than sun, sand and sex, and whereas most would stay the course for the summer, others would be on their way home within a few weeks, or in some cases, a few days.

As we were about to get sucked into another six months of manic summer I looked back on what had happened since the new year: I'd seen dolphins frolicking in the bay; Lefteris and I drank his prized Bushmills whiskey to celebrate Saint Patrick's day; a bowling alley opened in Travliata; Argostoli's traffic light system went live, and just what she could have done without so close to the start of the season, Rosa was admitted to hospital.

Rosa

Rosa being the strong minded woman she is discharged herself and was out in time to open Portside as the new season began. At first she took things easy, but because taking things easy wasn't part of her mentality it wasn't long before she was back into overdrive.

Originally from Athens, Rosa had lived in New York since childhood, where she met and married her ticket to paradise in the shape of her Kefalonian husband, Spyros. He had worked in one of the city's many Greek diners, while she had been a personal assistant in a busy Manhattan firm of lawyers, but on moving to the island their roles were reversed in an odd sort of way. She became the driving force behind Portside and controlled it with an iron fist, a keen eye and a big smile, and although Spyros didn't move into law he was an integral part of the taverna, but in more of a support role!

For most Kefalonian men, and he was no different, supporting meant sitting and supervising, ideally with a cigarette in one hand and a drink, preferably an alcoholic one in the other. However, in the middle of the season, their busiest time, Spyros's support role suddenly and dramatically changed.

Rosa's regular chef, without warning, decided he wanted more pay, although he was getting way above the normal rate for the job; it was blackmail, or at least attempted blackmail.

Rosa however, was having none of it, and told him, 'If you're not happy here then go.' So calling her bluff he did. His scheming though completely backfired because within seconds she'd found a rather reluctant replacement, and from that moment Spyros's position in the business suddenly became more than the supporting role he'd been used to...he was ushered into the kitchen with instant promotion to head chef.

Despite the quality, value for money food and her awareness of customer service, all of which was of the highest standard, she had a love/hate relationship with Portside. Summers for her, as for every working mother on the island, were a stressful slog, especially in the intense heat of July and August.

It was relief for Rosa when the end of the season finally arrived, because as well as being physically exhausted, she was also mentally drained. But with the long hot summer over she was able to wind down and look forward to spending quality time with her young family during the relatively calm months of winter.

Moving

Throughout the Spring, Makis, Minas and other assorted building tradesmen had been busy refurbishing Panagis's apartment (which Makis owned) next door. Our present home had become cramped due to the extra furniture we were accumulating, which included the television, a computer and a huge bookcase housing an ever increasing collection of books, CDs and DVDs.

Panagis had built a block of apartments next to Makis and was moving into one of them. Knowing that, we made a swift approach through Minas, who made his Father aware that we would like to move into Panagis's more spacious apartment when it became available.

We loved living where we did and couldn't have wished for a better landlord, he felt the same way about us as tenants, and although he had never told us in so many words (because there was still the language barrier), we'd heard it through the male voice choir grapevine.

With the refurbishment complete we moved in the middle of June, and in the days leading up to it most of my spare time was spent packing. I also visited the various utility companies to let them know the change of address; from number nine to number nine. The most interesting visit (from a man's point of view that is) was to the OTE office, requesting to keep the same telephone number. The young lady with the big smile and customary plunging neckline (there was no such thing as a company uniform) said it would take fifteen working days to transfer the number to the new line and would cost thirty five euros. With a big smile of my own I told her paying wasn't an issue, but waiting fifteen days was, explaining that having the internet was an essential part of my business.

Then, in a very seductive manner, she smiled again, leant forward, revealing all, then replied, 'I'll see what I can do for you.' Which she did, and within a couple of days of the move we were re-connected with the same number.

Panagis vacated the apartment just before the weekend, so on the Saturday I moved everything manageable over the metre-high wall separating the properties. The heavy gang, of Peter TZ and Malcolm arrived early the following morning to help me with the heavy and awkward items. Pam was working that day so Marilyn came and took charge of breakables, clearing and stacking shelves, and most importantly, making the tea. There was no heavy lifting for her, and being rather petite there was no climbing back and forth over the wall either. We all cracked on and by mid morning the move was complete. At about midday as I was tidying up there was a knock on the door; it was Makis the taxi, the missing member of the heavy gang.

'Ah Petros, am I late?' he asked, wearing his usual smile.

'No Makis, the others haven't turned up yet,' I grinned sarcastically. It was pointless questioning his late arrival, but I was curious, because he was normally punctual; which proves there's a first time for everything.

A Separate Bedroom

It was great to be living in a larger apartment with a separate bedroom, full central heating and the added luxury of air conditioning. The main entrance was at the side of the building and opened straight into the living room, but there was no black knocker. The path leading to the apartment was accessible through a wrought iron gate from the street and up a short flight of steps, then continued round the back to a patio which was overlooked by the ground floor bedroom and kitchen windows. The back door opened from the patio directly into the kitchen which had been completely re-fitted, but not re-tiled, because the yellow and white 'job lot' which we'd learnt to live with next door graced our new home. From the kitchen, a door opened into a small central lobby, from which the other rooms were connected; the living room, bedroom and shower room. Another much smaller door, positioned directly above the shower room door gave access to the tiny 'loft' space, which was ideal for storing suitcases and packing boxes; there was a water boiler up there too.

The compact double bedroom had new fitted wardrobes, with doors that opened into the room, which under normal circumstances wouldn't have mattered, but because the room was so compact it was only possible to fit the bed in one position, that was with the headboard under the window. There was a problem though; that was also where the radiator had been fitted…whoops. We pointed it out to Makis who immediately saw the funny side, gave us a huge smile and promptly phoned the plumber who came the next day and re-positioned it, the radiator, not the bed.

The shower was great. There were no steps or other obstacles to fall over when getting in or out of it, and no doors or awkward glass partitions to struggle with, it was a case of just pulling the curtain back and walking straight in. Compared to what we'd been used to, the living room was huge with the same fantastic views as next door. It was like living in a palace; we couldn't have wanted for more.

One Thousand Euros

Now we were living in a larger apartment it was time to buy some comfortable furniture. Lefteris said our landlord, The Gallery owner, had a suite for sale in his country house at Keramies, so I went to see it. There were two double sofas that would have fitted in our living room easily.

'How much?' I asked.

'One thousand euros.'

What! A grand for two second hand sofas! I wouldn't pay that for two new ones, and if pushed I'd sit on orange boxes.

'I'll give it some thought,' I said, and through Lefteris offered four hundred, hoping he might have gone half way. It was déjà vu; I'd been down this road before.

'No Baby, he wants a thousand, but he did say you can pay in instalments if you can't afford a single payment.' Lefteris chuckled when I told him what he could do with his sofas, not to mention the instalments.

After that nonsense, Pam and I went to the store the ex-pat population often referred to as B & Q (a well-known UK DIY Store) which was out of town on the Poros road. We saw a nice sofa and wanted to buy it, but the sales girl didn't know the price and told us to go back a few days later. I couldn't believe it, go back a few days later? The thing would be sold by then. What she needed was a season working for Rosa, where she'd learn some real customer service skills.

Eventually we bought a comfortable three seater sofa and matching armchair (the sort you sink in to) from Fran for a fraction of the price, and delivery was free. Spyros and I collected them from Lassi in his pickup truck. It wasn't the last time he'd be on removal duties, because later in the year we borrowed, courtesy of Portside, a dining table and four chairs, for the winter before eventually buying our own.

Winning

As far as things were going in the world of sport it promised to be a great year for the Greeks because they were hosting the Olympic Games, but things didn't look so good as far as international football was concerned. The national team were ranked as total outsiders in the Euro 2004 championships, with pundits, amateur and professional, giving them less than a hope of winning. However, a brave betting man would have made a small fortune if he'd known how things would turn out.

Portugal were not only hosting the tournament, but along with the Italians and the mighty French were amongst the favourites to win, and any likelihood of Greece lifting the trophy, as far as the passionate but pessimistic Kefalonians were concerned, was completely unthinkable.

A huge screen for the televising of Greece's matches had been erected in the Argostoli square by Makis the sound, while television sets in *kafeneions*, tavernas and homes all over the island were being checked for workability. The cabinet at Portside had been unlocked and the television installed as Football Fever spread through Kefalonia.

As the competition progressed, so amazingly did Greece, and the streets of Argostoli came alive with celebrations that at times resembled delirium, after each victorious match, but it was an air of despondency that descended on the town as the semi-final approached. The Greeks had been drawn to play France, the current World

Champions who, according to my Kefalonian friends were unbeatable.

I told them all, 'Nobody is unbeatable in football, and if Greece can get this far, they can beat the French and go on to win the title.'

Although I'm no expert on the game I do know a thing or two about self motivation and how to motivate others, and so too did the Greek's German coach, because after beating the French on a hot evening in July, his team then went on to win the tournament by beating odds-on favourites Portugal the following weekend.

We watched the match on the Portside television and even Rosa got excited. The final whistle was the signal for the celebration of all celebrations to start, when once again the streets of Argostoli became gridlocked with what seemed to be every car on the island. Vehicles of all shapes and sizes drove nose to tail at a snail's pace with horns blaring, flags waving and passengers hanging out of car windows and open tops. Fireworks lit the night sky as the obligatory display from the roof of the Prefecture offices got underway. Rockets headed for the heavens and explosions echoed off nearby buildings in and around the square.

The celebrations carried on through the night, but for those who missed them first time round there were more the following evening, although on a much smaller scale; with less noise, fewer people and no fireworks.

The Olympic Flame

Eventually the construction work in Napier's Garden was completed, but I wasn't totally convinced. The main pathways and central part of the gardens were a vast improvement on what had been there previously, but the perimeter paths were still the same mixture of grit, loose gravel and weeds! It was rumoured the project had run over budget and out of money, so maybe that had something to do with the unfinished bits... maybe.

The ornate wrought iron gates at the main entrance were painted black and gold and looked first class, while the historic, but vandalised bust of Governor Napier welcomed visitors as they made their way up the steep slopes and past the war memorial to the garden's focal point, The Bandstand, which had also been given the black and gold treatment.

Napier's Garden was the perfect setting for the arrival of the Olympic flame before it left for the mainland and its final destination, the Olympic stadium in Athens. The police in Argostoli had been out earlier that morning, and with the help of a mobile crane had removed all illegally parked vehicles from the route along which the relay of torch bearers would be running.

The flame arrives

Napier's Garden

A huge crowd had gathered and just after ten o'clock the final runner entered the gardens, ran to the front of the bandstand and lit Kefalonia's own symbolic flame. The lighting was a signal for celebrations, and after the mandatory speeches, a traditional dancing troupe performed around it.

The Olympic Games

Although there were no Olympic venues on the island there was a general interest in the games themselves.

Progress and preparation, especially of the Olympic Stadium, had been closely monitored by the local, national, and international media for months, and with only a few weeks to completion, questions were being asked as to whether the central show-piece of the games, with its revolutionary tubular roof structure, would be ready for the official opening ceremony. Everybody, other than the hosts themselves were having a field day fuelling the negative speculation, but the Greeks always knew it would be finished, and with a few days to the deadline it was finally unveiled to the world. The burning question in everybody's mind now was... how much would it all cost?

The whole Olympic project was reported to be hundreds of millions of euros in debt, a debt someone, somewhere, would have to pay back, but as with most previous Games of the modern era the bill would be passed on to the tax payer.

Although the world's media had been hyper-critical before, during and after the games, the Greeks themselves couldn't have cared less, because in their opinion their Olympic Games had been the most successful ever.

Another Christening

During our first summer on the island Pam and I had been to the christening of Clara, the grand daughter of Clara, who we still saw occasionally at the hotel.

Then on a blazing hot day in the middle of summer we

210

went to another. Spyros and Maren were having their young son, Lukas christened. Although the small cave church of Saint Gerassimos doesn't offer the grandeur of the Argostoli Cathedral (which was where Clara was blessed), it is equally as enchanting, and being so small there was an intimacy you couldn't find in a bigger church. Its location, on the Spilia road high above Lassi offers splendid views across the bay which the centre of Argostoli could never do.

The small church of St Gerassimos

On the afternoon of the christening the heat was intense. It was one of those Kefalonian days when the coolest place to be was indoors, so with that in mind, Irini, the proud grandmother, ushered everybody into the tiny chapel. We were wedged tight, like sardines in a can, and gradually, as the double effect of body heat and candle power took effect, the temperature steadily rose. There was no escape, indoors or out.

Of course, there were the usual last minute arrivals who not only expected to park directly in front of the chapel's door, but when eventually they did get parked, then attempted to push to the front of the congregation, but because people were so tightly packed there wasn't a hope of pushing anywhere.

The Orthodox christening is a lovely ceremony in which

the congregation are encouraged to take part, but it comes as a bit of a shock to the 'christenee' when the big moment arrives. It's not a gentle pouring of holy water over the forehead, oh no! The poor little innocent (unless it happens to be an adult christening) gets the full saturation treatment as he or she is taken from the arms of its loving parents by the priest and dunked three times into a font full of holy water and essential oils. As the infant looks up into his face, the holy man must appear to be the devil himself and not one of God's worldly disciples; Lord have mercy.

Up to that point the little lad had been angelic, not once a murmur, but as the holy water flowed over and around him, so too did the tears.

While on the subject of christenings and specifically the naming of Greek children, there is, as one would expect, a tradition to uphold. For example, if the child is the first born son he is named after the grandfather on the father's side, and if it's a first born daughter she is named after the mother of the father. After that it's too complicated to go into further detail. There are though, parents who completely buck the trend and don't name the child after anybody in the family, no matter whose side they're on. And that's when the shit really does hit the fan!

Strangers Bearing Gifts

Statistics were showing that The Diary was being read by a lot of people, which sometimes resulted in strangers bearing gifts. Although I'd more or less settled into the Kefalonian way of life, there were times when I'd post on the website some of the minor irritations of living on a small island; nothing major, just niggling little things, like not receiving the colour supplements in the Greek edition of the English Sunday paper. Another quirk was having to wait until the Monday evening before getting it.

In the season there was never a problem, as a handful of Lassi supermarkets sold the Sunday papers on Sunday should I ever get desperate. My local newsagent was conveniently situated in Rizospaston, sandwiched between the mini market and the chocolate shop. Lampros and Theo were the English speaking brothers working in what was another family run business, and would keep the paper for me providing it had been delivered from the main agent in the Lithostroto; it was the ideal arrangement.

In summer, as I didn't go to Lassi, I'd normally collect it on a Monday evening on the way to work. If it wasn't in, one of the brothers would phone the main agent, and if he'd got it, it would be collected and delivered to The Gallery; what a great service, but it was summer service only.

During the winter I'd call in on Monday evening as usual, but it would be touch and go as to whether it had been delivered on the mainland ferry (all newspapers came from the mainland, except local ones). So from one week to another, summer or winter, I was never quite sure if I'd get a paper or not.

Anyway, back to the supplements. It was not uncommon during the season for some diary readers to visit The Gallery and, after brief introductions and smiles, to hand over a carrier bag (usually with the W.H. Smith logo on the side) containing my favourite Sunday weekly, which, of course included the full complement of supplements. It was great, because the English edition would be more than enough to keep me in reading material for at least a week. It's remarkable how a little thought can give so much pleasure.

Summer in Rizospaston

During the balmy evenings of the high season, craft stalls were a common feature on the streets of Argostoli. In

213

previous summers they had lined the wide avenue between the south side of the square and the archaeological museum, but now, to everybody's delight, especially the businesses situated close by, they were re-located under the palm trees of Rizospaston, selling a variety of items ranging from jewellery and ceramics to fine art. The street took on a wonderful creative atmosphere and was closed to evening traffic, as most of the streets around the square were, to become a constant meandering stream of slow moving pedestrians.

Although I knew most of the artisans well enough to stop and talk to, two of the most colourful were artists from Belgrade; Dragisa (pronounced Drageecha) and his beautiful art-teacher daughter, Jelena (pronounced Yalayna). They returned to Argostoli every summer and I'd first met him a couple of years ago when he exhibited in The Teacher's House in Rizospaston, which was a popular venue for exhibitions.

His work was interesting, being neither abstract nor traditional, but was more or less an extension of his own personality. Wild eyes lit up a face that could have been carved from granite, and from which grew an unkempt moustache, beard, and a mane of straggly shoulder length hair, and there you had a guy who in every sense was the true Bohemian. The fact that he couldn't speak a word of English didn't matter, because we always warmly greeted each other with hand shakes and embraces, while Pam was smothered with hugs and showered with hairy kisses.

Jelena in no way physically resembled her extrovert father. She was a dark haired Balkan beauty whose smile and eyes radiated warmth, which, I somehow sensed cloaked a cool interior, and although her English was good, it was spoken in such deep sex filled tones that lesser mortals such as I went weak at the knees. I did everything possible to keep our conversations as lengthy as possible, even if it meant talking nonsense.

Jelena was as artistically gifted as her father. However, the opinion she had of people such as him and me, was that we were entirely selfish in our pursuit for artistic creation. To a certain degree she was right (note from Pam - 100% right!) because while Dragisa was creating the alternative in the name of art, she had drawn the short straw and prostituted her talent sketching head and shoulder portraits on the half lit footpaths of Rizospaston.

It really was a tough way to make money, as she and other portraitists worked the streets under the most difficult conditions. The lighting was subdued and there was the stifling heat, but worst of all were the overbearing spectators who crowded behind, and as close to the artist as possible, in an attempt to see the drawing come to life. Through all those claustrophobic distractions and against all odds the artist struggled to create a likeness of the subject, usually a child, who, after a few minutes of trying to keep still, lost concentration and became totally bored with the whole thing. And, if the truth be known, so did the artist, and while some, like Jelena, actually caught the likeness, there were others who completely lost it… and still expected to be paid. Those guys were really on a hiding to nothing and relatively speaking were working for peanuts. I wouldn't have done it for love nor money, but ultimately it was their choice.

Ban the Dog

As word spread round the neighbourhood that Napier's Garden had re-opened, the locals began their social gatherings again. The new wooden picnic tables were ideal and used frequently by a variety of visitors, which included family picnickers with their homemade goodies as well as an abundance of pizza eaters. Fast food was slowly but surely infiltrating the island as an alternative to traditional Greek cuisine.

It was a peaceful setting under the shade of the giant eucalyptus trees, while the downside, and unfortunately there was one, was that litter pollution was rife. The rubbish bins were far too small, especially for the pizza boxes, and quickly filled to overflowing. Given a hard task, the municipality did their best to keep the gardens clean and free of ordinary rubbish, but no matter how hard they tried they were always on to a loser. But a far greater hazard than the litter pollution, especially for the youngsters who played unaware of it on the grass areas, was the mess left by fouling dogs.

Ban the Dog notices had been strategically placed close to all entrances and were easy to see, and even easier to understand. There was a picture of a dog with a line through it, similar to the universal 'no smoking' sign, with white lettering on a red background printed in English and Greek that read, 'Dogs are not allowed'.

Dogs can't read, and because there were no barriers or gates to stop them they wandered in freely to do what comes naturally. What was unnatural however, was the number of local residents who could read, but ignored the signs and took their dogs in anyway, letting them loose to defecate anywhere, which unfortunately included on the grass areas where the youngsters played. From the point of view of the health hazard, the dog problem was far worse than the litter one, but sadly both were results of human neglect.

Bobbing

At the height of summer when the sea was at its warmest, not only were the island's beaches invaded in great numbers, but the shallow waters between Kiani Akti and the lighthouse, and in particular Fanari beach, were popular with early morning Bobbers.

Bobbing is a form of semi-stationary paddling, where the body is submerged up to the neck, and although Bobbers often had to bend their knees to achieve that (they were after all, standing in shallow water) they also had to have a good sense of balance to stop themselves from falling over.

As well as being a popular way of starting the day, Bobbing was also an exercise in social awareness, because, it seemed, the whole purpose of the exercise was to have a good chat with the person, or persons nearby, whose voices carried across the glassy water in the cool breath of early morning, Bobbing to their heart's content in time with the gentle swell of the crystal clear sea.

To Steki

As the islanders started relaxing after another scorching summer, the doors were about to close on what for us had become another regular eating place - To Steki.

As well as the bizarre interior, where the walls were painted with surreal images of the lighthouse and various other forms of marine life, there was also some of the most basic dining furniture imaginable. However, in total contrast to the eccentric interior, some of the best value for money food and wine in Argostoli was served, which only goes to show you can't judge a good taverna by its appearances; indoors or out.

I say that, because some months before we started eating there regularly, I'd refused to go in based on what I seen on the outside. The multi-coloured plastic flags that hung from the canopy overhanging the pavement, and the freezer that sat on the edge of it, the pavement not the canopy, were a definite turn off.

To Steki Ouzeri, Argostoli

It was another family business and was run by Irena's brother-in-law, and which she'd become involved in through marriage. Her brother-in-law, like most Kefalonian men, was happy to play the 'supporting' role and left the day to day tasks to the women, or woman, who in that case was the aforementioned Irena.

It came then as a big shock when he told her he was closing the taverna at the end of the summer. She however wasn't prepared to accept that and in the wake of his decision took the business off his hands to go it alone, a brave step for a woman living in a male dominated society. At the beginning of October as the season began to wind down To Steki closed, only to re-open straight away to let the builders in.

Irena's vision was to transform it into an upmarket taverna, but without upmarket prices, and was totally committed to the task ahead which would involve dealing with macho builders and the beast of Greek bureaucracy.

Although we hadn't known her long, it was long enough to know she was capable of doing it, and over the winter months Pam and I kept a discreet eye on progress as an amazing transformation took place.

An Early End

The season finished early for Pam and me because we were going to a wedding; at long last Bradley intended to make an honest woman out of Sarah.

Earlier in the year when the wedding had been announced our main concern had been how the flight from Athens to Luton would affect Pam's dodgy lung. The Greek doctors had imposed a flying ban which she understandably wasn't happy about, so she wrote to the lung specialist in the UK for a second opinion. His detailed and informative reply concluded that millions of emphysema sufferers fly with no adverse effects, and he saw no reason why Pam, who didn't smoke, and took regular exercise should be any different.

At the time of her grounding we had, or rather I had spoken to Costas (the taxi) about the possibility of doing the journey in the Mercedes.

'What a good idea,' he'd said, and couldn't wait to fire up the navigational aid again to show me how easy it would be.

In the end we didn't need Costas, as Pam was finally given the all clear to fly. A great time was had by all at the wedding. We met Brad's family for the first time, all of whom had flown to Edinburgh from New York, while at the ceremony I felt honoured to have been asked to read one of the passages.

Despite having a great time, I picked up a couple of injuries in the most bizarre circumstances, which had me walking with difficulty for weeks after. It was during the reception as I was dancing the Gay Gordons, when suddenly severe pain in both Achilles tendons forced me to stop, therefore bringing my evening of dancing to a premature end.

I limped painfully to the bar and asked for an ice pack, 'Sorry mate we haven't got any ice.' What, a bar with no ice, that's as bad as a pub with no beer. Although my injuries put a bit of a downer on things, there was however one massive up side to the whole trip; Pam suffered no ill effects from the flights.

Trade Training

Although the wedding was close to the end of the season I didn't really want to close The Gallery early, but to avoid it meant finding someone to stand in while we were away. The ideal person was Jennie who lived just round the corner and was a friend of Prue's who we'd met and got to know through the mutual friendship. It was fortunate Jennie was still around, because earlier in the year she'd left Kefalonia, but like so many others hadn't been able to stay away, much to my good fortune.

In fact, it was back in the earlier part of the summer that Pam and I, along with Prue had a farewell dinner with Jennie at the *Sto Psito* (pronounced Stow, as in stowaway, Puhseeto) taverna in Lassi.

She and Prue were an odd couple, a bit like Laurel and Hardy, not physically, and they didn't wear bowler hats, but it was just the way their banter worked. Jennie was the bossy 'big Ollie', while Prue gave back as good as she got; the typical Stan. Both were on top form that evening as friendly insults shot back and forth across the table, but the funniest of all was as we were leaving. It was one of those wonderful starlit June nights when a million pinpoints filled the sky, and the reflected lights of the Paliki danced on the black water. With our good nights and goodbyes said, Pam and I watched and listened as Stan and Ollie melted into the darkness to become part of the night.

Then Jennie's voice broke the silence, 'Peter, thank you for the picture.'

At which Prue retorted, 'How can you thank him, you haven't seen it yet.'

Shortly before Pam and I left for Scotland, Jennie came to The Gallery for some trade training when I showed her where everything was, the important things such as tea and coffee, and how everything worked, such as the cash register. But as there were no sales while we were away she didn't have to use it anyway.

A Reality Check

Although Pam and I weren't rolling in money, we looked after what we'd got and lived a fairly frugal but not uncomfortable lifestyle. Having to rely on what we earned in the season meant tightening our belts through the winter, especially during the months of March and April, just as a new summer season loomed over the horizon. It was of some consolation then that she qualified for Greek unemployment benefit which helped us through those six empty months off season.

The Gallery was a way of life for me and I loved it for what it was, and because of what I'd made it, but despite our winter economy drive the financial omens still looked grim. Over the past three summers takings had dropped, not dramatically, but enough to cause concern, and to make things worse the outgoings followed an upward trend; they were the overheads associated with any business. In my case the biggest was the rent, followed by the outrageously high TEBE contributions, which, despite the change of government still increased on an annual basis.

So, taking everything into consideration, and after a lot

of soul searching it was with deep regret that I made the decision to close The Gallery.

Since I'd been there Lefteris had become more of a mate than a landlord, and because of that I felt a deep loyalty towards him, but in business sentiment has no place, which in the past I'd suffered the harsh consequences of.

The more I thought about closing, the more I put it off, but Lefteris as usual came up with a solution, or at least he thought he had! Because of my low income he said it might be possible to suspend my TEBE payments for the winter.

'What a good idea,' I thought, and went to see Dimitris.

Now whether I'd misunderstood Lefteris, or whether he'd got it completely wrong, Dimitris was adamant that TEBE payments had to be paid in full and on time, summer and winter.

'B****cks,' Lefteris said, but Dimitris was right.

Something New

As a way of supplementing my shrinking income, Pam suggested something completely different in addition to my repertoire of Kefalonian paintings. Her lateral thinking saw the production of the highly successful Kefalonian calendars. She was the mastermind behind the idea and did all the necessary design, graphics, and assembly work at home, and by the time the calendars had been spiral bound they looked really good, very professional. And more importantly, people loved them, and more importantly still, people bought them.

Tipota (pronounced Tee pot ah)

Tipota to the Greeks, roughly translated, means 'it's nothing', which was a word I'd heard a lot, without actually knowing what it meant.

Having lived in Argostoli for over three years Pam and I were recognised and welcomed warmly wherever we went, especially in the shops and supermarkets. Pam had made some plain white curtains for The Gallery which I'd fixed above the windows with small pins, not only as curtains but as simple sun blinds; primitive but effective. She was making more curtains for the apartment with a more conventional way of hanging them, by using hooks and header tape. The materials were bought from the shop, Messari, (also known as The Brothers) who sold everything from carpets to underwear.

'I'd like to buy a metre of header tape,' she told Makis, the eldest brother.

'That'll be five thousand euros or nothing,' he said with a big smile.

'I'm sorry but I don't have that much in change.'

'OK *Tipota...*' Deal done.

Nikos, one of the friendliest guys in Argostoli owned the hardware shop 'Krystal' in Sitemporon. He too had a big smile and a ready handshake as part of his welcome. Having bought most of our smaller kitchen utensils and accessories from him the latest purchase was a small serrated kitchen knife.

'*Poso kani* Niko?' I asked.

Then the glow of the smile warmed his face, '*Tipota* Peter'.

Another man who found it difficult to take my money was Nick the jeweller, brother of Spyros (part of the same family as the Fok dogs). My watch had stopped, so Nick and his son Yiorgos, who like brother Nikiforos spoke good English, inspected it and fitted a new battery. Although Nick didn't speak much English himself, like most Kefalonians he understood more than he let on.

As he handed me the watch I paid him, then, placing the

money back in my hand, he said in broken English, '*Tipota* Peter, keep it in your pocket.'

We found unexpected kindness like that wherever we went, not all the time obviously, but that's how it was. So Pam and I adopted a simple philosophy: if we were spending money, where possible we'd spend it with people we liked and trusted.

I've often described the Kefalonians as warm and welcoming, but in so many other ways they were generous and giving too.

A Black Line

Graffiti increasingly continued to be a regular insult to the eyes around Argostoli, but we didn't expect it to encroach on our lives the way it did one morning. The White Panda, which was normally parked outside the apartment had been sprayed with a wide black line that ran along the driver's side from the headlight to the rear light cluster. It was a stark contrast of black on white. Fortunately the paint was water based and came off easily with hot soapy water and elbow grease.

The graffiti vandals had also been in Napier's Garden where everything there had been sprayed, including the war memorial, Napier's bust and the bandstand. Such was their fuddled brain power however, that they hadn't realised that spraying black on the black wrought ironwork of the bandstand, would never have the same impact as black on white.

An Amazing Glimpse into History and Chaos

As well as giving us the opportunity to get out and about generally, our white panda also gave us the chance to explore parts of Kefalonia's turbulent history. During the

2002 walkabout I'd had no idea that nestling in the foothills of the mountains high above the modern resort of Skala were the remains of what had once been a thriving community. Having since heard about it and knowing roughly how to get there we headed in an upwards direction from the square of New Skala. It was a gradual climb, and after about an hour of walking we were suddenly and without warning there, amongst the ruins of Old Skala.

Above us, hidden in shade was an olive press, a relic of past prosperity but, now rusting, it was almost hidden by the trees whose fruit would once have fed it, but after so many years would never again be harvested.

A rusting olive press in Old Skala

Up on the slopes to our right, scattered broken stone shells had virtually disappeared, forgotten in the side of the mountain. They would have been homes to villagers, but were now deserted and partially obscured by the rampant growth of uncultivated trees, bushes and wild grass.

Further along the track stood a stunning bell tower, battered but majestic, its rustic masonry a patchwork of filtered light that broke through the nearby trees. In comparison to the crumbling bell tower, and only a few metres from it, was the bleached stonework of the washhouse, and although damaged, the four semi-circular arches stood virtually intact on the square columns supporting them.

The communal wash-house, Old Skala,
Painting, oil on canvas by Peter Hemming

We spent a lot of time up there that afternoon, and heading back from the old village to the new, came across even more ruins; a church nestling almost unseen amongst the trees below us. It too had been almost devoured by over five decades of living growth.

That first visit to Old Skala had been profoundly moving, giving us an amazing glimpse into a lost world of history and chaos.

There were hundreds of isolated ruins scattered around Kefalonia, easily visible to the passer by, but the ruined villages were much harder to find. It was as though they had been purposely and discreetly hidden, perhaps as a way of covering up the pain and scars of the not too distant past.

Christmas

Argostoli was once again highly decorated for the festive season. The musicians were, as usual, out in numbers parading along the Lithostroto adding gaiety and song to the already joyful atmosphere of Christmas Eve.

The Argostoli Male Voice Choir on Christmas Eve

Later we went to Pub Old House, where, as well as enjoying the evening there was a collection to make. Pam and I had fancied some Harvey's Bristol Cream Sherry, just as a special treat, so in the run up to Christmas I'd tried to buy some in the supermarkets and cavas of the town (a cava is an off licence, or liquor store) but without any luck, so Mr Do-It-All sorted it for us, and it was good.

We saw Christmas in at the pub, but New Year, anywhere other than upstairs wouldn't have been the same, so once again we climbed the marble stairs. Later as 2004 slipped away to the dulcet tones of the choir, Pam and I looked back on some of the other things that had happened in a year of amazing highs, as well as depressing and unnecessary lows.

A guy came to The Gallery trying to sell me paintings; another came selling calendars; there was a bomb alert at the courthouse; I was asked to teach private art lessons, but couldn't because I didn't have a licence, to teach that is; we went to the regatta at the Koutavos Lagoon; a new road test certificate for the car was issued, legally; Stathis bought a new car and I started work on this book.

Bell Tower, Old Skala
Painting, oil on canvas by Peter Hemming

2005 – As One Door Closes Another One Opens

Happy New Year

Pam and I welcomed in the New Year with our friends upstairs, and unlike twelve months previously we were celebrating it together.

On New Year's morning once again the strains of brass music woke us as it drifted up through Napier's Garden from the streets around the square. Most of the day was spent with Tim and Maria at their home in Spilia. Maria's sister Margaret was visiting from Australia, and Isabel, who worked for one of Argostoli's local estate agents made up the six. Tim, being the perpetual football addict couldn't resist switching the television on for coverage of the English Premier League match that was being shown, and having no choice I had to watch it with him. There was a moment when I thought Maria, who said he was out of order switching it on, was going to slap him, but because it was the festive season, with goodwill to all men and women and all that stuff, she didn't.

Tim and I had watched a lot of football in various bars and cafés during the season, but it felt good to be watching it in the smoke free zone of their lounge instead of the smokescreen of an Argostoli bar, and as an added bonus Tim's drinks were free. After eating, drinking and generally having a good time we walked home which fortunately was all downhill and we settled down for an evening of more visual entertainment! We watched Captain Corelli's Mandolin, having fun playing 'spot the location'.

Other than the short walks to Spilia and back, our first real walk, in which we exerted some real energy was two

229

days later along the coast road to Fanari, at which point Pam turned back. Since the surgery she'd struggled with any sort of uphill slope, so the walk to the lighthouse was ideal for her because it was relatively flat, but going much further would have certainly meant a severe test. By turning back, the only significant climb was up through Napier's Garden and along our road, but by then she was almost home anyway. I carried on along the water's edge, and coming off the track, back onto the coast road, met Makis the taxi and his friend Dimitris. Dimitris worked as an installation engineer for OTE so as well as wishing him Happy New Year I couldn't resist the temptation to ask why connecting to the internet was so slow (broadband was still in the distant future, and the further from Argostoli you were the more distant it became).

'Peter, everybody knows it's slow, but no-one knows why, nobody in Athens knows either.' I don't know where in the equation Athens came, and it wasn't quite the answer I was expecting, but then sometimes getting a straight answer from anyone was like getting a 'yes' or 'no' from a politician.

A Casualty of the Civil War

Wherever we walked there always seemed to be someone to stop and talk to. Pam and I befriended another local character named Spyros - yes another one - it was probably second only to Makis as being the most common name on the island. We'd first met him one afternoon, sitting, idling the time away on the low wall at the top of the hill where the main road from Argostoli bends and descends towards Lassi (and is sometimes referred to as Lassi bank). He said it was one of his favourite spots and sat there often. Like a lot of other people, including me, Spyros loved that view. The light shone on the water and the dark Lassi headland cut into the sea, whereas the patchwork of distant greens on the Paliki played tricks, as the eyes adjusted in the dazzlingly bright sunlight.

Spyros was a Royalist and proudly wore a small pin in his lapel to prove it, but as well as the badge there was more gruesome evidence of his loyalty to royalty, because as a consequence, his 'good' right hand had been severed by his communist captors during the Greek Civil War. Like many other Kefalonians his face was full of character. Bushy side whiskers grew down each side of it meeting under his nose to form a huge moustache that almost, but not quite hid his warm smile; another trademark by which to recognise him was his black beret.

Although Spyros spoke little English, his understanding of it was good. He always greeted us in English and listened carefully to our pronunciation as we spoke slowly for his benefit. He too was blessed with the famed Kefalonian generosity and when he saw us dipped his hand into his pocket, bringing out an assortment of boiled sweets. Because of their different flavours, which weren't the usual greens, reds, blacks, and oranges etc. we thought they must be Kefalonian. Pam's favourite was ouzo, whereas I was a lobster man; with those sort of flavours it's possible they just could've been an island speciality.

Mechanical Crisis

We'd really got into the swing of frugal living and stretched our money so it lasted through the long months of winter, but every so often something totally unexpected dented the budget. The car needed new shock absorbers and we were left with no other choice, apparently it was a legal requirement so we grinned and bore it.   There wasn't a lot of grinning, especially when our trusted mechanic discovered a cylinder head problem as well. 'What next?' I thought.

In small island communities everybody it seems is related in some way, because whoever we spoke to just happened to be a cousin of someone else. It came then as no great surprise to discover that my mechanic's son was my lawyer, which was a real twist of good luck. His office was in Argostoli and because he also lived in Travliata, next door to his dad, it was nothing for him to drive me back to town after I'd delivered the car to the workshop. Then he'd kindly take me back when it was ready for collection. The arrangement was ideal, and unlike most solicitors there was no fee.

The Seeds Had Been Sown

The grass was growing under our feet which meant it was time to leave; but where to we asked each other. Spain? No, it was as hot there as it was in Kefalonia. Ireland? No, it rained a lot, but the Guinness was tempting! Back to the UK? No.

So after more deliberation and deep thought I suggested, 'Let's go to France.'

Pam was a dedicated Francophile and in her former life (that is, before she met me) had been part of a twinning group with Chambon sur Voueize, a village in the Creuse, a very rural area of central France, and although we didn't make a definite decision there and then the seeds had been sown.

Renting out our house in Swindon had become fraught with a multitude of problems verging on the unbelievable. The letting agent had turned out to be next to useless and had been invoicing us for the most ridiculous things. For example the latest was: we were billed ten pounds for the replacement of a broken light shade. The mind boggles! How does a light shade get broken beyond repair, and what's more, why did we have to pay for it? From then on we queried every payment, at which the agent got not only defensive, but stroppy too. As Landlords surely we had a right to know what was happening in our own home? But according to that agent, obviously not.

The straw that finally broke the camel's back though was when the water boiler packed up and the cost of a replacement was over a thousand pounds. There was a service contract which we thought covered eventualities like that, but it wasn't worth the paper it was written on, so we paid out. Unlike the lampshade the tenants couldn't be expected to pay for that; it really was down to us.

Later that day we walked to the pulpit rock and sat quietly in the sun while the sounds of the sea calmed us and helped to clear our minds, which it did. It was then we decided to sell the house.

Once In A While

Although I worked to a strict daily routine, Monday to Saturday, once in a while I'd clean my brushes and finish early. 'Pam, it's such a beautiful day let's go out for the afternoon,' was what I wrote in the text message (yes, as incredible as it seems, by then I'd learnt how to send, and receive them).

'OK,' her reply read, so we did.

The light was crystal clear with a sky as blue as I'd ever seen it when we left Argostoli heading northwards up the west coast road, stopping and starting whenever the mood took us. The famous Myrtos view was, as it had been on that first holiday excursion, amazing, so we parked up and gazed in wonder at the ever changing mood of the sea, relentlessly pounding the white stony beach. Further north I turned off the main road at the village of Vassilikades (pronounced Vassili karthez) and followed the signs for Agia Efimia, along what became known to us as the East Coast road.

Pam and I had first driven along it a few weeks earlier after a walk to Sia monastery, from where there were also beautiful, but almost unknown views of Myrtos. Unfortunately, on that day the weather closed in and on higher ground we drove in cloud which reduced visibility to almost zero, making driving extra hazardous on the wet roads. One option was to turn back, but I chose the lesser of two evils, and although not knowing the road, carried on to Agia Efimia.

Meanwhile, and on a day when driving was a pleasure, we could actually see how the road climbed and meandered to reach the top from where the most spectacular views were. We stopped at a small parking place to take in the panorama, where in the pure light Ithaca seemed close enough to touch, while the distant snow-capped mountains of the mainland were clearly visible.

Southern tip of Ithaca with snow-capped mainland mountains

As well as the natural land and seascapes one of the nicest things about driving the East Coast road was that it was virtually traffic free, even in summer, for which there was a perfectly good reason. Because the road was so narrow, especially through some of the villages, heavy vehicles, which included long tour coaches and larger lorries, found it impossible to get through; even driving a small car like ours could sometimes be difficult.

Thousands of visitors to the island would, unless they hired a car, motorbike or taxi, never experience that amazing journey, and therefore missed out on what for me was another part of essential Kefalonia. Driving along the coast from Agia Efimia to Sami that afternoon I thought we'd seen everything there was to see, but I was wrong.

It was after the long drive up the mountain coming out of Sami, and on the final descent to Argostoli, at the Valsamata turn, that the whole western sky ahead had turned into a burning orange inferno, which, reflected in the sea gave the impression of it being on fire.

Kefalonia boasted beautiful sunsets, but they didn't normally last long. That one though was an exception and seemed to go on for ever. It was still blazing as we crossed the Dhrapano bridge, so I drove along the waterfront and out of town to Fanari, stopping briefly at the lighthouse, which in that strange light glowed pink.

It was from the car park of the Olive Garden holiday complex high above Lassi that we watched the late afternoon sun eventually burn itself out, turning from a glowing red, through various shades of crimson before finally disappearing into the ink blue of evening. It had been another unforgettable Kefalonian experience and I never saw another sunset quite like that one. The East Coast road however would always be there.

Another Spyros

Although we'd driven round the Sami and Agia Efimia areas of the island, Pam and I hadn't done any walking there at all. All that changed in the Spring when we went for a long hike with Dee (Peter had an ankle injury, but was mobile enough to cook dinner, and promised it would ready when we got back).

Having parked close to the Drogarati Cave we set off on a big loop, taking in the villages of Haliotata, Poulata and Karavomilos. What immediately struck us all was how friendly the people were, as they waved and greeted us from their houses and cars.

One car did stop and a young Greek guy stuck his head out of the window, 'Good morning I'm Spyros, you're English, would you like a lift?' which we politely refused, and then struck up a lengthy conversation. After telling him where we'd started from, and where we were going he was momentarily lost for words, but his facial expression said it all. He thought we were mad.

'And how did you know we were English?' I asked.

He smiled. 'Easy – you don't look Greek. I studied in the UK and had a great time, that's how I learnt to speak your language.'

Greek men have a reputation for being great lovers, that's their opinion not mine, so I posed him another question.

'OK Spyro, you had a good time at university and you think the UK is a great place, so what did you think of our British girls, were they great too?'

The smile broadened and his eyes lit up, 'Peter I loved them, and they loved me, that's how it was.'

After studying at Sheffield and Guildford, the lure of the island brought him back home to the family-owned Sami Beach Hotel at Karavomilos. It is set in beautiful surroundings, looking across the bay from behind the giant eucalyptus trees that grow along the shoreline. He invited us to call in during the summer when the hotel was open, so we did. His family were charming people and always made Pam and me welcome whenever we called.

Spyros, as with many other Kefalonians wore two hats, a summer one for the hotel, and a winter one for his own property development business.

The Coffee Courier

Argostoli has enough colourful characters to write a separate book about, and one in particular, who also wore two hats, was Makis the coffee courier. Facially, like many, he'd been scorched by the harsh elements and was easily recognisable by his thinning black hair which was greased to his ebony coloured scalp. His clothing was fairly distinguishable too, he wore either black or white.

Not many of the town's businesses had in-house coffee making facilities, so workers either called into the nearest coffee shop for a takeaway, or used one of the few that offered a door to door delivery service.

One such café was a couple of doors up from Mia's salon, adjacent to the entrance of the tax office, and was run by a big friendly guy called Nick; it was from there that Makis delivered. Of all the coffee couriers in the town he was reputed to be the best, and legend has it that he had never spilt a drop, and more importantly had never had any serious collisions with anybody, or anything. Incredible, because there were unseen obstacles around every corner. It was fascinating to watch him skilfully threading his way through the pedestrians along the Lithostroto on his small blue motorbike, while at the same time performing an amazing balancing act with a look of pure concentration etched into his dark face; using one hand to carry the tray of drinks, as the other controlled the all important steering and braking.

Although his tray was custom made for coffee on the move, it wasn't exclusive to motorbikes, because the less famous foot couriers, mainly the guys working at The Bell Tower, used the same design. Four lengths of metal were fixed to the raised sides (raised to stop the drinks slipping off) of the circular tray, and were joined at the top by a large metal ring that formed the handle.

And Makis's two hats? As well as being Argostoli's king of the coffee couriers in the mornings, during the summer he worked the afternoon reception shift at the White Rocks Hotel in Lassi.

The End of an Era

One morning I bumped into a rather distraught Clara who, almost in tears, went to great pains to tell me that Panagis had sold the hotel, and because she was so upset, I didn't ask why he'd sold it. There was a time and a place for questions, and that wasn't one of them. She was a familiar face to regular passers by, in and out of season, and walking past the Star was never the same after she'd gone. It was the end of an era, but there were so many happy memories to look back on.

Only a year or so before selling up Panagis spent a fortune refurbishing it, and one day as I was passing he dragged me in to show off his 'new hotel', which was how he described it. It had been totally transformed, and had I been taken inside blindfolded it would have been impossible (once the blindfold had been removed of course) to recognise it as the Cephalonia Star that had briefly been my home.

'Peter,' he said, after proudly showing me round the once familiar bar and the rest of the ground floor, 'I'll show you your room, the one you stayed in, can you remember which one it was?'

'Yes Panagis I can,' and led the way. Imagine then the look on his face as he turned the key and opened the door.

'Yes, what do you want?' came an angry voice from the darkness.

'*Signomi*,' was Panagis's embarrassed response as he quietly pulled the door to, then stepping back into the corridor he showed me to another room, but that time he knocked on the door before opening it.

Diana

Pam and I met Diana (real name, Yiota, pronounced Yotta) on our first Kefalonian holiday. Her taverna of the same name, Diana, not Yiota, was near the bridge with unobstructed open views across the water to Dhrapano and the mountains. On that first visit we had no choice but to go in, it was almost impossible not to. The open sided taverna was on one side of the narrow footpath, while parked cars were on the other; the imposing figure of Yiota stood like a one woman barrier somewhere in the middle.

With a big hello and an even bigger smile she proved impossible to pass, but her strong arm tactics didn't bother or offend us, after all we were on holiday with plenty of time on our hands and thought, 'What the heck, we've got nothing to lose, let's give it a try.' Which we did, and loved it.

The low cane chairs with their deep cushions were comfortable and the chilled freshly squeezed orange juice was a treat in the heat.

Diana's Taverna in 2001

Not long after arriving in 2001, Yiota spotted me walking past the 'winter headquarters' of Taverna Diana, which were situated across the road from the summer haven.

She greeted me with hugs and kisses, along with her familiar, "Ello my love 'ow are you?' and the unfamiliar, 'come, 'ave a drink, I pay.' (The Kefalonians do have wonderful memories, considering they see thousands of people during the course of the summer.) Despite my protests I was dragged inside and treated not only to coffee, but breakfast too. It was like returning home after spending years in exile.

She was always the same and never took a penny from me, saying with a big smile, '*Tipota*, my love.' I thought things would change after Pam arrived, but they didn't, because she received the special treatment too.

A couple of summers later Yiota closed up in Argostoli

and moved to Trapezaki which was a bad move, at least from a business point of view, because as summer visitor numbers steadily fell, she, like almost everyone else relying on seasonal trade, especially in the outlying villages, felt the pinch.

Then early this year she returned to the capital and re-opened at the other end of town, across the road from the Lixouri ferry port, which proved to be not only a brilliant location, but more importantly a great taverna.

The new Taverna Diana

Only a few days before opening she saw Pam and me walking past, 'Ello my love,' she greeted us both, 'soon I am open, you will come and eat with Yiota,' which we did and it was just like old times.

The new Taverna Diana had been completely renovated and the smart interior décor was a touch of class. The proof of the pudding however is always in the eating, and that evening there were no complaints (and no bill) as we walked away completely satisfied after once again receiving the Diana VIP treatment.

Because of its location, the taverna offered a feast of entertainment. To sit at one of the front tables and watch the docking and unloading of the Lixouri ferry opposite was a must, as chaos and pandemonium broke out only a few meters away for what really was a very good live comedy show.

Links

'My name's Brian and I'm opening a bookshop in Argostoli, I've seen your website and read the diary on a regular basis. My own site is being built and once it's up and running I'd like to link with yours.'

That's how the guy introduced himself on his first visit to The Gallery. I've never seen anything wrong with coming straight to the point, and had it not been for his strong Belfast accent it would have been easy to mistake him for a Kefalonian. Brian though hadn't been the only person wanting to link. My site had also been seen by other local businesses including the Mouikis holiday company who also wanted to link. Brian had spotted a niche in the market, and his bookshop, appropriately called The Bookmark, filled it perfectly, and in time would go from strength to strength. The majority of English speakers on the island had, until The Bookmark opened, relied generally on the jumble sale, the internet, or swapping with each other for reading material. He had not only plugged a huge gap for the ex-pats, but also for many of the English speaking Greeks who were beating a path to his door.

At no cost, website links were another lucrative business opening for me, and Brian became a good mate into the bargain.

Old Karavomilos

The villages that had been shattered by the earthquake were fascinating places, not for any sombre or macabre reason, but for what they represented, a part of Kefalonian heritage that had been lost in time.

Vlahata (not to be confused with the village of the same name straddling the main road south from Argostoli), known also as old Karavomilos, was, like old Skala situated in the foothills of the mountains and because we missed any obvious signposts, it was, on our first visit quite difficult to find.

The familiar spread of overgrowth was evident as nature continued to claim anything that didn't move. There were huge ruined mansions, once homes to the wealthy, as well as other more modest remnants that would've housed the less well off. The earthquake however, made no distinction between classes, wreaking havoc and terror for the fifty three seconds it lasted. The ruined villages were now classless, as what had once been dwellings now resembled nothing more than masonry skeletons and piles of rubble. Inevitably, everyone suffered the same fate; abandonment, homelessness and in some cases death and bereavement.

As well as dwellings, every other type of building had been damaged in some way or other, giving no clues to their past identities. Three walls stood on the site of what would have been a very beautiful church. Traces of faded blue paint, like patches of sky, clung to the outside walls, and where the exterior rendering had peeled away was now exposed Venetian stonework. The inside walls were much the same except for two arched recesses where the original frescos were still clearly visible and intact, even after years of exposure to the harsh Kefalonian elements. And the timber roof joists? They had collapsed and were long gone or lay like corpses where they had fallen.

Old Karavomilos was another poignant reminder of a bygone age.

Introductions

An invitation to spend an evening with Stathis and Irini, unless for a special occasion, a name day celebration or something like that, was quite unusual, so it came as a bit of a surprise when Irini phoned and asked us over. Yet despite the formality of this particular invitation we knew the evening would be anything but formal. We also knew there would be some good humour over a glass or two of wine once we got there.

Because it was such a nice evening we walked the scenic route, through the special place and along the coast road. Passing Spyros's *spiti* (Greek for home and pronounced Speety, as in sweety) I saw him feeding the chickens, he saw me too.

'Ah Petros, how are you? Come round to the house.'

'OK Spyro, but we can't stay long, we're going to Fanari.'

He appeared not to hear, or if he had, hadn't taken any notice. It was the first time he'd met 'my wife', and on introduction repeated her name several times, breaking it down into three syllables; Pam-el-a. Once we got indoors there were more introductions, but that was left to me, so I introduced the women to each other, Dimitra, unlike Spyros didn't get her tongue in a twist.

Just before leaving home I'd phoned Irini to say we were on our way and would be there in about forty minutes. However, events beyond our control were beginning to overtake us and the original plans for that evening turned on their head. Having sat down for no more than a few minutes Dimitra passed a bowl of sweet fruits across the table to accompany the two glasses of wine that Spyros had poured for us.

He had opened a bottle of Troianata (pronounced troy, as in toy, an arta, which is a village in the mountains near the monastery) Robola, and holding it to his eye proclaimed, 'Petros, this Troianata is the best,' and to prove a point we all lifted and chinked glasses.

'*Yiammas*,' we chanted loudly, in exactly the same way the Kefalonians do.

As Pam and I finished our drinks we gave each other the wink as a signal to leave, but it was too late, because Spyros had re-filled the empty glasses and once again the famous Kefalonian hospitality was about to move into overdrive, and from then on we were helpless. For all intents and purposes we may well have been tied to the chairs.

'Thanks Spyro, but don't forget we're visiting friends at Fanari and we really must be going soon,' I half heartedly protested, but it fell on deaf ears and he lifted his glass once more.

'*Yiammas* Petros and Pam-el-a.'

Fanari could never be described as the most over populated place on the island, and once he'd worked out who we were going to see, Spyros went to great lengths to tell us he was in the same class as Stathis at school.

We'd almost finished our wine and tried not to make it look too obvious that we had to get away, but once again we were pipped at the post. Dimitra had switched the gas on and loaded the pan with oil which was a signal for Spyros to top our glasses up again. As the wine flowed, the conversation got livelier and then the food arrived, a plate full of frankfurter sausages and eggs… each. What could we say? Nothing. I couldn't even protest my vegetarianism, well

I could, but considering the circumstances it wouldn't have been very polite.

Feeding us was another island custom. Visitors to a Kefalonian house for the first time, (even though I'd been before) are offered a drink and a light snack, usually a biscuit or a piece of cake, whereas in our case the offering bit didn't come into it, we had no choice. And what we were about to tuck into was slightly more than a light snack.

By now, and because a few glasses of wine always helps to loosen the tongue, the conversation was flying off in different directions before I remarked on the longevity of the Kefalonians, the men in general, Spyros in particular.

'Petros I have lived so long and it is down to the natural things in life, good meat, fresh fruit, vegetables, olive oil and red wine,' (even though we were drinking white). Then he smiled and with a twinkle in his deep dark eyes carried on, 'And of course Petros there is one other reason why I have lived so long..' There was a slight pause before he uttered the next word, '...sex,' at which Dimitra burst out laughing. It was amazing stuff, like something from a classic comedy film and we were part of it. But it wasn't comedy, he was serious.

After finishing our 'meal' and drinking even more Robola, it really was time to go, but if our hosts could have had their way we'd have been there all night. Since our arrival, it had started to rain, so as we were leaving Spyros lent us a huge black umbrella, the sort golfers use, but without the bright colours and advertising, then at last we were finally and unsteadily on our way.

Although Fanari wasn't that far, with the amount of wine we'd drunk it was everything we could do to hang on to the umbrella as the gusting breeze threatened to take it and us skyward. Just before leaving Spyros and Dimitra I'd phoned Irini again to explain the delay and that she'd get the full story once we got there… if we got there.

Being Greek, she and Stathis fully understood and we all had a good laugh as Pam and I re-capped the previous couple of hours. It was late by the time Stathis drove us home, and good that he'd offered, because after drinking more wine with them, walking would have been difficult. Being the practical joker he is I was surprised he hadn't come up with an excuse for not taking us, like something was wrong with the car, and sending us on our way only to drive along and pick us up a few minutes later. If our roles had been reversed I would have, although they would probably have phoned for a taxi.

Into the Modern World

There was only one Post Office in Argostoli which most of the time was packed, and because queuing didn't apply to some Kefalonians, getting to the counter sometimes became a bit of a lottery. That was, until the Post Office became part of the modern world and introduced a ticketed queuing system. It was easy to use, and more or less foolproof. On entering the building, the machine was just inside the door on the left, and by pressing a button it issued a ticket with a number on it.

Above each cashier's desk was an electronic numerical display, and once a customer had finished, the cashier flicked a switch and the next number appeared along with the sound of a buzzer. Then when the number on the display corresponded with the number on your ticket it was your turn; simple.

There was no doubt about it, the new scheme was much better and meant the previous free-for-all was a thing of the past, and not only that, seating was provided for customers as they waited patiently.

There was another benefit. Customers no longer had to wait around if they had other things to be getting on with, for example, some quick shopping. There was though always the chance of miscalculating the timing and getting back to find your turn had gone; that meant drawing another ticket and starting again. As well as introducing the ticketing system, the hours of opening were extended, from a two o'clock closing time to a more convenient four pm.

The first time I queued using the new system I saw our postman Makis who uncharacteristically was looking rather out of sorts.

'Hi Maki, you don't look very happy today what's the matter, oh, and I haven't seen you for some time have you been on holiday?'

'Hello Peter, I'm OK. I am around, but the day before yesterday I had a day off, and yesterday we were on strike.'

No wonder he wasn't happy. Makis, like most workers in the public sector, had a job for life, even though he wasn't particularly well paid, and strikes, although considered to be a legitimate and common form of protest in Greece were an unwelcome inconvenience to the customer and usually achieved nothing, while at the same time leaving the striker well and truly out of pocket.

It's All Free, Drink And Eat As Much As You Want

With 'Clean hearts and good intentions' the Greek Orthodox Church begins the period of Lent with what's known as Clean Monday. As well as starting the forty days fast, which is the way the Greeks clean their souls, outdoor celebrations such as kite flying, music and dancing are an essential part of that special day, many of which are performed on the island's beaches and open spaces. One of the most spectacular kite flying displays can be seen on the huge expanse of beach at Skala, where hundreds of gaily coloured kites lift off in a heavenly direction.

Locally, Gradakia beach in Lassi was the place to see the kites, whereas dancing took place in the school playground opposite the Montenero taverna. It had been the regular venue for years, where there was more than enough space for the performers and the appreciative audience who turned up to celebrate with them.

Although I'd asked around no-one knew what time the celebrations started, so not wanting to miss anything we arrived at midday but there wasn't a soul in sight, even though tables and chairs had been set out, so at least something was due to happen sometime, but we still didn't know when that sometime would be. There was no point in hanging about so we walked the short distance to Prue's and enjoyed a cup of tea with her. Jennie was with us, and once she and Prue started the banter Pam and I sat back to enjoy every minute, as it flew back and forth like verbal salvoes. After the tea we headed back for more entertainment.

While we were at Prue's a small audience had gathered in the playground so we sat and waited for something to happen; nothing did so we got up to leave.

As we were walking away a voice boomed across the playground, 'Hey, where you go? You can't leave yet.' It was Makis the sound. He came over, greeted us, then guided us to the refreshment tables.

'Help yourselves,' he said, 'it's all free, drink and eat as much as you want, and don't worry, the musicians will be here soon, it will be a good afternoon.'

Eventually the musicians, and more people, did turn up, by which time the gathering had swelled to create a real party atmosphere. We were glad we went back, because the food was good, the wine exceptional and the entertainment first class.

A Road Test?

As far as Kefalonians are concerned Lixouri is Lixouri, and it doesn't matter whether they're talking about Vatsa, Atheras or the town itself, because when they say Lixouri they are broadly referring to the whole peninsular; the Paliki.

We still enjoyed it there, but the time had come for me to go on official business, and there were fewer things more official than road testing the car, the English equivalent is the M.O.T. (Ministry of Transport) test.

Pam made the appointment and was told to be there at eight o'clock. So having caught the seven thirty ferry, I arrived at the testing centre, a short drive away, at a few minutes past the hour, only to find half the island forming a long line of cars; it looked like everybody was booked in for the eight o'clock appointment.

The testing procedure was painfully slow as each car moved forward at a snail's pace, and I soon found out why. There were no clerical staff working that day which meant the technicians had to double up on admin duties, and although the road test itself didn't take long, as with any government department there was always more than enough paperwork to complete.

Eventually it was my turn. The emission test, the first check, was over quickly, but just when I thought I was on a roll everything stopped to complete the paperwork. Then after a lengthy coffee break work resumed, and remarkably within minutes the test was over. Much to my surprise there were no checks on lights, wipers, screen washers or seat belts, and a slight flaw in one of the tyres went completely unnoticed. The car was passed as suitable for Greek roads with a new blue sticker fixed to the rear bumper to prove it.

Training

Pam went to Corfu on a pre-season training course for a few days, but unfortunately after landing at the airport she discovered her luggage was missing. It was though, a temporary inconvenience as the belongings were delivered to her the following morning. But the bizarre thing was that there hadn't been an incoming flight to Corfu since hers, which meant the luggage had travelled with her all along and had been at the airport overnight.

While she was away the government announced an increase in the rate of VAT with immediate effect, and because my cash register needed updating to display the new rate I was desperate to find an engineer to re-calibrate it. My bloke had completely disappeared so Lefteris once again pointed me towards his man, but for whatever reason he still wasn't interested in taking my money.

The law stated that all cash registers had to show the new rate and only licensed engineers were authorised to make the adjustment. Makis (who worked in the pub during the winter) recommended another Makis and told me where to find him. On meeting the other Makis there was instant recognition; he was a member of the choir and knew me as a friend of Stathis, and as well as being more than helpful, he did the cash register work free of charge. As the saying goes; It's not what you know, it's who you know… sometimes.

The Unsuspecting Tourist

As another new season approached, the local grapevine was once again reporting that visitor numbers would be down, and although the hand-painted stones (like paperweights) that I had made, and calendars had helped to boost my income, there was another scheme that might help to keep the cash flow healthy in a roundabout sort of way.

The Taxi Brothers, along with almost every other cabbie in Argostoli made regular runs to the airport which gave them direct contact with tourists, that was, in addition to their core business of local work, and the occasional long distance 'fare'. Like me, taxi drivers had overheads, and with the price of fuel forever increasing were always looking at other ways of making an extra euro or two.

I remarked to Costas one day in a rather flippant sort of way, 'Costa, why don't you and Makis do taxi tours around the island for tourists?'

'That's a great idea Peter, why didn't we think of that ourselves.' I smiled and said nothing.

Guided tours were an excellent way of getting an overview of the island, but not all summer visitors cherished the idea of sitting on a coach to be told when and where they could, or couldn't stop. There was also the added complication of understanding the guide, because not all of them spoke recognisable English. The alternative to an excursion was to rent a car, a motor bike, a scooter or even a pedal cycle, but some of the island's road surfaces were less than perfect. Frequent pot holes, huge rocks, as well as the occasional goat herd were constant hazards for the unsuspecting British tourist who not only found it difficult driving a hired vehicle, but also had to drive it on 'the wrong' side.

Hiring a taxi, especially a luxurious air conditioned Mercedes, was an affordable option to car rental and eliminated any stress driving might cause, by letting the taxi driver take it all. It was also a way in which the hirer could have a say by planning their own tour and going where they wanted to go.

The Taxi Brothers thought my idea was great, and because they knew the island's history and geography inside out would make the ideal guides, so we put together a plan that would benefit us all. Pam took photos of them with the taxi and designed 'Taxi tours' posters, some of which went in the cab and others went on display in The Gallery.

In return for my services Costas and Makis put Gallery posters in the car and pointed people in my direction. It was a brilliant example of reciprocal back scratching.

Beer and Lots Of It

Through the winter, Lefteris and I had talked about the forthcoming season, and being aware there would be fewer tourists we knew it could be a long dry summer, for him especially. I suggested that he might try poster power, and knowing how successful it was for me he agreed.

'OK baby, I'll give it a go.'

He was already using posters to advertise live music nights at the pub, but there was too much information on them for attracting tourists. What he needed was a poster with instant impact; something with a bit of oomph. He gave Pam and me carte blanche to completely re-design them, so we did. They weren't dissimilar to my own, even down to the map, after all he was only next door. Big black block letters stood out on the light background and the first eye catching word people saw was 'pub', which was enough, because to most visitors 'pub' meant only one thing; beer, and lots of it.

Needless to say not everyone read the posters properly, especially the opening times, which were 8pm till late. It was not uncommon then to see excited punters turning up in the middle of the morning expecting to relax over a cool beer, only to find the garden gate padlocked and the windows securely shuttered. Finding the Pub closed was a real disappointment, especially as most people had worked up a thirst by walking from Lassi; and while some came the direct route, over the hill, others took the long way round, along the coast road.

Pub Old House posters were successful, and as a favour to Lefteris I stapled some up at the same time as I did my own poster runs.

A Mansion

Through the winter Pam and I had been keeping a discreet eye on how the former To Steki was being slowly ('slowly' being the key word) transformed into a gourmet's delight. As one might expect it was all a bit stop-start and there were times when it looked as though the whole project had come to a standstill judging by the lack of activity.

The ouzeri had been popular with locals and tourists alike, but if Irena's new taverna wasn't open for the beginning of the season there would be those who would forget what was there before and go elsewhere.

The good news was that work was progressing, even though, more than once Irena had to get her hands dirty as a way of keeping things moving, as well as chasing up builders to get on with their work. She was after all, a woman in a very macho world, but looks can be deceiving! Her femininity hid an inner toughness and she wouldn't be given the 'run-around' by anybody.

As Easter approached, opening deadlines were set, postponed and re-scheduled. It was nail biting stuff right up until the delivery of the dining furniture, which, as well as being indoors was also located outside on the pavement. After months of hard slog there were big smiles and congratulations all round, and we were only too happy to be her first customers for the grand opening on Easter Saturday, just in time for the breaking of the fast.

The transformation was remarkable. The old ice cream freezer had gone, the leaking canopy was replaced with a new waterproof one and the plastic bunting no longer fluttered in the breeze. Indoors, the walls were half textured with a blend of golden stone and rendering that had been painted to match it, and there wasn't a sign of sea creatures anywhere. The kitchen, which previously had resembled a chef's worst nightmare, had been completely demolished and replaced with a modern state of the art one, which was absolutely essential if the staff were to cope with the demands of the increased business the new taverna would attract. Irena had promised the food would retain its high standard, which it did, and the wine, particularly our favourite, the house red, was very drinkable.

The interior of Arhontiko

On that opening evening it was warm enough to sit outside; so we did. The new tables and chairs took over the footpath, with a narrow aisle between them for pedestrians, even though the majority, certainly the Argostolians, often promenaded in the middle of the road oblivious to everything. It struck me as odd how tavernas, restaurants and *kafeneions* got away with taking up so much of the public footpath in that way. They all did it, so the only thing I could think of was that their licence must have been a special one. After all, there was a licence for everything.

That first evening was superb as we enjoyed our first meal at the newly named *Arhontiko* (pronounced Arkonteeko, which translated means mansion) where the extensive menu offered a wide choice of traditional Kefalonian dishes with more adventurous Mediterranean cuisine. Arhontiko was a revelation.

During the winter as work had lumbered on, Pam had kept a photo diary which she made into an album and presented to Irena on that opening night. The whole thing was very emotional, and as tears welled up in her eyes she couldn't thank us enough for our support.

Tipota Irena, *tipota*.

For us it was a pleasure, a token gesture of our lasting friendship.

The Glass Bottom Boat

Ever since first meeting Captain Makis, back in 2001, he'd been trying to persuade me to join him, his family and friends for the annual May Day cruise on the Glass Bottom Boat, and this year he was successful.

The May Day voyage was a precursor to the long hours of summer sailings and was by invitation only. It was also the last chance Makis and his crew would have to really unwind before the hard slog of the season dictated their lives.

The regular crew of the Glass Bottom Boat were all Kefalonian except for Yvonne, who was English, and known as the 'star behind the bar'. Nick and Christos were general deck hands and did virtually everything to keep the G.B.B. seaworthy, which included looking after the ship's parrot. They all worked seven long days a week, unless trips were cancelled, which could be for a number of different reasons, but was usually due to bad weather. There was a relaxed but disciplined atmosphere on board, but every member of the crew knew they were on to a good thing working for Makis, because not only was he a fair man, he paid well too.

It was a bright sun-drenched morning when family and friends set off from the Argostoli quayside heading for Vardiani island. The highlight of the voyage was the sighting of dolphins as they closed in on the boat and swam alongside for some distance. Once moored up at Vardiani I spent most of my time on the outside deck sketching, relaxing and generally soaking up that unique G.B.B. experience.

Having heard so much about the Glass Bottom Boat, at long last I'd finally tried it and wasn't disappointed. It really was a great day out.

Drip

Even with all the dams, barriers and flood defences known to man, when water is on the move it's difficult to stop, so when I heard the unmistakeable sound of dripping in the shower room one morning I knew our water was on the move when it shouldn't be, and there was only one place it could be coming from.

The roof space was exactly that, a space for crawling and storage only. A midget would have problems moving about up there because it barely measured eight feet by five, and was hardly three feet high. After getting our cases and bags out I alerted Makis, (in sign language of course) by using the word 'problemmo', a variation on the English pronunciation that everybody understands.

It was, as I'd thought, a leaking boiler, so he turned it off at the mains and promptly phoned the plumber, '*Signomi* Maki, *avrio.*'

'*Avrio*' means tomorrow, and is one of the most common

words in the Greek vocabulary, especially in Government offices, which was where I first heard it when I arrived in Argostoli.

Fortunately for us, Makis was a man who made things happen, which was one of the reasons we liked living there, but as he turned the water off I thought, 'Oh no! No water again.' I needn't have worried though, because the plumbing system had a number of independent stop taps which meant if one was switched off, the rest of the supply wasn't affected and worked as normal. The bad news however, was that because the boiler was out of action we were without hot water, which meant cold showers.

As promised, the plumber came the next day, squeezed into our storage cupboard, and with some grunting and straining, and I suspect, some Greek swearing, repaired the boiler.

Tom's Back

As the first week of May heralded the start of another season, it was time to look back at some of the other things that had happened locally during the earlier part of the year. The Go Kart track opposite Oskars taverna was dug up and became part of the enlarged sewer works; the Katavothres café was refurbished and was no longer an eyesore; in Argostoli, red and white cones were bolted to the roads to stop vehicles parking too close to the corners; and Thomas booked another holiday.

Unlike the last time he gave advance warning. It was great news and I really looked forward to seeing him again. On my advice he changed the original accommodation booking from over the hill at Spilia, to a more convenient location in Lassi next to the Princess Hotel, which was close to all amenities and convenient to the main beaches. Once again he came with Guy, but to avoid the high season temperatures they came in May. On that second visit he had more respect for the sun, and although it's a lot less fierce in May, it still has teeth.

Cobblers

Dimitris (the smooth operator) opened his own tailoring business at the far end of the Lithostroto and soon established a sound reputation by providing a good value-for-money quality service. As well as benefiting from the local grapevine, he also took a leaf out of my book, using poster power as a way of advertising.

Heading back towards the centre of town from Dimitris's shop, and tucked away up a side street between the Lithostroto and Vergotis street was another useful tradesman with bespoke skills; a traditional Cobbler. Although there were others in the town his work was first class, and more importantly he spoke English, albeit with an accent mix of American and Greek, which really wasn't surprising, because he'd lived in New York for many years before returning to settle on the island.

Without a doubt he was the King of the Cobblers and, like Rosa, had brought the American service mentality back to Kefalonia with him. It didn't matter whether he was repairing trainers, sandals or Sunday best shoes, it was all quality work and nothing was too much trouble. He was a great find.

That Language Thing… Again

It's a known fact that learning to fluently speak and fully understand a foreign language is difficult, but reading and writing it can be even more daunting, because there's so much to trip up on.

Some of my Greek friends were still trying to convince themselves, and me, that English was easy, so with that in mind I quietly chuckled as I walked past the cluster of waterside tavernas near the bridge one morning, having spotted a sign that read: 'Today's specials.. meatballs and flies'.

Another elementary blunder often seen on chalk boards outside more than one of the bars in the town advertised, 'Draft beer sold here'.

The English language easy? I don't think so; it's difficult enough for the English people.

Expert Advice

Despite the loving care and attention 'my' roses received (the ones outside The Gallery that is), by the beginning of May they had shrivelled up and were all well and truly dead.

'Great,' I thought, 'no more watering for me.' That wishful thinking however was short lived, because my gardening chores were just about to start again thanks to my neighbours Grigori and his wife Elizabeth who took it upon themselves to dig them up and plant new ones. The good thing about them getting involved was that watering duties were shared unequally between us, and it wouldn't all be down to me, there was no weeding either, not that I'd ever bothered anyway; Elizabeth did it all.

But there was, should I have needed expert advice, a professional in town. It was at about the same time the new roses were planted that I became friendly with Winston, a fellow Englishman. He was the head gardener, curator, manager, head everything really, at the Botanical Gardens which were tucked away out of sight at the southern end of Argostoli. He was a mine of information when it came to things that grew, having formally trained in horticulture and gained tropical plant experience working on the Eden Project in his native Cornwall before moving to Kefalonia.

A Point of Law

Since the children's summer playground first appeared, more rides were added season by season to make it not only bigger, but unfortunately, louder; loud enough in fact to wind Lefteris up, and Piero even more so.

Piero owned the Pizza Restaurant next door to the pub, and during the summer evenings diners were able, or, according to him, unable to enjoy their meal outside in the shade of the overhanging trees. He claimed the noise and close proximity of the expanding playground was having an adverse effect on his trade and decided to get it moved. Between them, he and Lefteris sought legal advice, then for a few days playground construction was put on hold as a point of law was checked. Piero though, not being satisfied with consulting a lawyer took it one step further and went to the *Dhimos* (the Town Hall, pronounced Theemoss,) hoping they would do something, but of course they couldn't, or more to the point, wouldn't.

After legal consultations it was concluded there was nothing anybody could do, the playground was legal and construction went ahead. Within a week all rides, including the highly popular red dragon were working normally, but

Piero still wouldn't let sleeping dogs lie and petitioned the local residents, who, like the *Dhimos* weren't interested.

It was then that I asked him, 'Piero, if the playground is illegal, as you seem to think it is, why should there be a need for a petition? Just accept what the lawyer has told you.'

That went down like a lead balloon and our relationship, which had always been a bit on the cool side hit an all time low, and from that moment on hardly a word passed between us.

I'd been living with the playground since opening The Gallery and didn't like it anymore than he or Lefteris did, but I knew that getting anything done, or even changed, especially when it involved lawyers and the thorny world of bureaucracy, would cost a fortune and take forever. It was for the very same reason that Pam and I had never taken legal action against the Greek National Health Service since her treatment, or lack of it.

Kick the Cat

I arrived home from work one lunchtime to find a small cardboard box outside the door with a note attached to it. That time the handwriting was legible and the words read, 'You English like pets, look after this one. Thank you.'

Against the odds, lightning had struck twice, and although not exactly on the same doorstep it was certainly in the same manner, so preparing for the worst I tentatively opened the box and peered inside. There was a cat, but thankfully not a real one. A practical joke no less, and it wasn't Stathis!

On our Christmas visit to Glasgow in 2001 one of Sarah's friends had given her the cat as a present. It was covered with real rabbit fur, and she being a strict vegetarian, recoiled in horror at the sight of it.

After a bit of fooling around we decided to give the cat a name, 'You'll have to keep it as a pet and we'll call him Kick the Cat,' I said, and with that impromptu christening he left my foot and flew across the room. At that point we all had a good laugh, but she definitely didn't want him, and neither did we, but under mysterious circumstances he ended up in our luggage.

Since that Christmas, Kick has clocked up thousands of air miles travelling between Greece and the States, as Sarah and Bradley between them have done everything possible to place him in our care, and we likewise.

They'd been on the island for a week's holiday and knew about my episode with the real kitten, and decided Kick should have a new home, and knew exactly where that new home should be. Unfortunately with all that fur he'd never cope with the Kefalonian climate and was therefore destined to collect more air miles. Not long after his visit to the island, and after a cunning collaboration between me and Jason, their Best Man, Kick made his next public appearance at Sarah and Bradley's wedding reception.

Enough is Enough

I often refer to Kefalonia as paradise, but paradise or not there were times when litter pollution was completely over the top. 'Enough is enough,' I thought, and because I felt strongly about it I decided to take action.

At the time, Napier's Garden had become a second home for litter louts, because as well as dogs' filth, general rubbish accumulated there on a daily basis.

I paid local taxes and felt entitled to complain, so one morning, I called in at the *Dhimos* and did just that, expecting a hostile response but receiving instead a polite, 'Thank you for your troubles,' from the man behind the reception desk. He also assured me that every effort would be made to clean up the gardens as soon as someone was free to do it. It's a known fact that getting things done sometimes took a little longer (a fact that most of my Kefalonian friends were always reminding me of, usually with a wry smile) but that time it wasn't the case.

The following morning Napier's Gardens received the full treatment, as a cleaning gang arrived and removed all the rubbish, restoring it to its former glory.

Energy

Kefalonia is an island of outstanding natural beauty with stunning scenery at almost every turn, but sooner or later something, usually of man's design or making has the potential to destroy that beauty forever. That something happened on the mountain ridge across the water from Argostoli. As the weeks passed, fifteen white wind turbines appeared, one by one, standing in line like soldiers to attention. It was bad enough that they had to be built there at all, but why did they have to be white? What was wrong with sky blue, as camouflage?

There is a belief that wind turbines have their place in the world of sustainable energy. In a semi rural environment, yes, but up there on the skyline, not really.

Jazz at The Philharmonic

I enjoyed the walk to and from The Gallery along Rizospaston, and occasionally kept an eye on the big double doors of the Philharmonic building, where posters advertising forthcoming events were displayed, and although they were always written in Greek, the word jazz was universal and meant only one thing.

It was summer, when concerts were commonplace in Argostoli, with most of them specialising in traditional Greek or Kefalonian music. Jazz at The Philharmonic was as rare as snow in August and seemed too good to miss.

The featured band, 'Spark Blue', was a trio of young musicians, playing piano, drums and electric bass. Spark Blue! They should have called themselves Electric Blue because that's exactly what their music generated. It was a form of fast tempo, highly charged Latin jazz, producing a tapestry of pure high voltage sound. Those three guys blew the roof off the Philharmonic, it really was unbelievable stuff, and what's more they were right in there with it, the musicians and the music together as one.

It was a free concert and I'd expected the auditorium to be packed, but it wasn't, because unlike the jazz, the poster power hadn't been quite powerful enough! That concert was a total contrast to some of the bizarre outdoor rock gigs taking place during the summer, which in most cases were pretty dire, sounding more like a mixture of amplified distortion and feedback rather than audible tones.

Quite a shock then for anyone sitting down hoping to relax over dinner in the square, only to be serenaded by an assortment of heavy metal wannabees.

Fake!

Dragisa and Jelena were permanent fixtures in Argostoli during July and August, but they weren't the only Serbian artists to hit town that summer. There was another visitor from Belgrade who visited The Gallery, and as well as liking my coffee he also admired my work, at least that's what he said. He painted too, so there was much to talk about. It turned out that for him painting was only a hobby, and being a dentist by profession meant he didn't have to struggle to make a living from his art, as most full time painters do. Jelena (herself a teacher in Belgrade, didn't have to work the streets of Argostoli either) branded him a fake.

He was exhibiting at the Teacher's House. The paintings were very precise, similar to the Dutch painters of the 17th and 18th centuries, but oddly enough none of them were for sale, perhaps that's why Jelena thought he was a fake.

Argostoli was a vibrant town during the summer and I was meeting people from around the world, people whose outlooks on life were varied and interesting. But the vast majority were nomads, always on the move, and just when I thought I was getting to know someone really well they moved on. Even my football buddy Tim had moved back to Australia.

'Friends of The Bridge'

Early in the summer a hole appeared in the road surface of the bridge close to Aristafani's *kafeneion*, and when I looked down into it, the hole, not the *kafeneion*, it was clear that most of the supporting masonry had collapsed and disappeared into the water below. Structural engineers inspected the damage and declared the bridge unsafe, closing it with immediate effect.

Red and white plastic tape (the sort commonly seen around roadworks) was tied across the road at both ends of the bridge as a way of stopping vehicles crossing it, but that proved to be totally inadequate as cars drove straight through it, and within minutes red and white strips of plastic fluttered in the breeze like streamers at a carnival.

After more inspections the engineers closed the bridge until further notice, and so as to let everybody know how serious they were, the Municipality replaced the plastic streamers with new vandal proof metal barriers. The new barriers were shaped like mini football goalposts, painted yellow and concreted into the road (no-one had considered access for emergency vehicles) but in time they too fell foul to the vandalism of the mindless minority.

Once news spread that the bridge had been closed indefinitely there was a public outcry from the villagers on the Dhrapano side, because now the only route to Argostoli for all motorists was by using the recently improved and resurfaced road skirting the lagoon. Despite the protests, driving that extra distance was really no big deal because heavy vehicles had been driving that way for years, it just meant drivers would have to allow a few more minutes for the journey.

However, from a pedestrians' point of view walking across the bridge without fear of injury was something that hadn't been possible for years, and other than the odd motorbike and pedal cyclist it was completely safe.

The closure brought conflicting rumours as to how long it would actually be closed. Some, especially the pro-driving lobby hoped that it was only a short term measure, whereas the environmentalists and 'friends of the bridge' were optimistic it would be forever. Just being closed at all was something of a relief for the many fishermen who risked life and limb, not to mention a good soaking, as they perched precariously on the bridge's low walls with traffic driving dangerously close to them.

Fishing in the UK is regarded by some as a serious sport, while for others it is a relaxing pastime, but for those guys in Argostoli it was a necessity, because the fish they caught was guaranteed to end up on their dinner plates. The permanent closure of the bridge would ensure a part of Kefalonia's heritage would never collapse under the weight of continual and unnecessary traffic.

From Hawkers to Gypsies

Hawkers and Gypsies were regular visitors to The Gallery, but they never ventured inside the door, because I wouldn't let them, especially if there was more than one. They were always trying to sell something, anything; from Chinese paintings to glossy calendars, nothing I really needed.

A stern *oxi* was enough to see them on their way, but if that didn't work I just looked blank, with both arms outstretched and the palms of the hands uppermost (just as a Kefalonian would) then I'd ask, in Greek of course, '*Milate Anglika*?' It never failed, because none of them ever did. Then it was their turn to give me the blank stare before quickly moving on.

The guy who took top marks for gall pulled up outside The Gallery one evening in a shining red open top sports car, and because he was dripping gold I thought perhaps he was coming in to look at the paintings; wrong again.

Without getting out of the driver's seat he began in broken English, 'I work on the ferry to Italy and don't have enough money to pay for my room, would you like to buy…,' but before he could breathe another word I'd cut him off in mid sentence.

'Sorry mate, but I haven't got any money either, we're all in the same boat.' I hadn't meant the pun to be offensive, but he, like the hawkers and gypsies got the message anyway, my outstretched arms had worked again.

The End

Financially, the season had been a disaster, caused by a combination of ever increasing overheads and a significant drop in takings, so it was time to close The Gallery and move on. Last year any thoughts of closing had only been embryonic, because deep inside I was really hoping business would pick up, but it didn't. On top of everything else the building was falling apart and in desperate need of serious repair, which in itself would cost big money... money I hadn't got and although there had been no more serious flooding, the ceiling was showing signs of damp, with paint flaking off it, off the walls too.

Lefteris had always been a good listener whenever I needed help or advice, and because of that I felt a special loyalty towards him, but loyalty doesn't pay the bills and once the decision had been made there was no turning back. And when I did tell him he wasn't surprised, it was as though he'd been expecting it.

The alternative to The Gallery was straightforward enough; having made tentative enquiries I'd rent studio space and exhibit for the summer.

It was though, with a heavy heart, but no regrets, that at the end of October I walked away from The Gallery for the last time and moved into The Studio.

A Change Is As Good As A Rest

A few weeks before finally closing I took a break and went to the UK. Pam kept herself occupied in The Gallery, while at the same time doing some painting of her own, and I don't mean painting and decorating. As well as indulging in the artistic side of life she also enrolled for free Greek language lessons, courtesy of the bottomless pot of EU funds that Greece seemed able to dip into with ease.

The Municipality organised the classes and applications were invited from non Greek- speaking E.U. citizens working on the island. Pam submitted her application then, for some weeks, heard nothing more, so she chased it up.

'We'll let you know, but there is a problem, we don't have any teachers,' she was told, which I thought was a bit arse about face in anybody's language; does it not make sense to line the teachers up first?

The classes eventually started but she gave up after a few lessons. As a language teacher herself, learning 'parrot fashion', which was how the lessons were taught, was certainly not the best way to learn a language, and certainly not from a lecturer in archaeology!

Also, while I was away Pam attended a presentation in Lassi promoting the book 'Odysseus Unbound', which gives an interesting and informative insight into facts relating to geological and seismic movements within the island over past centuries. Based on research and evidence, the author, Robert Bittlestone, disputes whether 'modern' Ithaca can be the same one Homer wrote about.

Pam and I had been invited to the presentation out of courtesy as Robert had used material from my website (with permission of course). As a token of his gratitude he presented Pam with a signed edition of the book, which incidentally, makes for some very interesting reading. He also visited The Gallery, but unfortunately I was still away and as a consequence I never got to meet him.

Planning

Within a couple of days of moving into The Studio I was ready to start painting again. It couldn't have been a better location, situated in the middle of town overlooking the busy Sitemporon Street and conveniently placed for everything. What's more, if I needed pharmaceuticals, or more importantly, mosquito repellent, I was directly above Vassillis's pharmacy opposite the Mouikis hardware store.

Prior to me moving in it had been a real studio apartment, the furniture was still stacked along the communal corridor. I had at one point thought about keeping the bed, with the idea of moving away from traditional Kefalonian paintings to specialise in 'life' studies. Pam however, was adamant that painters and their nude models made more than just art; she'd made her stand so the idea never got off the ground.

The Studio really was ideal and suited all my needs. There was a combination of good strip lighting and natural light that flooded in through a huge sliding double glazed window. As added security, as well as being a shield against the afternoon sun there was also a single sliding shutter.

Whereas The Gallery's main feature had been the bar, The Studio had a balcony overlooking the street below from where I could hear and see most of what was going on in it. Now I was set up with working space it was time to find an exhibition venue.

'Could I hit the jackpot again?' I asked myself. 'Yes I could,' but *'Siga, siga'*, it would all happen in due course.

Official Paperwork

To coincide with moving to The Studio, there was official business regarding the closing of The Gallery, which wasn't a simple matter of locking up and handing the keys back to Lefteris, oh no. Dimitris and Eleni took control once again, and she, in her usual efficient manner guided me once more along the winding road and slippery slope of bureaucracy. As I was no longer a bona fide business the cash register became surplus to requirements and was de-registered by the ever obliging Makis. There were more visits to the tax office, but for signatures only, and Eleni arranged payment of my outstanding VAT bill. Once the crossing of the T's, the dotting of the I's, and after the signing and stamping had been completed, Dimitris then gave me the best news of all. According to his calculations I'd overpaid TEBE contributions and he said there was no need to pay any more until I started exhibiting in 2006.

Flash and Grab

Since coming out of hospital Pam had been determined to live as normal a life as possible, even with a dodgy lung, and for most of the time she did. During the summer she woke early and swam before going to work, and if she didn't swim she'd do her best to get a walk in, with or without me. Neither of us had ever felt threatened by walking alone, but back in the summer there were a couple of unexpected incidents that surprised us both. Pam was on one of her routine 'out and back' walks to the lighthouse, and had just passed the Katavothres on the way back, where the path is a bit secluded and runs between some small trees and bushes.

Approaching, she saw a bloke, and thinking he was having a pee thought no more of it (because some Kefalonian men did it anywhere) but she did slow her step. However, it wasn't until she got close up that she realised he wasn't peeing at all, then to her surprise and disbelief he turned full frontal and flashed her. Her surprise was that he actually did it, the disbelief was the size, as he stood holding on with both hands before dashing off.

Afterwards, when I asked would she recognise him again she answered with a smile, 'Well no, not his face anyway.'

My close encounter came one Sunday lunchtime as I was walking home from Rosa's. Crossing the road at the top of the square a guy in a grey Passat pulled up. My first thought was that he was asking for directions, but he was in fact offering me a lift. It wasn't far to walk so I wasn't particularly bothered, but by the time I was across the road he'd opened the passenger's door, and thinking no more of it I got in.

'Centro Security *parakalo.*' (Centro Security please.)

'*Endaxi,*' (OK) he nodded and smiled.

He stopped at Centro, but as I was about to get out of the car his hand came across and grabbed me, 'Whoops,' I thought, 'this guy's got a problem.'

Then in one swift movement my right hand grabbed him by the collar, while the other guided his groping fingers from between my legs, then looking him straight in the eye I said, 'No you f…..g don't mate!' and I knew exactly where to put the stress. Although the 'f' word is universal I wasn't quite sure whether he'd understood me, but judging by the look on his face he had, and backed off straight away. Once I was out of the car, he drove up the Lassi road, and that was it, end of problem.

Those were very rare and isolated incidents and nothing similar ever happened to either of us again. We weren't particularly bothered or worried, and it certainly didn't stop us from walking, alone or together.

More of a Challenge

As Pam regained her former stamina and strength she had one big challenge and burning ambition, to walk up Aenos again, so she did, and I went with her.

To the summit from the entrance of the National Park, which was where I left the car, is a continuous climb, and on that day it took us about an hour and forty five minutes. The view from the top was still as breathtaking as it had been that day with Stelios. Despite a scattering of clouds a fresh breeze was whipping over the summit so, to avoid it we picnicked in the shelter of the trees and banking. As we ate, drank and chatted, it became obvious how cold it was getting, but only by walking out from our shelter did we realise why.

The clear views of only a few minutes earlier had disappeared to be replaced by dense cloud and a plummeting temperature; suddenly it was time to go, and fast.

On the way down I made the flippant comment, 'You know, Pam, this is really a boring walk,' and in places it was. The views would have been spectacular had they not been screened by the endless numbers of pine trees, the famous Abies Cephalonica, that grew on both sides of the track.

'Yes,' she replied, 'it is, but for me it's not so much a walk, it's more of a challenge.'

Which of course it was, and more importantly, one she rose to.

Health Insurance

At about the same time as closing The Gallery I was desperately trying to get my European health card which I'd applied for some weeks earlier from the TEBE. It's a form of health insurance for EU citizens travelling within Europe but outside their country of residence. In cases of necessity they are covered by it for emergency health care costs. As time was relentlessly moving on, getting mine had become a priority, because in December I was travelling to the UK and then on to New York.

The week before I was due to leave I went to the TEBE again hoping the card would be there, but Maria, who spoke some English and had always been helpful to me over the years said, after searching through my file, 'Ah Peter, it is not here, come back on Friday,' which I did, and again the following Monday. 'Peter I am sorry, but you will have to come back later in the week because your card is still not here.'

'Maria I'm flying to the UK in two days time and from there to New York, I won't be back until the New Year.'

Smiling, she wished me a safe journey, a Happy Christmas, and because she still couldn't find my card offered a temporary solution. Maria had a brief meeting with her boss to explain my situation (I think), then invited me to join them, where I was handed a sheet of paper endorsed with a TEBE stamp and some handwritten scribble that I assumed was a signature.

Maria, who had been translating for her boss then said, 'There Peter, if you have any problems show them this, and when you come back in January your card will be ready.'

December 8th

We were spending Christmas in New York. Pam had become a grandmother in October and couldn't wait to see her first grandchild, Daniel. She flew the direct route from Athens, while I went the long way round via the UK.

December 8th was the twenty fifth anniversary of John Lennon's murder and Thomas, the ever aspiring guitarist and Lennon addict, was playing a set of his songs at a tribute gig in one of Swindon's music pubs.

It had been a long, long time since I'd seen or heard him play 'in concert', and that was way back when he was at junior school. So whereas Pam was the proud grandmother, I was an even prouder father, because Tom's interpretation of the rock icon's songs was superb. A couple of days later I headed for the Big Apple with his music ringing in my ears, it had been a worthwhile and very emotional detour.

Tom plays Lennon

Pam got her grandmother fix and a good time was had by all, but because of our different flight schedules we arrived back home with twenty four hours between us. We were however re-united, although somewhat jet lagged, on New Year's eve; just in time to enjoy the celebrations upstairs.

The year had seen the closing of The Gallery, but that wasn't all: Zebra crossings were introduced in Argostoli (which totally baffled pedestrians, and confused motorists even more); ramps were introduced for the disabled; some of the main streets were resurfaced and plans were unveiled for the building of a new improved road to Poros.

2006 – A Full Circle

While We Were Away

We'd always known our landlord Makis was a star, and while we were away he gave us further proof of it.

A couple of utility bills arrived for us that he kindly paid in our absence, because he knew late payment would result in a fine, and being out of the country for whatever the reason was no excuse.

There was still unfinished business at the TEBE concerning the health card, so I went to collect it. Seeing me, a smiling Maria went straight to the file and got it, while at the same time wishing me a Happy New Year.

Around the centre of town, improvements to the ramps for the disabled had been made, especially those close to car parking spaces. Metal barriers were bolted to the road in the hope they would deter motorists from parking too close, therefore causing great difficulty to those who used them. Sadly there were still drivers who ignored the barriers, and continued to cause grief by blocking the disabled access with their haphazard parking. Haphazard parking would be something I saw a lot of from The Studio balcony.

Epiphany

Last year Pam and I missed the Epiphany celebrations, but this time round we were lucky enough to get a close up view from the deck of the Glass Bottom Boat. It was a beautiful start to the day as the snow sparkled on the higher mountains, reflecting the clear blue of a typically bright Kefalonian morning sky.

When we arrived at the quayside a few people were already on board, and as the cabin filled everybody was asking the same question, 'Where's Makis?'

Nobody knew, but he eventually appeared, and in his unrushed, unconcerned manner made coffee for passengers, crew, and of course, himself.

The harbour waters closer to the bridge are very shallow in places and Makis was concerned about 'bottoming out' (getting stuck on the mud), but after some expert navigating from his first mate Nick, who hung over the side for a clearer view, we arrived just in time for the fireworks and cross throwing ceremony.

Epiphany in Argostoli

Once it was over we headed back for the quayside, well, at least in that general direction but not quite, because once we were in deeper water Makis opened up the throttle and headed for the open sea. Approaching the Katavothres, any signs of the blue skies that had graced the morning earlier were replaced by angry looking storm clouds, which we were heading straight in to. Upon entering the darkness, like Hobbits into Mordor, a fierce electrical storm was at its height and huge hail stones rattled the steel roof and deck to give the distinct impression that we were sailing into battle and not bad weather.

Following us closely into Lixouri harbour but none the worse for the weather, came the ferry boat with the Bishop on board, and because there was no bridge or specially decorated platform in Lixouri to throw the cross from he stayed on the passenger deck, and sheltered by a roof of umbrellas threw it from there. Blink and you'd have missed it, as most spectators who were parked along the harbour front did, as they peered through misted up windows of parked vehicles.

As the Glass Bottom Boat departed for home, the storm cleared as quickly as it had started ensuring a pleasant and incident free journey, but even with the bad weather it had been a good morning and one we would never forget.

A New Church

For our first driveabout of the New Year Pam and I returned to Old Skala, and what a shock. As we approached the village the silence of the still morning was broken by the unmistakable sound of heavy machinery as a mechanical digger excavated what looked like foundations for a new building.

I'd always been under the impression that Kefalonia's ruined villages were sacred, untouchable, and that it was taboo to even think about building in any of them. Yet on reflection, the land belonged to somebody and would no doubt have been in the same family for decades, centuries even, which meant it was their right to build if they wished, subject of course to the relevant planning permission! My thoughts were based on the fact that in all the old villages I'd been to there had never been a sign of new build work anywhere, either to replace or renovate any that still stood.

'So,' I asked myself, 'was the shock of the new a sign of things to come?'

Walking on further, the noise quietened until we could hear a pin drop, there wasn't a sound, not even birdsong. It was, once again a very moving experience to feel the deserted silence and tranquillity of Old Skala.

Approaching the wash house and bell tower, that tranquillity was once again shattered by the sounds of more building work, and of all things, they were building a new church. Maybe, in time, the whole village would be resurrected.

Away from Old Skala, the rest of Kefalonia was becoming one vast construction site, as grey concrete shells sprang up everywhere, like mushrooms from a carpet of heavy morning dew.

'Could it go on forever?' I wondered. 'Surely one day the bubble will burst!'

A New Television

Stathis's television was on the blink, and although it sat on a level table the picture itself was on the tilt, so we decided to buy a new one.

Having bought most of our electrical goods from Mouikis, the 'white goods' store, we went there again, browsed around and saw a nice grey set. Spending time wandering in and out of different shops comparing models and prices wasn't on our agenda, but out of curiosity we tried 'B & Q' again, but had no more success than when we'd tried to buy the sofa, so we went back to Mouikis.

I knew the owner, Makis, quite well and we quickly

came to a 'best price' agreement, shook hands and the deal was done.

English and French

Although Pam had given up the teaching assistant's role at the *frontisterio* long ago, she still kept her hand in and taught English and French privately. Irena's daughter Margaret had opted to study French at school, and like most pupils took extra lessons over and above the curriculum as a way of supplementing her class work, so Pam took her on.

The arrangement was that Margaret came to the apartment where she and Pam used the kitchen as an improvised classroom.

I used to sit in the living room with the door closed doing my best to shut out Margaret's moans, groans and shrieks of, 'Oh no, Pam, no more verbs,' as she struggled with the masculines and feminines and other intricacies of the French language. It sounded funny but wasn't, as I one day would find out.

Pam's other pupil was Spyros, a local entrepreneur, who wanted to improve his English, which, with Pam's help he did. He owned a highly successful printing business in Argostoli, and through that business, as well as his social circle, had built up a library of contacts and friends, one of whom was Takis.

Takis and his brothers Andreas and Makis, along with other members of the family, ran a successful car hire and holiday agency business from their head office in Lassi. The family though couldn't do everything themselves and occasionally hired outside expertise, and one, thanks to Spyros's introduction to Takis, was Pam. She already had summer job offers on the table, but hadn't made a decision on any of them, so the tempting prospect of additional part time hours during the remainder of the winter, which Takis was offering, made his an offer she couldn't refuse, so she didn't.

In the meantime I was busy arranging summer exhibitions.

Summer Exhibitions

Although I'd last exhibited at the Bell Tower over four years ago, it still held special memories for me and was uppermost in my mind as the venue for a series of summer exhibitions. I chatted with Eric, who was as enthusiastic as I was, in turn he phoned Katherina there and then to arrange a meeting. At that meeting she listened intently to my proposal and saw the benefits for everybody. Whereas I'd be busy exhibiting and selling paintings, many of my visitors would in turn become customers of the Bell's Café, keeping the guys there busy serving drinks and snacks; that was the plan.

Since the 2001 exhibition Katherina's role had changed, and although still overall responsible for the *kafeneion* she asked me to liaise directly with Lena, who was now the café manager; which I did. Lena and I discussed formalities and she was more than happy for me to deal with Eric, George and Spyros on a day to day basis; it was just like old times.

So it was settled, dates were confirmed and that was it, I would exhibit there for the summer.

Horta

Horta is a rich green vegetable that grows abundantly wild around the island, where the pickers (or to be more precise, cutters, because horta, like lettuce has to be cut with a knife) were a common sight when it was in season, which seemed to be all year round. Horta is an ideal starter to most meals, but is best when soaked with fresh lemon juice, olive oil and accompanied by a nice tomato salad. However, there was a snag! To fill a carrier bag was laborious and time consuming, and what's more, once the contents of that bag had been boiled or steamed the leaves shrank to give about enough for two average sized servings; that was the snag!

Pam and I loved horta and would have tried our harvesting skills if we'd known how to tell it apart from the other greenery, but not having the trained eye of Kefalonian women we would probably have ended up with a bag full of assorted weeds. So for us, buying it from Cardiff was still the easy option as it did away with the strain and backache that bending and cutting would've caused.

A Little Puzzled

The famous panoramic view of Myrtos from the lay-by above is always spectacular, however, the neck craning view looking up from the beach is equally so in its sheer scale, as the towering cliffs, a stratum of multi-coloured rock and natural growth, gives the impression they're disappearing into the sky.

Pam and I had only been on to the beach once before and felt it was time to go again. I parked the white panda at Diverata before we strolled leisurely down the steep, twisting road, beach bound. At about half way we were confronted by a huge herd of goats who looked both confused and curious at the unusual sight of two people walking (unusual, because virtually everybody drove to the beach) towards them, but as we got closer they scattered, scampering to the safety of higher ground. If we'd been driving they would probably have sat stubbornly blocking the road risking life and limb, as goats do, but Kefalonian goats had the knack of moving at the last moment, therefore avoiding the inevitable crunch.

Pam on Myrtos

Although there was bright sunshine, it was a cold, clear January day. We relaxed, listening to the never ending rhythm of the breaking waves washing over the smooth pebbles of the huge beach, which, except for us was deserted then, suddenly, we were no longer on our own.

Appearing as if from nowhere, a man and his two dogs, oblivious to us, walked straight past to the water's edge. I expected the dogs to bound headlong into the foaming surf, but exactly the opposite happened. They sat as still as statues, quietly and obediently, as their master stripped completely, then without giving it a second thought dived in. We were amazed, because there had been no tentative dip of the toe in the water, and although we were warm in the shelter of the rocks the sea must have been freezing, but if it was he didn't notice and swam for a good fifteen minutes.

Once he'd dried and dressed, the three of them walked back towards us, at which point I couldn't resist the temptation to try the beach chat up line again.

'How was the water today?'

'Well, it's a little colder than yesterday, but it was fine.'

'What, you swam yesterday as well?'

'Oh yes, I swim here everyday, but not if it rains,' and with that they were gone. I was impressed, but a little puzzled as to why the rain should stop him, and then the penny dropped: if it rains his clothes would get wet.

That afternoon was similar in one way, but totally different in another to the Ursula experience years before, insomuch that they were both extraordinary cameos; the difference was that she had kept her clothes on.

Cold Showers

During the winter bad weather was common in certain parts of Greece, and that included Kefalonia. There were severe gales, torrential rain, snow storms and on the higher mountains temperatures dropped dramatically to well below freezing. But in the time we'd lived there it had never affected us enough to worry about it, and thankfully any downturn didn't last too long; famous last words.

Towards the end of January fierce storms, far worse than we'd ever experienced, battered the island, and the constant howling of the accompanying winds woke us during the night. It was impossible to know if there was any damage so we snuggled under the covers and did our best to get back to sleep.

After getting up the following morning the first sign of the aftermath was that we'd lost all power. That really was bad news because the apartment was all electric which meant we'd be without hot water, there'd be no heating, and worst of all, no cooking facilities. The good news was that at least there was still running water even though it was cold, and not knowing how long we'd be without electricity I clenched my teeth, shivered, then reluctantly turned the tap for another cold shower.

After my baptism by cold water I phoned Stathis for an update on how good or bad the news was. It was worse than bad he said, and furthermore, most of the island was without electricity, and in some of the smaller mountain villages there was no running water either, and how long it would last for was anybody's guess. The manager of the National Electric Company in Argostoli was a member of the choir, so Stathis no doubt would have a hotline to his office from where he would relay further updates.

I followed my normal morning routine and headed for town. The first serious sign of damage was in Napier's Garden, where, although none of the trees had been completely felled, many had lost branches. The wind was still howling, and walking along the waterfront was out of the question as water cascaded over the quayside, partially submerging the footpath and road.

As well as flooding and the loss of electricity there was considerable damage to parked vehicles, caused by falling roof tiles. It was only by sheer good fortune that the storm had been at its raging worst during the night when the town was sleeping, because judging by the scattered debris, human casualties would have been high had it happened in daylight hours when people were out and about.

Stores selling gas appliances did a roaring trade and within minutes of opening everything that produced a blue flame had been sold. Another wave of panic buying quickly followed, and was sparked off by the news that power would be off for at least a week. The rush that time was for generators and the diesel fuel that powered them. We didn't bother with either, because we had an ample stock of candles for lighting, and Marilyn helped out by lending us a camping gaz ring on which to boil water and cook food, albeit only soup. Then after a couple of days, and once the shops had re-stocked, we bought our own burners and lights.

As the extent of the island's damage was fully realised it was found the storm had caused much more than was first thought. Power lines and the poles that carried them had fallen like nine pins in the high winds and now there were teams working round the clock, struggling in difficult conditions to repair them as quickly as they could.

Then one morning as the crisis showed no visible signs of improving, we sat drinking tea with Prue, who, as only she could, came up with this question: 'Now there are windmills on the mountain generating electricity, why do we have to be so long without it?' A valid point, but one nobody seemed able to answer.

With no heating in the apartment an air of dampness, like an invisible mist, descended within it. We kept the windows open during the day in the hope that producing a through flow of air would help, but unfortunately it didn't. We found the best way of insulating ourselves against the damp was by wearing extra layers of clothing which trapped warm air between them. Our strategy for keeping warm was both simple and effective. We wrapped up and walked as usual, and as our body temperatures rose the trapped layers built in a form of central heating, which we topped up with hot soup soon after getting back indoors. After eating, we did what almost everybody else did (except for those with generators who were able fire up their televisions), we kept our layers on and went to bed early.

Those living conditions didn't last long and five days after the storm, just as life was returning to normal, the navy turned up to help out. A huge warship steamed into Argostoli harbour with large generators on board, which, we understood were earmarked for the 'essential' services. Better late than never.

A couple of months after the storms, the consequences of the blackout conditions and those early nights appeared in the town! Numerous women in the same state of early pregnancy were making tracks to the ante-natal clinic at Argostoli hospital; the January storms had caused a mini baby boom and had they been nationwide, then Greece's shrinking population problem would have been solved, and it would have all be down to a few nights without the television.

And those cold showers? I'm not sure if they're of any more benefit than a hot one, but I found them exhilarating and, since the storms, I have followed a hot one with a cold one; now that's a real wake up call.

Storm Damage

I consider the tiny village of Assos to be the jewel in Kefalonia's crown, and judging by the number of people who flock there every summer, strolling along the picturesque harbour and sitting in one of the waterside tavernas to drink frappé or sip chilled beer, thousands of others think so too, but of all those visitors, I often wonder how many have ever been up into the castle grounds.

A week after the storms and when the island's power was restored Pam and I went to Assos. Driving along the west coast the recent storm damage was clear for anyone to see, yet despite the landslides and fallen rocks the road was clear of any major obstacles. It was on the exposed mountain slopes where the real damage had been done as large numbers of trees lay like corpses, motionless victims of the fickle power of nature.

One such victim, a huge pine tree had fallen and lay completely blocking the main track from Assos village to the castle, and because there was no way round, over or under it we detoured along a narrow lesser known cliff path that is precariously high above the sea and enters the castle by a side entrance close to the ruined jail. Once inside the massive stone walls, we re-joined the main track that passes close to the Visitors' Centre.

I always found walking through the grounds of Assos castle slightly bizarre, because over the years I'd never seen any other sign of life there (other than the odd goat or two) and considering it's supposed to be a Visitors' Centre, I'd never seen any visitors either. Work appeared to have been abandoned years ago when the project was in its later stages, and all that now remained were discarded building materials which gave it a feeling of emptiness, and not one of 'Visitors Welcome'.

During its construction heavy vehicles had used the track, which was the only access to and from the village, and the longer work had gone on the more it had deteriorated. In places the subsidence was serious, to the point of being dangerous, highlighting the need for urgent and essential repair work.

The latest project within the castle grounds was the building of a narrow stone road which started at the main entrance and ended at the Visitors' Centre.

Building anything up there defies logic, but does provoke one valid question, 'What purpose does a Visitors' Centre serve in such a remote and isolated part of Kefalonia?'

I love Assos and regard the castle and the unspoilt beauty within its walls as one of the most precious and beautiful places on the island, and feel that every possible effort should be made by those with the power to do so, to stop any further deterioration and destruction before it's too late.

One immediate solution would be to ban all unauthorised traffic. People wanting to visit the castle grounds who are unable, or unwilling, to walk, could, and should be encouraged to use a lightweight (electrically powered) mini-bus owned and operated by the municipality controlling Assos. That sort of scheme would open the castle up to summer tourists, who, because of the high seasonal temperatures, not to mention the steep climb, would never give walking up there a second thought. The Visitors' Centre could then be opened and used for what it was built for, with the addition of a small café and a museum of local artefacts as added attractions.

Now I've been off on my tangent I'll get back to the day we were confronted by the fallen tree.

Having reached the Visitors' Centre we walked on, past the church and through the olive groves to the end of the grass path which opens into a small clearing high above the sea and with views stretching northward along the coastline. Paradise beyond belief.

Because most people believe there is nothing beyond the Visitors' Centre they don't bother venturing any further, which is possibly why it remains free of any serious litter (except for an abandoned car, yes, even up there) that often blights other beauty spots on the island.

The village of Assos is the paradise that everybody knows, whereas the northern tip of the castle is its best kept secret.

Fire

We were quietly having dinner one evening when the rumble of heavy vehicles caused the windows and doors to vibrate. I looked out into the darkness in time to see two fire engines with flashing blue lights disappearing up the road.

'Oh no, Pam I hope the woods aren't on fire.' So not wanting to miss anything I was up and away and through the door like a shot. Approaching Mrs. Flowers' house I looked up through the pines to see the small single storey house where Pink lived seriously ablaze, but he was fine. I saw him running round the crowd of onlookers, one of whom was Denis, and he was as excited as Pink.

The following afternoon Pam and I walked that way to have a closer look at the damage, and found only the walls intact of what was otherwise a charred and blackened shell, everything else had been completely destroyed.

Pink

The burnt out shell belonged to Denis's family, which is why he was so excited, and the saving grace was that the family didn't actually live there.

Like many other Kefalonians Denis's family kept a guard dog, and whereas some were allowed to run free in the confines of the property they guarded, most, like the unfortunate Pink were shackled to short chains, therefore severely restricting any serious freedom of movement which made their roles as guard dogs useless. All any would-be intruders had to do was give them a wide berth. After his brief taste of freedom Pink was chained up again to guard the burnt out shell.

When Pam and I first met Pink his coat was a beautiful off-white colour, similar to that of a polar bear, and when walking past him we always said hello. It was only natural then that he became friendly towards us, so friendly that he jumped on the roof of his kennel and allowed us to stroke him, while at the same time whimpering and struggling to break free in his desire for lasting affection, and of course, lasting freedom. That's one hell of a guard dog!

However, it wasn't long after we'd met Pink that Denis painted the kennel red, but instead of using a waterproof gloss paint, he used a water based emulsion. Then slowly, and especially after rain, the kennel began to lose its original colour. That's because it was being transferred to, and, unfortunately for the dog, absorbed by his fur, which had gradually turned the colour by which we knew him.

Talking To The World

Since we'd first lived on the island Pam and I had kept in close contact with our family, friends, and people we knew, through email, the telephone, and by conventional letter, the so called snail mail. Generally the Kefalonian postal service was good, especially if mail was leaving the island, but anything coming in always took a little longer to be sorted and delivered; not a lot, two or three days maybe.

Worst of all though was when anything had to pass through Greek customs, which in our case wasn't very often, but there's always a first time for everything.

Pam was awaiting delivery of a camera lens that had been posted in the States some weeks before, and because it was taking so long she became concerned and queried the delay at the Post Office. It had definitely left New York, but when she told the guy at Argostoli his reaction was to raise his eyes and hands in typical fashion, heavenwards, and say

292

there was nothing he could do and to try the customs office at the port. They couldn't help either but told her to contact Athens, so with Stathis's help she did.

After a lengthy conversation with Athens customs office he came off the phone only to confirm what we already knew; yes, there was a delay and she shouldn't expect delivery for at least three months. It was, in fact, delivered a few days later, but the overall time taken from posting to delivery had been about three months, so at least they'd got something right.

At about the same time as the lens delay, verbal communication took a quantum leap when we discovered the internet phone service, Skype. Skype is a way of talking to people through the magic of computers, free, or at least if not for free, then certainly at much cheaper rates than most Telecom companies were charging. At around the same time that we discovered Skype Pam bought a new computer. We knew Nikos, a pub regular, who not only sold and serviced computers but he also came with Lefteris's highest recommendation.

Nick and Pam met to discuss the possibilities, the technicalities, and more importantly the price. She was happy with her new purchase and for a couple of days was busy uploading, downloading and doing whatever other loading there was to get everything working, whereas my thankless task was hiding and tidying the cables and leads.

We'd recently been connected to the Kefalonian version of broadband which was still in its infancy, and although not the fastest connection in the world, it was far superior to the previous dial-up system, and light years ahead of my days in Exelixis. With so much technology at my fingertips I had at last lost my internet virginity.

Bird Flu

Bird Flu of pandemic proportions was spreading across Europe with disastrous results, so to protect the migratory and residential bird species in Argostoli, the lagoon footpath was closed to the public. A red and white plastic barrier, identical to the ones used on the Dhrapano bridge, was 'stretched' across the entrance to the narrow wooden footbridge opposite the tennis courts. It was an attempt to protect pedestrians and birds who might have been in contact with the dreaded virus, but just as the barrier on the bridge had been, the new lagoon one too, proved to be every bit as ineffective. The good news was that after a few weeks, Europe was declared a bird flu free zone, and what was left of the barrier was removed, and the footpath re-opened to the public.

Over a relatively short period of time a number of changes had been made along the banks of the lagoon, the best, and most aesthetically pleasing was the demolition of the roadside buildings and workshops that had stood for years almost opposite the bus station. Once the land was cleared and levelled it was tastefully landscaped and paved.

The demolition also made it possible to complete the unfinished footpath that now runs continually from the Dhrapano bridge to the copse of eucalyptus trees at the lagoon's southern end.

The lagoon had many moods and was one of our favourite walks, especially in the early mornings of high summer. We were determined not to give up walking altogether, but because of the scorching heat in July and August it was impossible to take our usual afternoon exercise. The only way to 'beat the heat' was to wake early and get out before the sun rose, and despite still having a variety of walks to choose from, the lagoon was very special early in the morning, especially as far as Pam was concerned, because the walk was flat.

Koutavos Lagoon, Argostoli

To sense the unseen rising sun colouring the sky with warm dawn glows of golden pinks filled us with a feeling of unbelievable calm, and as it slowly appeared from behind the mountains the still grey waters were gradually washed, like a watercolour painting, with colours of morning light that gradually spread to the town and beyond.

Those early mornings at the lagoon were the perfect start to the day.

Bullshit Baffles Brains

Computers and the internet were a new concept to many Kefalonians, and as with many other things, they, like me, adapted to the changes slowly. It came then as no great surprise that some of them were being ripped off by smooth talking, slick mouthed salesmen posing as computer experts who targeted small local businesses extolling their own virtues when it came to the design and building of websites, while at the same time charging a hefty fee for their services.

Bullshit baffles brains, and some hard nosed Argostolian businessmen, usually so astute when it came to

295

money matters, fell as easy prey to the smooth talkers who did the baffling. I was fortunate insomuch that Deb and Pam knew exactly what they were doing when it came to improving and updating my site, and they weren't charging for their expertise.

Websites are a great way of generating business, which was only too evident in my case, and because I was linked to the main search engines, anyone anywhere looking for an artist in Argostoli found me, and what's more, they didn't have to have my name or web address to carry out the search, as was the case with the unsuspecting locals.

The scammers, for whatever their reasons (probably because they didn't know how) weren't linking their clients' sites to the all important search engines, which was about as useful as being lost at sea without a radio.

One person who'd been taken for a ride on the website roller coaster was our friend Nick (the guy with the goats) and he only found out about it by chance. He was having problems with his email and had asked Pam's advice. It was then that she discovered the scam and broke the bad news to him, while at the same time explaining how search engines worked.

Vivian Villa

Nick and his wife Vivian owned Vivian Villa, a block of 'superior' holiday apartments and rooms. He was quick to point out that their property was possibly the only accommodation in Argostoli, the island even, where the toilets were fitted with 'western plumbing'; hence the term superior. It simply meant that loo paper could be flushed away instead of having to 'store it' in a pedal bin until the plastic bag liner was full enough to dispose of into the nearest wheelie bin.

Nick was a cousin of Makis our landlord, and we'd met him at the first name day celebration upstairs (the one when we thought we were going up for dinner). Nick and Vivian had lived in New Zealand for several years, which is how he knew about 'western plumbing' and both spoke good English. But he was another of those who went to great pains to tell me that I must speak Greek, and what's more, he told me how to do it successfully.

'Peter,' he'd say with a smile, 'to speak Greek you will have to learn one new word every day.'

'Some chance of that Nick,' I said with my own smile.

The Great Escape

As well as helping Vivian with the running of the apartments Nick spent a lot of time tending his goats in their settlement amongst the olive trees near the Italian Monument. Despite living away for so many years he was still a true Kefalonian and eccentric enough to prove it! As a way of thanking Pam for helping with the website he offered her a kid goat.

'No Nick, Makis would never let us keep a goat in the apartment.'

'It's not a pet Pam, it's for you to eat.'

'Thank you but Peter's a vegetarian.'

'You can freeze it.'

'My freezer is the tiny bit at the top of the fridge. It's very kind of you, but I'll have to say no.'

Then as further proof of his Kefalonian blood line he claimed the goats were bi-lingual, English and Greek with a twist of Kiwi thrown in for good measure.

Despite being beautiful animals they still gave off the distinct pungent goat aroma which hung in the air even when they were out of sight. But they, just as Pink had, got used to us talking to them through the wire fence, and answered back with little goat like replies which we recognised as English! With that in mind I thought there may have been some substance in Nick's bi-lingual claim after all.

It was on one of our frequent walks to the monument that we found the boundary fence to their grazing pastures damaged, and quickly realised they'd all escaped. Following a fresh goat trail wasn't difficult and we eventually found them near their compound happily munching olive leaves; there was only one problem though… the trees they were munching didn't belong to Nick. We would have phoned him, but neither of us had our mobiles, so the only way to alert him was to walk down the hill to Vivian Villa which would take about twenty five minutes, so we started walking.

Having reached the crossroads at Maistrato, who should come speeding towards us in his white van but Nick, with Vivian in the passenger seat. I'd lived on the island long enough to know there were some Kefalonians who, when behind the wheel of a vehicle travelling at speed, could be a little, or a lot, crazier than normal, even more so when their goats were feasting on someone else's olive trees.

Taking that into account, and my life into my hands, I stepped into the road and frantically waved at him to stop, and whereas most people would, he didn't, but just returned my wave, Vivian smiled, and I quickly got back on the footpath. He had no intention of stopping and just because I was in the road made no difference. Pam and I were gob-smacked, and watched the van disappear up the hill towards the monument, so we turned round and followed it.

By the time we reached the compound, wet with sweat and out of breath, the goats had been rounded up and were safely locked away. Nick then explained that his neighbour had phoned him earlier, but he did thank us for our trouble, then with one of his characteristic chuckles apologised for almost running me down.

Portraits

I loved painting Kefalonia, and it didn't matter what the subject was, landscapes, seascapes, trees, goats, buildings, anything, because when something caught my eye I'd turn whatever that something was into a painting.

Most Kefalonian men are blessed with striking features that are full of character, and although I don't consider myself to be a portrait painter, every now and then I liked to have a go. My first serious attempt was one of the honey seller at Kastro. He used to sit with his jars of honey at a table in the front garden of his house, passing the day away and greeting passers-by who would be on their way, either to or from the castle.

His face looked like it could have been 'carved in stone', and as well as possessing two of the most common Kefalonia male characteristics, a strong jaw and a pronounced nose, he also had dark deep set eyes, which were protected from the bright scorching sun, not by a huge sun umbrella or the latest designer shades, but by a cloth cap. A white, cleanly trimmed moustache contrasted sharply with his weathered skin, which over the years had turned the colour and texture of parchment. After finishing it, the painting of the 'Honey Man' was hung on The Studio wall along with the other work, the intention being to exhibit him at the Bell Tower in May.

With all the comings and goings along The Studio corridor I soon realised the offices of the pharmacy were at the other end, and I was soon on speaking terms with most of the women working there, as well as Vassillis, the owner. Some spoke good English and within a few days of moving in they became curious about me, stopping to peer through my open door. It wasn't long then before one stood in the doorway for a little longer than usual.

'Come in and have a look,' I said, which she did, and when she saw the Honey Man there was a surprised gasp, 'Peter, it is the father of my friend, I will tell her,' and down the stairs she went.

Minutes later the two of them came back. Her friend was another of the pharmacy females, and looking at the portrait she whispered, 'Oh Papa.'

It was obviously a very emotional moment for her, then after a short pause she asked if it was for sale, which it was, and then they left. A few minutes later Vassillis came in.

'Peter, you have a painting, which I believe it is the father of one of my girls, how much is it please, because I would like to buy it?'

'But Vassillis she has already asked me... '

'That doesn't matter, I want to buy it for her because it is very special.'

Which he did. Portraiture is a very lucrative form of art, and the Honey Man was the first of my Kefalonian portraits to be sold.

Odysseus Unbound

Not only did the book Odysseus Unbound make fascinating reading, but through its pages Pam and I discovered parts of the island that we never knew existed. Two in particular, Koumaria and Agia Sotiras were close to each other at the northern end of the gulf of Argostoli. Neither was signposted from the main road, so finding the exact turning for each was a bit hit and miss, but we got there eventually.

As usual, when walking the unknown we prepared ourselves by filling rucksacks with food, water, sun cream and waterproof coats, not because of any rain, but they were useful to sit on, especially if there were ants around, which was more often than not; big black ones.

The trail to Koumaria began as an asphalt road, but within a hundred metres or so became a typical rough, but walkable track that meandered and dropped steeply to the sea. The afternoon light sparkled and danced like diamonds on the water far below, while the distant Paliki resembled a patchwork carpet, ranging in colour from the lightest spring greens to the darkest umber.

We zigzagged towards the golden strip of sand that was in fact Koumaria, and had almost reached it when I noticed another track leading off to our left.

'Pam, we'll have a walk along there on the way back,' I said. Because it was exposed to strong southerly winds, over the years the Koumaria shoreline had been partially buried beneath a collection of flotsam, jetsam and other assorted junk, hence making it a beachcomber's dream, or, in the other extreme, an environmentalist's nightmare. Sitting on the beach (but not amongst the junk) the feeling of solitude was strangely fascinating, because once again it felt like we were the only people in a long lost forgotten world of our own. There was nothing, nobody, just us and nature.

On the way back we did detour along that other track, and what a find! There was a wooden jetty to which a small blue boat was tied, and from our vantage point high above it looked like it could make the perfect painting, but I needed to get closer.

The thought of risking life and limb hadn't entered my head, 'Pam, I'm going down.'

'Are you sure? There's no path, no track or anything, just be careful,' she replied, unable to hide her concern.

The track, or what there was of it, was quite narrow in places, and in others completely overgrown with rough bracken, that with difficulty I managed to scramble through and over. A goat, an animal usually so sure of foot had somehow become ensnared in the branches of an overhanging tree and its skeletal frame hung motionless above me.

'Whoops,' I thought, 'that's ominous,' then scrambled on and down, reaching the bottom with a few scratches but in one piece.

In a small cave, which was impossible to see from the track above and whose entrance was almost hidden by more overhanging branches, were remains of another unfortunate goat scattered on the dirt floor. Despite the macabre find, it was a fascinating place, and after wandering round for a while I called to Pam, beckoning her to come down and share it with me, but knowing how much she dislikes climbing, knew she wouldn't.

Agia Sotiras is only a short distance from the main road which turned out to be another gem, one of the many that we came across, sometimes by chance and good fortune, other times planned. Agia Sotiras, like the 'secret' cave round the corner of the bay was also hidden by the steep overhanging hillside as traffic on the west coast road passed a few hundred meters above it.

As we approached another small breath of civilisation, a man on an ancient tractor cheerfully greeted us. He was busily cultivating his olive trees and vines, but he wasn't so busy that he couldn't stop to talk and introduced himself as Nicolas, and we were only too glad to oblige him in conversation. After a few minutes of interesting chatter that was in danger of going on forever, we left him to his work and walked towards the small white church overlooking a narrow strip of shingle and sand.

Two small wooden rowing boats and a larger red and white traditional fishing boat had been dragged over the narrow beach onto an adjoining grass area, where in the lee of the nearby headland they were sheltered from the prevailing winds. Those boats, like the one round the corner made a painting too.

Unlike Odysseus I never did get to Ithaca, but later in the year an Ithacan came to the Bell Tower. We talked a lot, but said little about painting, then eventually I broached the subject of the speculation relating to Ithaca.

'Yianni (John) what do you think about the theory that modern Ithaca isn't the same ancient Ithaca depicted in Homer's writing?'

His reply came straight from the handbook of Greek philosophy. 'Peter, it will take many years for anybody to prove that theory convincingly, so in the meantime we'll continue to live with the myth.'

A Newspaper for English Speakers and Readers

With regard to following Kefalonian news on a daily basis most English speakers were in the dark, unless they could read Greek, and more importantly understood what they were reading (or of course they could listen to local gossip, ex-pat gossip that is!). Unfortunately that's where I came unstuck, because although reading Greek wasn't such a problem, understanding it was. Keeping up to date with the National news was easy enough, because there were two English printed publications; a weekly, The Athens News, and the very informative daily, *Kathimerini*, sections of which were also available online.

As well as being an artist, my friend Kosmas, along with his wife Kiki, compiled and published a local weekly newspaper which, understandably was written in Greek. After telling them about the lack of local information available to English speakers they were interested, even more so when I pointed out the viability of an English addition to their Kefalonian edition; so it was agreed. They would publish a pilot issue with topical articles that would interest ex-patriot readers.

When I told Brian he suggested that Bookmark could be the main retail outlet; and my role? I was the guy in the middle trying to pull it all together. It was a good idea and everybody was up for it, but unfortunately the initial euphoria quickly lost its momentum. Running a successful business took up much of Brian's time and energy. It was the same for Kosmas and Kiki. For them there would be the additional work of editing and translating, and although they both spoke excellent English and could translate it themselves, it was time they could ill afford. So, what with one thing and another, including the coverage of the forthcoming local elections, the project never got off the ground. I was disappointed the idea didn't become more than just that, an idea, but unfortunately things were beyond my control.

In the meantime Pam and I still kept up with local news as we always had; from the communication centre at Fanari, The Athens News, *Kathimerini* and the odd piece of ex-pat gossip.

Hand in Hand

Pam and I enjoyed celebrating with the Kefalonians, especially the christenings, which I compared to the coming of Spring, because like Spring's new growth the Baptism is a celebration of welcoming new life onto God's earth.

However, life and death go hand in hand, and where there is a beginning there will ultimately be an end; a funeral is the end. It's the final page in the book of life as we know it. Although I'd seen a number of funeral processions in Argostoli, albeit from a distance, there had never been any temptation to join the procession as many of the locals did. It was considered to be a mark of respect, not only for the deceased, but for the bereaved family also.

One of the friendliest characters I'd met since coming to the island was a taxi driver known to me only as 'big Makis'. He wasn't called that for nothing, it was a fact. He was a big guy, with a big personality and an even bigger smile to match, and whenever he saw me the greeting was always the same, 'Hello my friend, how are you today?'

He'd visited the UK often and talked fondly about the country, the people and their hospitality. Makis, because of his warmth, and especially being a 'cabbie', had made a lot of 'tourist' friends over the years and said to me more than once, 'I love the British because they are always so polite and friendly.'

It wasn't only Makis who said it, but other Kefalonians often made the comment too (about being polite and friendly that is) and I was never quite sure if it was a criticism or a compliment; they could never understand why we said 'please' and 'thank you' so often.

I was walking through the square one afternoon and found it totally deserted, and thought, 'Where is everybody, and where are the taxis?' It was April and the rank was empty which was unusual for the time of the year, and even more so for the time of day, it was only five o'clock. Then minutes later as I reached the Lithostroto the missing taxis mystery was solved, they were parked 'en masse' in front of the Court House.

Walking on I came across a large crowd gathered round a hearse in front of the church, many of whom were the town's taxi drivers, including Costas.

'Hello Costas, what's happening, why are all the taxi drivers here this afternoon?'

'Peter, you know Makis, the big guy. Well, he was in

Athens recently, at the hospital, and it seems there were complications and he died.'

By nature I'm an inquisitive sort of bloke, but I didn't ask how or why, it wasn't the time or place. In an instant his words took me back in time to Pam's hospital experience and I shivered at the thought of what could so easily have been. She though, unlike the unfortunate Makis had walked away from it.

Easter at Piniatorou

Easter at Fanari was cancelled because Stathis and Irini were away, but we were invited by Spyros and Dimitra to celebrate with them at Piniatorou instead. There was a large family gathering in which we were total strangers to some, but familiar faces to others, nonetheless we were welcomed warmly by all.

The Easter Barbecue with Dimitra supervising

As well as the traditional roast lamb, there was goat, both accompanied by huge containers of home grown vegetables which of course, included horta, and needless to say there was more than enough wine, red and white, to wash it all down.

Spyros and Dimitra between them had cooked the meat over open fires whose embers glowed in shallow trenches that had been specially dug for the occasion.

We thoroughly enjoyed ourselves that afternoon, and then, as the shadows of early evening lengthened we felt it was time to leave. After the endless farewells and thank yous, for coming, and for inviting us, we strolled arm in arm to the pulpit rock to enjoy the last of the sun as it sank slowly in the western sky.

We were still feeling the effects of the Easter feast when we got home so decided to siesta, just a short nap to re-charge the batteries. Four hours later we woke, cleaned our teeth and went back to bed and slept till next morning; that was some siesta, some Easter.

Easter is a special time for the Kefalonians, and because we'd become used to celebrating it with them it became very special for us too. They opened up their homes and hearts to welcome us as friends not just guests, and although we tried to reciprocate the same generosity it wasn't the same and we often wondered why. I think it was because we were only visitors to their culture and they knew that just like the boat people, we were only passing through, although it did take us a little longer.

Ultimately it's down to the Kefalonians themselves; their warmth and welcoming nature is legendary, unless the two are abused, and then, as an English friend living on the island made the comment to me more than once, 'Peter, the Kefalonians take no prisoners,' and he would know. He married one.

All Inclusive

Through the winter a new development had been taking shape on the eastern shore of the Paliki which from a distance looked pretty grim.

If I'd thought the wind turbines were a disfigurement of beauty, they were beautiful sculptures compared to what could easily be mistaken for a Mediterranean style prison camp, but, what was, in fact, an all inclusive holiday complex. Controversy had surrounded it from the word go, and as the completion date approached another major row broke out concerning the access road… there wasn't one.

Local gossip had it that the owner of the land the road was to pass through was having a problem deciding whether to sell it or not, or at least not for the price he was being offered. Subsequently, a number of meetings were held and he was finally persuaded to change his mind. To every problem there is a solution and eventually the road was built.

It was the May Day holiday and once again I was on board the Glass Bottom Boat with family and friends heading for Vardiani. On the way, Captain Makis took great pleasure in sailing as close to the uncompleted holiday village as possible, therefore giving those of us on board a chance to see how the latest concrete blight was contaminating the shoreline of paradise.

An Exhibition

With only a few days to go before the start of another holiday season there was more paperwork to complete before I could move into the Bell Tower officially. The boring and frustrating wheels of bureaucracy were turning again which meant it was time to 'get legal' once more, but thankfully it was far less painful than it had been when I opened The Gallery.

As well as having all the necessary documents for me to sign, Eleni showed me how to fill in the pages of the transfer book. Transfer book? The transfer book was another Tax Office novelty designed to confuse and bewilder; it was in effect, a record of artistic movements! Any artwork being moved from The Studio to the Bell Tower and back (a distance of about 300 metres), whether oils, watercolours, drawings or whatever, the contents of each journey had to be recorded and categorised for Tax Office records. It was crucial that all work being transferred corresponded exactly with sales receipts which were recorded in another book - the receipt book.

Although it was all mind boggling stuff I quickly became adept, knowing that one wrong slip of the pen would have meant Tax officials coming down on me like a ton of bricks. Eleni was impressed at how quickly I'd learned to use it, but I told her paperwork was easy, it was computers I had problems with; she smiled. In reality, none of the paperwork was exactly rocket science, although it was all written in Greek, and as incredible as it seemed there was even more paperwork in addition to the reams of 'getting legal' documents.

Tax Office regulations required a completed contract between the Bell Tower and me outlining terms, conditions and exhibition dates; it was a formality and straightforward enough. Exhibitions would be held for two weeks in every four, starting in May and finishing in October, and although the contract didn't say so, those dates were flexible. With everything completed it was time to move in.

Hanging paintings is more complicated than it would appear, and although the exhibition space at the Bell Tower was small, about twenty-five square metres, the works had to look balanced, which, after a bit of juggling they did.

The Bell Tower Exhibition

Posters were, as they had been in the years of The Gallery, displayed in the usual places with some very important additions locally; very locally!

During the summer The Bells *kafeneion* served drinks and snacks outside in the Cabana square, where customers could sit and relax under huge sun umbrellas to watch the world go by. Locals went about their day to day business rubbing shoulders with tourists who strolled in the laid-back ambience of the Lithostroto.

Those very important additions locally came in the form of extra advertising. Pam printed half size posters, which were laminated then placed along with the menus on the *kafeneion* tables, indoors and out. As well as 'table publicity', by far the most important advertising 'prop' of all was the 'A' board which had been specially made and stood just outside the entrance of the Bell Tower.

Looking Back

As another season dawned I looked back at the highlights of the past winter: we'd bought a full size cooker; Thomas was accepted at East London University to study, of all things, Fine Art; Portside was fitted out with wooden decking; and Mister George's store had a complete re-fit, which, unlike previously, became a pleasure to visit.

That Language Thing Yet Again

Although I was learning new Greek words and phrases, but not on a daily basis as Nick had suggested, I knew fluency would never become my strong point, which my Kefalonian friends, after years of badgering were still quick to pick up on. However, there were those who had language difficulties of their own, English difficulties that is and Vlassi, who I'd known a while was one of them. He also bucked the Kefalonian trend, especially when it came to dress and appearance. He was much shorter than the average Kefalonian, which made him very short, and a long flowing mane of black hair hung down his back, making him look even shorter than he actually was, and I was never sure if he owned a razor, because a permanent shadow of dark stubble gave his face a well weathered look, and he would never have won prizes for being Argostoli's best dressed man.

Baggy jogging bottoms peppered with rips and tears, and a thick woollen pullover were his usual winter wear, but as the weather warmed, the pullover was discarded to be replaced by an assortment of well worn tee shirts. His dress sense could best be described as casually comfortable.

Vlassi's girlfriend Eleni, on the other hand, didn't wear jogging bottoms, or stubble, but she was as casual as him in a 'hippy' sort of way. Beads and bangles cascaded from her neck and wrists, whereas the usual plunging neckline and tighter than tight trousers, or jeans, were tastefully replaced with flowing silk blouses and patterned cotton skirts, and to complete the picture her long dark hair was tied with silk ribbons; she also spoke English very well.

During the summer Vlassi and Eleni had a stall in Rizospaston from which they sold interesting and unusual craftware, some of which had been brought back from India where they sojourned for part of the winter.

When they weren't away in warmer climes, or trading in Rizospaston, they sold mainly clothing and small items of soft furnishing from the back of a beat up white transit van, the hippymobile, which was parked a short distance along the street from Cardiff.

I was walking along there one morning when Vlassi unexpectedly appeared from a nearby *kafeneion*, and grabbing my arm said, 'Peter, *ella ella,'* (which is pronounced how it's spelt, *'ella'* means 'come').

After dragging me to the van, he jumped in the back and produced a rather grubby dog-eared exercise book then excitedly flicked through the pages, pointing to each one.

Moments later Eleni appeared, and as he continued to flick the pages, which were covered with a mixture of Greek and English writing, she explained that he was learning English and she was his live-in tutor.

It was obvious she was doing a good job too, because a couple of days later a beaming Vlassi greeted me in perfect English, 'Good morning Peter, how are you today?' I didn't pursue the conversation, knowing that with our limited linguistic skills we'd have both ended up in knots.

Nick the Icon

Because of the summer exhibitions I got to know many of the business owners in and around the Cabana square, if only to nod to, but the one I became familiar with most was Nick, who I labelled Nick the Icon.

The Bell Tower was sandwiched between two shops, one sold lingerie and sexy underwear, while the other, in total contrast specialised in religious symbols, selling anything connected with the Greek Orthodox church and in

particular Saint Gerassimos; that was Nick's icon shop.

I hadn't been at the Bell Tower more than an hour or so when I descended on him in his cave of holiness, and introduced myself.

'Good morning, I'm Peter and I'll be exhibiting my paintings next door during the summer, and because we're going to be neighbours I thought it would be a good idea to introduce myself.'

We shook hands, or to be more precise I was locked in a vice-like grip, and before letting go he smiled, 'Welcome to the Cabana square Peter, let's hope it's a good summer for us both.'

Nick was a Greek Canadian, having spent some of his formative years in Montreal before coming to live in the mountain village of Faraklata. He too was from the Kefalonian mould, short, powerfully built, and although losing his hair, which in the main was very un-Kefalonian, he'd made up for it by growing a full moustache. We got on famously and shared some great moments, especially sitting together on the step outside his shop, where, just like the patrons of the Bell Tower, we relaxed and watched the world go by.

Although I'd introduced myself to Nick I didn't bother visiting the sexy knickers shop, knowing if I was spotted going in, or coming out, there were those who would put two and two together and reach the wrong conclusions.

Another Exhibition at the Bell Tower

During my two week break in July Prue moved into the Bell Tower and filled the void with a show of her artwork. I was only too pleased, and along with her daughter Kate, helped with the hanging, and by the time the pictures were on the walls the exhibition looked superb. One painting in particular, a blue black toned watercolour of Foki Bay stood out from the rest, so much so that Pam and I bought it.

'Prue we want to buy the Foki bay painting.'

She wouldn't believe us and replied in her own down to earth modest way, 'No, you're not kidding me, do you really?'

We weren't kidding and she was delighted, or to be precise, full of beans. It's a beautiful painting, and is one of the many reminders of the happy times we shared with her.

She'd only recently been discharged from hospital in Patras after a short stay, which was why Kate, who lived in the UK was around to keep a daughterly eye on her. Unfortunately, only a couple of days after opening her exhibition the doctor in Patras phoned, summoning her back for more tests. After that call everything happened so quickly. We met at the Bell Tower, dismantled the exhibition and early the following morning she was on the ferry coach to the mainland, and that was it. Within the space of twenty four hours she was back in hospital. Considering the circumstances she was so calm, but that was Prue, always very positive about everything. It's true to say she was more concerned about her animals than herself, but she didn't have to worry because we kept an eye on them.

The doctors hadn't given her any idea how long she'd be there, but she thought it would be no more than a few days, which in fact it was, although Pam and I thought it would be longer, knowing what we did about her illness. We also suspected Prue knew more than she let on, because things weren't quite as simple and straightforward as she'd hoped, but nonetheless it was good to see her back home so soon, and for the time being life carried on as normal.

More Furniture

We were more than content with the furniture in the apartment and it really was a comfortable home.

Yes, indoors was fine, but it was the plastic tables and chairs on the patio that concerned us; they'd seen better days and needed replacing. The original white chairs had, over so many summers in the sun become brittle, cracked easily and were dangerous to sit on, the dangers of painful plastic splintering were real. When they became irreparable Makis consigned them to the wheelie bins and they were replaced with some second-hand brown ones (which I think originally were red) from the Lassi apartments, but they soon went the same way as the white ones.

So the time finally came for us to splash out and buy our own. I'd looked around some of the shops in town but saw nothing with a realistic price tag, so Pam, whose Greek had come on leaps and bounds explained our intention to Makis, who not only understood, but because he occasionally bought plastic furniture for his Lassi holiday apartments, knew where to get the best deal.

Nothing more was said until one morning a few weeks later when a voice from the upstairs balcony called out, 'Pamela ella.'

315

It was Makis, who was going shopping. Five minutes later Pam was in the van heading out of town with him on a shopping trip, returning later with a set of table and chairs in a dark shade of green. We'd learnt lessons with the previous ones and were determined to protect our new set from the sun; first by covering the table, then placing it along with the chairs in the shade, and it worked.

Fran was a frequent visitor to the apartment and more than once had done a great demolition job on our plastic chairs, yes, more than once. She had the habit of leaning back on the two back chair legs, which was virtually guaranteed to result in the unmistakeable sound of cracking and splintering plastic under stress, followed by a big smile hopelessly disguised as guilt and, 'Oh dear Pam, sorry.'

To avoid any further plastic disasters we always reminded Fran to lower herself gently into the danger zone.

Fresh Figs

A basket of green and black figs

It was on that out of town shopping trip that we became hopelessly addicted to fresh figs. On their way back Makis and Pam stopped off at the Lassi apartments for coffee, and while there he filled a carrier bag with freshly picked figs from his plantation and gave them to her.

Not only had Makis introduced us to the delights of

fresh figs, but he also gave her a demonstration there and then on how to eat them, which is basically to pop the whole fruit, excluding the stalk, into the mouth and chew. After the crash course in figgery, he also told her to help herself to as many as she wanted at any time. Which she did.

It's My Father

One afternoon back in the spring as Pam and I strolled along the shore of the lagoon I saw a man sitting in one of the towering eucalyptus trees. He was wedged between two massive boughs that formed a natural V, looking extremely relaxed and very much at home; it was as though he'd been there forever. I recognised him as an Argostoli local, but what was more important from my point of view was that he, just like the Kastro honey seller had a very paintable face.

'Pam, I'm going to paint that guy, you've got the camera, take his photograph quick before he moves.'

'If I point this camera at him you know what'll happen, he'll jump out of the tree and run like hell.' She was right, because if he'd known what we were up to the natural pose and spontaneity of the moment would have been lost forever.

'Yes you're right Pam, I'll stand with my back to him, then all you have to do is to pretend you're taking a photo of me but aim the camera over my shoulder and get him, that way he'll never suspect a thing.'

Which is exactly what we did and he was none the wiser.

It turned out to be a great painting of remarkable likeness. One day as I was working on it my landlord, Marilena, on one of her frequent 'head round the door' visits to the studio said, 'Hey Peter, I know that man, his name is Gerassimos.'

'Well who'd have thought it,' I said with a smile, 'just

another one of the many.' Makis was duly hung in the Bell Tower along with portraits of other locals.

One Saturday morning in the middle of August a woman came up the spiral, looked round and stopped in front of Gerassimos just as if she'd been turned to stone. Then after studying him for a few minutes she chatted to me briefly, wrote some comments in the visitors book, politely thanked me and left.

'Um, OK,' I thought.

About an hour later a man came in and he too spent some time scrutinising the same painting. I was more than curious and couldn't resist the temptation, 'Excuse me, but do you know that man?'

'Yes,' he replied, 'it's my father-in-law,' and disappeared down the spiral.

That evening as Nick and I idly chatted on his step the same woman from the morning visit walked past and casually turning to me said, 'Hello Peter,' then she disappeared inside the Bell Tower.

'Do you know that woman?' Nick asked.

'Yes, she came in this morning.'

'Well you'd better get off your backside and up those stairs, she's probably coming back to buy a painting, go on get up there.'

Never one to mince his words he then gave me a hefty shove to help me on my way. By the time I'd got upstairs she was standing in front of Makis again, so I quietly walked over to her.

'Excuse me but you were here this morning, and now I'm really intrigued because a man came in after you left and he too spent a lot of time looking at it. Who is that man in the painting?'

Then with a great big smile she replied, 'Peter, it's my father.'

I told her the story of how the painting came to be, and she smiled again. After talking some more she shook my hand, paid me, took her painting and went down the stairs for the second time that day. It was an amazing chapter, and one of many, which only goes to show how a smile can sometimes say more than a book full of words.

An English Girlfriend

Since our first meeting, Ingrid had become a good friend and on her annual holidays to Argostoli she still turned heads, especially men's.

Just before the start of the season Panagis at El Greco asked if I would do him a special favour.

'OK. Pano, so what's the favour?'

'Peter Hemming,' which was how he sometimes addressed me, 'on your website you could post the favour I want. I would like an English girlfriend, a good woman,' he smiled.

'No Pano, a good woman is the last thing you want,' I replied. 'What you really need is a bad one, the bad ones are the best.' He smiled again.

He was a Kefalonian bachelor, and because of the high ratio of males to females, competition was fierce when it came to coupling up. As I mentioned earlier, Makis the Taxi, himself a bachelor reckoned that the ratio was five to one.

'OK Pano, that's not a problem, consider it done.'

But he wasn't quite sure if I was serious or not. Pam posted the request on the website along with his photograph and waited for the response.

Nothing happened until one evening in August when a stunning short haired, blonde woman walked into El Greco and sat at a table near the front windows.

As Panagis approached her with the menu she smiled, asking softly, 'Are you Panagis?'

'Yes,' he said, slightly caught off guard.

'Is it true that you are looking for a nice English girlfriend, only I saw your message on Peter Hemming's website.' As soon as she mentioned my name he saw through the plot and realising he'd been set up burst out laughing. A few minutes later Pam and I joined Ingrid and thanked her for being such a good sport, and when Panagis came over I apologised for not being able to find a bad English girl for him and asked if a nice Norwegian would do instead. He smiled, but once again he still wasn't quite sure if I was serious or not.

Right up to the end of the summer he never did find his 'nice' English girlfriend, but Ingrid had found him charming.

Local Elections

The period of residency that qualifies ex-pat Brits for voting in the local elections is one year, so with that in mind we registered and waited for the big day.

Two elections ran simultaneously; one to elect a new Mayor for each island municipality, the other to elect a new Kefalonia Prefect. The Prefect was god, the man everybody answered to, and who in Napier's day would have been the equivalent to the Governor. The Mayor, like the Prefect, is powerful, and along with that power he also, and quite understandably has many friends.

On voting day Pam and I went to the polling station which was in the school opposite Napier's Garden, a convenient short walk from home. As we queued to vote a familiar voice drifted over my shoulder, 'Hello Peter, how are you?' It was Petros, who Nick the Icon had introduced me to in the summer, and who was a regular visitor to his shop, but not necessarily to buy anything religious. Nick was not only an icon seller, but he was also heavily involved in politics with a fiery passion, and had been a driving force behind Petros in the last General Election campaign, and subsequent victory.

After voting, as we walked home Pam asked, 'Who was that man you were talking to back there?'

'That's Petros, he's a good friend of the Icon's and lives in that house behind high walls at Piniatorou. He's an MP in the Greek government, the island is his constituency. Why?'

'I just wondered,' she said.

It was a quick count and the new Mayor of Argostoli, representing the socialist Pasok party (as did his predecessor), was announced the same evening. The vote for the Prefect hadn't been so decisive and a second poll took place the following weekend which also resulted in a Pasok victory.

Politics in Greece has a lot to answer for. A recent countrywide survey found that when the country is politically active it is sexually inactive as the urge for sex drops off! It went on to say that coming together takes place on average twice a month, down from a healthy four times. No wonder the population was shrinking!

Those figures were based on averages though, and personally I thought they'd be the other way round, with the pleasures of carnal knowledge far outweighing the excitement of televised political broadcasts and Go Go dancers in the square.

Summer's Over

As the end of October approached so too did the end of another season, and as the number of visitors dwindled many tavernas and gift shops closed for the winter. And as tourist numbers dropped the temperature dropped too. But it could never have been classed as cold, not really cold, not like English cold, which was why many tourists took advantage of the late summer warmth, at least during the day when the sun was still up. The Kefalonians though felt the cold and had been wrapping up in their warm clothes since the beginning of September, just as if winter had already arrived.

I was approaching the end of my first summer at the Bell Tower and everybody there had warmed to me, and I to them, it was a mutual feeling, a family affair.

As a token of gratitude I presented them with a painting (not one each) of the Bell Tower, a small 'leaving' present so to speak. There was a brief ceremony in which I gave a short speech, with an interpreter standing by, and in return, but totally unexpectedly I too was presented with a thank you gift, a set of beautiful handmade Kefalonian glassware.

Then in the blinking of an eye the summer exhibitions were over. The season had generally been good and as well as meeting a lot of interesting people, I'd become re-acquainted with old friends and made new ones along the way, but financially there had been nothing to shout about... again. It had been all downhill since 2002, the first year of The Gallery.

Money, What's That?

Even without falling visitor numbers, I knew I'd never become a millionaire with the money I was making selling paintings, but I always lived in hope. There are however, people around who believe art isn't a money thing and that we painters do it for love, which, as Lefteris would say is b****cks; painters, like everybody else have to live, love never paid the bills.

I've also been told that artists, whether they're writers, dancers, actors or whatever are never truly content or satisfied, which I can definitely relate to. I'm my own biggest critic and always looking for ways to improve, then I question myself again; because just what do I mean by improvement?

There is always something to aim for, but the problem is that I don't really know what that something is, maybe one day I'll find out.

A Holiday

Despite the beauty of Kefalonia and the way we'd become attached to it, the decision had been made; the summer of 2007 would definitely be our last on the island. The planet was warming up, Greek summers were getting hotter and Pam, almost three years on, was still suffering the after effects of her surgery, although to look at her she was the picture of health, but the heat and humidity was playing havoc with her damaged lungs. I'd never been a sun worshipper so the thought of leaving the island for a kinder climate didn't really bother me, and although it was definitely next stop France, we still didn't know where exactly.

Living near the sea still had its appeal, so with the rugged beauty of the Atlantic coast in mind we decided to holiday in La Rochelle on France's west coast.

Everything, including accommodation had been booked online, but a few days before we were due to arrive the French rail unions announced a one day strike, which coincided with the day we were travelling from Paris to La Rochelle... by train.

Pam was in regular contact with Pascale, who, as well as living and working in Paris had bought an apartment in La Rochelle. She gave Pam regular updates on the strike, which turned out to be token and not total, meaning there would be a train service, although greatly reduced.

After flying into Paris we stayed overnight within easy walking distance of Montparnasse station, from where the La Rochelle train departed. Due to the industrial action there was a choice of only two that day, one at 7am, the other at 3.15 in the afternoon. Although getting up at some unearthly hour to catch a train wasn't my idea of a holiday, there was no doubt that catching the early service was the better option, so after leaving a grey and foggy Paris we arrived in sun drenched La Rochelle by mid morning. There were other advantages to the early departure, the main one being that it gave us the rest of the day to settle in and get our bearings, and with Patrice as our guide we couldn't have been in better hands.

During our holiday we explored most of the town and surrounding countryside, as well as scanning local estate agents' windows, a pastime the English seem to enjoy, especially when they're on holiday.

La Rochelle is a beautiful town, with colourful marinas, harbour side cafés and medieval battlements, there was even an Irish pub. But as charming as the town was, it wasn't for us and neither were any of the smaller towns or villages that nestled along the coast.

We arrived back in Kefalonia in the knowledge that in a year's time we'd be heading for France again, but where to was still anybody's guess.

More Strikes

The Greeks, like the French, have a militant Trade Union movement and as a consequence irritating strikes in the public sector were frequent. Workers in private businesses however, and especially the smaller family ones, carried on regardless having no union to turn to, and they still had to make a living. Sadly, every nationalised department was riding on the band wagon of industrial unrest.

As a way of justifying their actions and at the same time trying to keep a high profile, the unions held occasional rallies in Argostoli, but they were poorly supported because no-one seemed to know they were taking place, which was all down to the lack of Poster Power again. When asked what the strikes hoped to achieve the union's response was, 'They are for better conditions,' which, in a nutshell, meant they wanted more money.

All government employees, no matter how well or how badly they performed had jobs for life and anyone getting fired was unheard of, so what better conditions did they want?

Teachers seemed to strike more often than most, but in all fairness they were poorly paid considering their responsibilities.

The latest dispute was over the use of mobile phones in the classroom, by pupils that is, teachers didn't count. Another recently published survey found that 74% of children between the ages of twelve and fourteen owned a mobile phone, the other 26% rented them. As a way of improving standards, teaching and learning, the education minister banned the use of all mobile phones in the classroom, but the teachers' union immediately responded by declaring the ruling undemocratic.

'It can't be done,' they said, 'because it will be too difficult to implement.'

The decision had been taken at the highest level in an attempt to improve the education system for the long term benefit of Greek society as a whole.

Will the unions say that can't be implemented either?

Moving Out

I was used to seeing my pharmacy friends on a regular basis as they popped in and out with their *kalimeras* and warm smiles, but it all came to an end in October when Vassillis took his harem and relocated to a recently refurbished premises just a short walk up the street.

The builders moved in almost as soon as the pharmacy doors closed for the last time, and although the majority of work was downstairs they were also working in the former offices at the end of the corridor. Within days, and after some heavyweight demolition the pharmacy became unrecognisable, but thankfully there was no major disruption for me, although it was difficult to completely ignore the noise that is synonymous with building work.

Dust was my main concern, and keeping it out of The Studio my main priority. I put my technical hat on and made improvised door seals, I also kept a feather duster handy. Eventually the doorway at the end of the corridor was bricked up, which was great news, because not only were noise levels greatly reduced, but it meant I could put the feather duster away.

No sooner had the work started than it signalled increased chaos in the street below, because as well as the normal traffic hold-ups caused by shop deliveries and double parking, builders' vehicles - which included huge skips - created even more havoc than usual, for pedestrians as well as drivers. Tempers wore thin and at times were pushed to the limit. Honking horns and raised voices indicated that traffic had once again come to a standstill, tailing back out of sight along the most congested street in Argostoli. To say it was a nightmare would be an understatement, because even before the builders arrived the problem was gradually getting worse not better.

With the possible exception of the waterfront road, Sitemporon was the busiest street in town. Businesses lined both sides of its entire length, so whatever parking restrictions there were, if any, were totally ignored during opening hours. Double parking was a normal practice that the traffic police fought a continual losing battle to control as they stood and shook their heads, threw their hands in the air, put their whistles back in their pockets and gave up; either by turning a blind eye to it all or by walking to another street, preferably one where the traffic was moving, or better still where there was no traffic at all.

Sitemporon from the Studio balcony

They couldn't dodge the issue forever and occasionally made attempts to move offending motorists on. A loud whistle blast was the signal that they were out and about and was a warning local people knew and understood. At the sound of the whistle, parking culprits emerged from shop doorways protesting their innocence, even though they were obviously guilty, before driving away totally fed up because their shopping trip had been disrupted, only to double park somewhere close by.

Parking tickets were rarely issued and within minutes of the police leaving, Sitemporon returned to its normal chaotic state.

In the years of living in Argostoli I was still finding it hard to understand the *'then pirazi'* (it doesn't matter) mentality of the Kefalonians, even though I tried. Perhaps it was the culture thing again, and being a Northern European was really the difference. I'd grown up conditioned to a sense of law and order, which, from what I was being told by pessimistic and disgruntled English tourists was breaking down back in the Motherland, and had become far more serious than double parking, whistle blowing, frustrated arm waving and builders' skips.

Out of the Ordinary

As Christmas approached I thought of doing something different as a seasonal greeting for the family: so I starred in a movie!

Pam was always experimenting with her camera, so she recorded a short video with it on Christmas eve, of me thrashing about in the water at the pulpit rock. Through the coughing and spluttering I could be heard yelling 'Merry Christmas'... that was the greeting. The air temperature was warm, but the sea, putting it bluntly was very cold (*poli krio*). It took four 'takes' to get it right and although I wasn't in the water long, it was long enough to anaesthetise those vital parts of a man's anatomy that feel it first, and most.

Meanwhile back in the UK Pam's Mum was poorly, so just after Christmas she went to see her, which for me meant that, with a little help from my taverna friends I'd be looking after myself again.

After strolling along the Lithostroto on New Year's Eve I called into El Greco for dinner, and while there had an interesting talk with Panagis's sister Katherina, who lived and worked in London. Her English was excellent, but she explained that it hadn't always been the case, especially when she first moved to the UK.

'What was the problem Katherina?'

'Oh Peter,' she sighed, 'I should have studied the Cambridge syllabus at the *frontisterio*, but at the time it was much more difficult so I chose the easier Canadian alternative instead.'

Sometimes, looking back at the decisions we've made in our lives and the way they affect our futures it's easy to see the mistakes, we agreed, but no matter what, it's always much more important to learn from them.

Some hours later in the warmth of Pub Old House, as the last minutes of the year silently ticked away I thought about Katherina's struggle with the English language. Then I looked at my own struggles, the ones I'd encountered and successfully triumphed over, before coming to, and since arriving in Argostoli.

The Obelisk, Argostoli
Painting, oil on canvas by Peter Hemming

2007 – *Chronia Polla*

A Bag Full of Oranges

Since the turn of the millennium Pam and I had missed seeing the New Year in together three times. As the world slowly spun into the new century she was trekking in the Himalayas, 2003/4 was spent in the gloom of a hospital in Athens, and this year she was in England. That left me to do the rounds of greetings on my own.

New Years day dawned bright and clear as the sea glistened like liquid silver, melting under the strong morning sun. Walking along the coast road to Fanari I couldn't help but notice how abnormally low the tide was, lower in fact than I'd ever seen it. Irini said she hadn't noticed any difference, and Stathis wasn't around to ask, he was in Argostoli celebrating with the choir; so I put the low tide to the back of my mind for a couple of days.

Walking on from Fanari, my next 'greetings' stop was at Spyros and Dimitra's. I was almost there when a voice from the olive groves close by sounded,

'Peter, *ella*,' at which Spyros's brother Nick appeared from amongst the trees.

We walked the short distance to his house from where he produced a large carrier bag full of home grown oranges, then handing them to me said, 'Happy New Year Peter, these are for you and Pam.'

'Thank you Nick, and a Happy New Year to you too, please give my best wishes to Lula (Nick's wife) and the boys.'

Then, with the bag of oranges I laboured up the lane to Spyros and Dimitra's just as they were about to leave on the BMW. There were the customary handshakes and kisses before he said, 'Ah Petros, good morning, Happy New Year, where is Pam-el-a?' I explained without going into too much detail, and because they were going out I thought that would be the end of it, but it was only the beginning.

'Petros, we are going to Argostoli to the family to eat, you will come.' It wasn't a question, he was telling me; but we wouldn't be going three on a bike surely? I explained why I'd got the oranges and suggested taking them home first and then meeting up with him later. Having said it I kicked myself, knowing that an arrangement like that would be fraught with complications. Kefalonians, at least some of the ones we knew weren't the best in the world when it came to giving directions, because for some odd reason the journey usually started at the Post Office; but Spyros had a better idea which was totally uncomplicated, and the Post Office didn't get a mention.

'No Petros, I will take Dimitra and then come back for you on the bike, please wait here.'
The ride to Argostoli went without a hitch and Spyros kept a sensible speed knowing I was having a hard time on the back, doing a balancing act with the oranges, and despite getting the odd face-full of tobacco smoke I arrived safely and in one piece.

Once inside the house I recognised most of the family from the previous Easter gathering so there was no need for any 'getting to know you' formalities. I was treated like one of the family, and the buzz of chatter was once again a lively mixture of English and Greek.

It was a great afternoon, and thanks to chance and the kindness of Spyros and Dimitra's family I had been plunged headlong into another Kefalonian New Year, although completely different to the celebrations of previous years.

I left in a slight alcoholic haze, struggling with the oranges along the short but torturous uphill walk home, where after a brief nap I converted most of them to juice; there was no four hour siesta that time.

Solved

The low tides had really aroused my curiosity, so I raised the question with a few people who I thought might know the cause. So far the winter had been mild with hardly any rain, so perhaps it was something to do with Global Warming, which seemed to take a fair share of blame for almost every other anomaly concerning the weather and the way it was affecting the world's climate.

Nikiforos, who loved the sea and spent most of his time in it said the recent and unusually strong north winds had caused sea levels around Argostoli to drop, but once the winds stopped they would return to the normal level. The only flaw in his theory was that the winds, which had never been that strong anyway, had dropped days ago to become nothing more than a gentle sea breeze.

I was in the shop telling the Icon about it when Spyros (the dentist) walked in, so I quizzed him. He confessed that he hadn't noticed anything out of the ordinary and really didn't have a clue what I was talking about, whereas Nick, with a puzzled look on his face shook his head in disbelief.

'Perhaps there's been a strong underground tremor and the sea bed has opened up,' I suggested, at which Spyros tentatively nodded and said,

'Yes, that's a possibility.'

But Nick was more than sceptical.

'Peter, you are definitely becoming Kefalonian, you're crazy.'

He was having none of it, although for once he was at a loss for an explanation of his own.

Costas (the taxi), usually a font of philosophical wisdom, knowledge and wit said the low levels were caused by barometric high pressure, but when I pressed him to be more specific, he couldn't.

There were others who I'd thought of asking but it was pointless, knowing I'd end up with a hundred and one different answers to the same question.

Eventually tide levels returned to normal and no more was said.

Moving Back Home

Thump, thump, thump. That unmistakeable sound of heavy machinery pounded my brain as I lay in bed early one January morning, and whatever it was wasn't far away, and because there were no signs of it stopping I took a look outside the back door to see exactly where it was.

When I first moved into Piniatorou Street, Minas and I had been neighbours, but he moved out some time later and went to live in Lassi. Since then he'd always talked about coming back and building his own home; that thump, thump, thump was the signal that he was returning to Argostoli and the building of his new home had just started.

At the far end of our building a digger was excavating foundations for an extension that would eventually end up as part of an additional storey that was going to be built on top of the existing apartments of his parents. Minas would move into it once the work was completed. The views from this new apartment would be truly amazing. It was no ordinary extension however, because incorporated into it was a garage at ground level with an integral lift shaft which would be ideal for moving not only furniture, but baby transport too, when that time eventually came.

Pam and I were dreading the disruption, which we knew from past experience would be inevitable judging by similar construction projects in the neighbourhood on and off since we'd lived there.

The concrete frame of the new apartment was completed quickly with the minimum of fuss and delay, and caused us no problems whatsoever. It was the morning that the bricklayers arrived that the problems started.

Rarely did builders work anywhere off proper tubular steel scaffolding (i.e. with safety rails, toe boards, protective sheeting, and clips that held it all together), and those bricklayers were no exception. The normal practice was to work off the concrete roof, thus doing away with conventional scaffolding, but when they did use it, primitive makeshift wooden framed platforms and uprights were lashed together with wire and rope that would never win major safety awards.

Unfortunately for us the bricklayers were working off the roof of Makis and Soula's apartment which meant we had to put up with 'bricklayer's shrapnel', those sharp pieces of brick, or concrete block, that showered down and littered the patio in the process. Equally dangerous was the cement and sand mix, splattering like bird droppings, not only across our patio, but also over the clean washing that Pam had hung out earlier that morning before the bricklayers arrived. What a mess! Pam was less than amused and Soula wasn't laughing either, she was furious.

I'd never seen or heard her get really angry before, but that morning the air turned a deep shade of blue as she gave those bricklayers a good tongue-lashing, she then apologised to us and rewashed our clothes. Later that afternoon

Makis cleaned the patio down with a brush and hosepipe.

The following day was the calm after the storm. The last thing those guys on the roof wanted was to incur more of Soula's wrath, but as a precaution we didn't hang any washing out until after two o'clock, which was when they finished work for the day.

A New Mechanic

Finding a good tradesman can often be a bit hit and miss which is why personal recommendations are usually the best way to go about it. Whether it's a plumber, an electrician or in my case a mechanic, because while Pam was away the car wouldn't start. Yes, finding that elusive right man, or woman, is a universal problem and applies not only to Kefalonia.

Costas the Taxi, who had previously worked as a mechanic, checked it over, scratched his head, asked me to turn the ignition key, then said, 'Peter, I think I know what the problem is,' and unlike the low tides he was able to tell me, and I'm sure what he'd said was right, but it was all in technical jargon and went completely over my head, so I was still none the wiser. Our usual mechanic couldn't come to Argostoli, and towing the car up the hill to Travliata was out of the question. It was then I had the brainwave, I'd ask Lefteris, he was bound to know someone.

I was walking to the pub when I had yet another brainwave. Irena had recently had work done on her car, so I did a swift left turn into Arhontiko. She'd used a guy called Spyros whose workshop was on the industrial estate, not far from the Botanical Gardens, so I took his number and phoned him.

It wasn't many minutes after the call that he arrived and looked at the sick Panda, pinpointing the problem straight away, even before opening the bonnet, then seconds after turning the key he said, 'Peter it's a sensor, and I'll have to order one from Patras. When it arrives I'll come back and finish the work, it won't take more than a couple of minutes,' which it didn't.

Because of his excellent service Spyros became our new mechanic, and because he spoke good English there was never any need for an interpreter.

Welcome Home

Towards the end of January Pam came home. Sadly her mum had passed away and she'd stayed on for the funeral. Needless to say, her New Year had been totally different to mine.

Checkmate

During last year's summer exhibitions I realised there was not only normal *kafeneion* business at The Bell Tower, but the back bar was also the meeting place of the local chess club who took it over en-masse for their evening practice sessions. Generally they were a friendly bunch and I got on with them well, all that is except one, that was a guy called Makis. One evening I arrived upstairs to find him using the exhibition space as a classroom, where he was tutoring a young lad.

Naturally I was upset and within seconds there was an exchange of strong verbal abuse, Greek from him, English from me. I called downstairs for Yiorgos to come and sort it out, and although he tried his best, Makis (the chess) wasn't listening which led to an even stronger and louder two way tirade that deteriorated rapidly into a verbal brawl.

Later that week I met Katherina and Lena, who assured me that any future chess lessons would take place either on the next floor up, or preferably downstairs, which they did.

House Clearance

So far it had been a busy year. Pam spent almost a month in the UK, then in the middle of March we returned for a two week visit that involved a mixture of business and pleasure. The hassle of letting out our house had finally got to us so we put it on the market, but before placing it with an agent it needed emptying, with some items going into storage and a house clearance company taking what was left.

It's common knowledge that in England, house purchase, along with divorce and bereavement are the most common causes of stress. Over the years Pam and I had been through all three and by the end of the two weeks we were not only stressed but completely exhausted.

We did though have enough energy to lift ourselves for two celebrations; one was Pam's birthday, the other Clare's wedding which were both on the same day.

On our journeys to and from the island to the mainland we normally travelled by coach and ferry, but because we were almost dead on our feet, flying back from Athens offered the much easier and less tiring option.

Upon landing at Kefalonia a mini bus drove us the few yards from the plane to the main entrance at the front of the terminal building.

'Pam, this VIP treatment isn't normal, something must be wrong – what's going on?' She agreed, and a few minutes later we found out what it was. While we'd been away a huge tremor had caused extensive damage to the underside of the terminal roof, but at least the carousel was working and our baggage arrived intact.

Le Tour

Mention the word tour in Kefalonia and one of the first things that comes to mind are holiday visitors climbing onto air conditioned coaches for a ride taking in the beauty spots of the island, but there was another very different tour that had nothing to do with tourists or air conditioned coaches. It was the sixth Tour of Kefalonia, an international cycling race (which was what the advertising blurb led us to believe) starting and finishing in Argostoli; so Pam and I went to watch the finish.

Conditions were perfect, cool, dry and little wind, for what was a testing circuit of the island. After leaving Argostoli the peloton headed along the west coast road to Diverata before making it's way across country to Agia Efimia, then onto Sami from where the toughest part of the course started; the climb into the high mountains. Once out of the mountains the field headed back to Argostoli along the main south road where they took a left at Peratata to eventually enter the town from the Lassi direction to complete a small loop which brought them to the Dhrapano bridge where they turned left onto the waterfront road for the mad dash to the finish.

So as to get the best view of the final bunch sprint we stood on the corner where the riders turned left off the waterfront road, with the theatre straight ahead, before immediately turning right to finish in front of the Prefecture.

In 1998 Pam and I had been in Paris for the final stage of Le Tour (the eye watering Tour de France) and were expecting the Kefalonian version to finish somewhere along those lines, well, not eight gut-busting laps exactly, but at least some sort of eyeballs out sprint! We were disappointed then, because there was no frantic heads down, bums up and elbows out in that final dash for glory. Instead, as the riders passed our vantage point their nonchalant peddling motion was no more than what runners would call a jog, so gentle in fact, that they weren't even out of breath and were still casually chatting away as they crossed the finish line, probably without even knowing they had.

Zigzag

Anyone with knowledge of Kefalonia, whether as residents or regular visitors, will no doubt have noticed the pronounced zigzag track that snakes up and over the mountain from the village of Dilinata; it's unmissable and can be seen for miles.

Not content with conquering Aenos, Pam was up for another challenge and planned to walk not only up the zigzag, but over the top and down the other side, with Dee for company.

'That's madness,' I protested, 'you're both crazy, you haven't got maps or compasses, what's going to happen if you get lost, and what about the heat?'

Although it was only April the weather had turned hot, but even so it was obvious I was wasting my breath trying to talk them out of it, they'd made up their minds and nothing, least of all me, was going to stop them. Even Pete, usually so laid back about most things thought they were stark raving mad, but he still drove them to Dilinata (I'd have made them find their own way) and once he'd found the start of the track, which wasn't easy, wished them good luck and went back home to prepare the evening meal.

Local rumour has it that once over the top the track takes a straight course to finish in Agia Efimia; the reality is totally different. The track makes many twists and turns to end up in many different places, as the two adventurers found out, and although the zigzag was steep it was in fact the easiest part of the trek, at least they couldn't get lost on it. Upon reaching the other side however, there wasn't a signpost in sight. There were though two good shepherds who pointed them in the general direction, the key word being general.

The other side!

Eventually, because they were travelling downhill both Pam and Dee assumed the path they were following was the right one, and without being really too sure, stuck to it. It was then, more by good fortune than judgement that after half walking, half scrambling over fallen trees and down the rocky remains of a dried up stream they eventually ended up in Old Karavomilos, which to Dee's amazement, not to mention her relief, Pam knew and instantly recognised.

In the meantime, and some hours after dropping them off Pete drove to Sami, but because of weak phone signals couldn't make contact with either of them, so he settled down to enjoy a beer in one of the waterside tavernas and waited for them to contact him. He was half way through it when his phone rang, which turned out to be the SOS call he'd been expecting, some six or so hours after seeing them on their way.

He finished his beer, followed Dee's instructions and headed for the mountains where he met Dee and Pam wearily trudging along the road between the old and new villages of Karavomilos.

On their way home Dee asked, 'Pete, how's the chicken doing?'

'Oh no,' he muttered under his breath.

In his haste to become a one man rescue team he'd left it roasting in the oven and was only too aware that by the time they got home it would be burnt to a crisp; but all was not lost.

Because there was no mains gas supply in Argostoli anyone wanting to cook with it had to use the bottled variety, which was what they did. Fortunately for us, some time after starting out on his mercy mission the cylinder ran out, but even more fortunate, there was a full replacement container in the cellar.

That same evening two tired women with heavy legs joined two fresh men for a wonderfully cooked roast chicken dinner.

Postscript - On that morning as they started out on their marathon hike Pam noticed a newly built road winding its way into the mountains, so a few days later we drove up to see where it went. Starting near the chapel at Lamia the new road headed north, and considering it was only a mountain pass it was asphalt surfaced and as wide as the average dual carriageway, at least to begin with. After the first couple of kilometres the asphalt surface became rolled hardcore, expertly prepared for the final tarmac topping, so there was no cause to worry about damaging the underside of the car. Undeterred then I drove onwards and upwards.

Reaching the top and starting the descent, the surface became less predictable, at which point I thought about turning back, but as I was about to, another asphalt topped road turned off to the right so I followed it, and although I wasn't quite sure where we'd end up I did have a good idea.

Not for the first, or last time, we were in the lap of the gods and trusting our luck!

The asphalt lasted for about fifty meters, before turning into a typical narrow concrete mountain road which in places was barely wide enough for one vehicle, but by that time it was too late to turn back.

There have been moments in my life when I've thought, 'Whoops, I shouldn't have done that,' and as I slowed our little Fiat down to almost crawling pace I realised that was one of them. The thought of turning back crossed my mind again, but it was impossible, there was only one way to go, and that was forward and down, perilously avoiding pot holes and bumps. As the slopes on Pam's side of the road became steeper and the ravines deeper she tried her best to ignore them by looking straight ahead, while I used all my powers of concentration to negotiate the tightest of hairpin bends. It was round about then that I noticed how quiet we'd become, as not a word had passed our lips since the turning then in one of the quietest moments I thought the unthinkable, 'What if we meet something coming the other way,' and in an instant broke into a cold sweat. It would've been the ultimate nightmare, so I hoped nothing would, and thankfully nothing did.

After what seemed like forever, our mountain ordeal suddenly ended in the village of Makriotika, just off the main road between Agia Efimia and Diverata, where we sighed sighs of relief and started talking again.

I guessed Diverata was where the new road finally came out, but didn't bother driving there to find out.

Wonderful Memories

It was a Saturday morning and I was in the jewellers talking to Nikiforos when my phone rang.

'Hi Pete it's Kate.' I said a quick goodbye to Niki,

headed for the door and braced myself for what I knew was coming next, then after a brief pause her voice came through again, 'Pete, she's gone.'

Over the last few weeks Pam and I had been in regular contact with Kate, and although it was the call I'd been expecting for some days there was still that horrible cold empty numb feeling after I'd taken it.

Kate had called to tell me Prue had passed away. She'd been diagnosed with liver cancer some months before, which we all knew was terminal. Even so, she was as positive then as she had ever been throughout the whole period of the illness and bravely prepared herself for the inevitable.

Looking back there was one particular morning when we sat together in the studio doing our best to talk about anything other than her illness, but I sensed it was uppermost in her mind and over the obligatory cup of tea she poured her heart out.

The specialists had recommended chemotherapy, which she was totally against, so I asked her why.

'Pete, I know the stress of it all would be too much for me, and although there isn't much time left in my life, at least what there is I want to enjoy as much as I possibly can.'

Then with a huge smile she said there had been a slight glimmer of hope and told me what it was. Olive leaves boiled in water, drunk as hot as possible were supposed to be a miracle cure for liver cancer, and because there was no shortage of them, especially near the caravan, she tried it.

'How did it go Prue?'
She grimaced and smiled again, 'Pete, I've never tasted anything so foul, ever, so I've given it up.'

A few days later I'd walked into Lassi and called to see her. It was her turn to make the tea, which she gladly did, and as we sat enjoying it I looked out at what had become affectionately known to Pam and me as 'Prue's view'. I suddenly realised that within a few weeks there would be no more sitting here enjoying the company of our dear friend, and at that moment of realisation it felt as though I was the one who was dying. As I held back the tears and fought to keep my emotions from spilling over it was apparent I was falling apart; yet that afternoon Prue was as calm as a clear day.

Shortly after, at the beginning of February, for the last time she left the home that had meant so much to her and travelled to the UK, but before leaving she asked one last favour of us.

It was no big deal to feed her cats, we'd done it before, but we knew that this time would be the last. As she'd instructed, we gradually reduced their helpings, 'By doing that they'll learn to look after themselves.' And she was right, because within a week, on our last visit, the food had gone and there wasn't a cat in sight.

All that was left was an empty caravan and wonderful memories.

The El Greco Project

About three weeks before the start of the season Panagis phoned.

'Peter Hemming will you come to see me and my father, it's not important, but please call into the taverna soon.'

It sounded important, and just for him to say it wasn't meant it was, so I went to see them straight away.

Slipping my coat on I said to Pam, 'Won't be long,' to which she responded with one of those 'are you sure?' looks as I closed the door.

Between serving customers and delivering pizzas a high level meeting took place between Pano, Andreas and me as we discussed the latest El Greco project. There had been a few in recent years which had brought about several changes to the taverna, some good, some not so.

The best had been to replace the front windows with full length folding double glazed doors that opened fully and proved to be ideal for those hot summer evenings. Then at the other extreme there had been an ill fated installation of seductive subdued green lighting, which was about as seductive as sleeping with King Kong. Awful! Andreas in his wisdom quickly reverted to the normal bright white lights before completely losing his regular customers, most of whom had stayed away in protest. They slowly returned once word spread that he hadn't completely lost his sanity.

It was just before the green light experiment that the chef left, but instead of turning out to be the disaster everyone thought it would be, it was in fact the best thing that could've happened, because Anna, Pano's mother, took over in the kitchen and the difference was immediate, proving to be a great move. Good wholesome, value for money food was El Greco's trademark and the locals knew it; so with new lights and a new cook they were more than happy.

Anyway, back to the meeting. The reason I'd been summoned was because Andreas was erecting two new signs outside on the front of the taverna and wanted me to design and paint them. One was to be written in English, the other in Greek, both with red lettering on a green background.

At first I tried to back off, explaining that it was a totally different type of painting to what I did, and it really was a job for a specialist sign writer. However, neither of them was listening and after they'd filled my wine glass for the umpteenth time I finally gave in and said 'Yes'. I told them what materials to buy and once they'd got them to phone me, thinking that would be the end of it, but it wasn't.

A few days later Pano phoned and the following day work started.

My workshop was the wonderful 'garden in the back', that summer hideaway where delightful authentic home-made Greek cooking is served. Greek yes, except for the odd pizza, or the wonderful Poutsin El Greco (formally Poutsin Italien), a dish of fried potatoes in a tomato and herb sauce covered with melted cheese.

My sign writing début turned out to be more straightforward than anticipated. Pam printed stencilling templates off the computer, which I cut out and taped into place on the signs once the base coat was dry. The red lettering complimented the green background and the finished signs looked good; everyone was happy.

El Greco Taverna, Argostoli

'Peter how much do I owe you?' Andreas asked.

'Andrea, you always give me glasses of wine when I come for my takeaway pizzas, and when Pam and I eat here Panagis always brings extras, please, you don't owe me anything, you are my friends, and anyway I don't know how much to charge.' It was true I didn't, but he insisted.

Eventually I plucked a figure out of my head fully expecting him to haggle, but he didn't, and paid me not only what I'd asked for, but there was a substantial extra on top.

Warm and welcoming, kind and giving. Once again I was moved by a Kefalonian's generosity.

The final twist in my brief sign writing career came shortly after finishing them, which was just as the season began.

I was walking home from The Bell Tower one lunchtime when Panagis called me over, pointed to the blackboard on the pavement, and asked, 'What can I write on the board so that more people will come into the taverna?'

'Give me some chalk and I'll show you.' I wrote on it in big letters, GREAT FOOD, GREAT VALUE.

The Last Time

My last May Day voyage on the Glass Bottom Boat turned out to be memorable for no other reason than 'Karaoke John' was on board. He was an all round Geordie entertainer who had lived on the island for a number of years, playing in bands, doing discos and of course, karaokes, and on that day he was determined to get everybody, including me, into the party mood. I've never been a karaoke fan and up until then had never taken part in one, but as we started out on the return voyage to Argostoli after another relaxing day at Vardiani, all that changed.

As the music played and the wine flowed, everybody, especially the children, who incidentally, hadn't been taking part in the wine flowing, were having a great time, then suddenly the fingers were pointing at me.

'Come on Pete,' John said, and using all his powers of persuasion, with Tim's help (Tim being Yvonne, the star-behind-the-bar's nephew, and a member of the crew) dragged me to the microphone for my karaoke début.

The first number was a rendition of the Dion hit, 'The Wanderer', in which I partnered John, but it was all I could do to sing and keep a straight face at the same time. As the lyrics flashed across the screen my thoughts turned to the English comedy duo, the Two Ronnies, who some years ago had sent up the Status Quo cover version, and re-titled it, 'I'm Very Fond of Her', in such hilarious fashion on British television. Once the applause for John and me had died down it was Tim's turn to get in on the act, and together we roared through a throaty version, complete with growls, of The Troggs hit, 'Wild Thing'. What a way to end the day.

After mooring up, shouts of, 'See you again next year Peter,' rang in my ears. As yet, news of the move to France hadn't reached the crew of the GBB but when it did they would be as surprised as anyone.

An Outlet For My Work - again

To coincide with the start of the new season I was offered an outlet for my work through a new Art Gallery that was due to open in the centre of Argostoli.

The seeds had been sown one morning in Mr. George's shop where I was being served by a young lady who not only spoke excellent English, but also happened to be Mr. George's daughter Denise, (pronounced thee-o-neecia). The gallery in question was hers, and at that time was in the latter stages of refurbishment and once it was open she wanted me to exhibit there. After talking it over I sensed a feeling of mutual enthusiasm, so we exchanged phone numbers and I left the store feeling quietly optimistic.

It was the usual gallery/artist relationship, whereby she took a commission and sold the paintings; all I had to do was keep her supplied.

Three Hundred Cups Of Coffee

As well as the outlet for my work, quite a few other things coincided with the start of the season. The return bus service (for the season only) from Argostoli to Lassi resumed at the end of May; cruise ships appeared, as did the passengers, swarming into the town like bees round a honey pot, and the skies came alive with the sound of chartered planes, which to anyone relying on tourism for a living was like winning the lottery.

But as important as any of those things, at least as far as we were concerned, was that Portside had opened again. Rosa's first evening was always special as Pam and I were part of a handful of regulars who turned up for it. Prue had been part of that group, and although she couldn't be with us in body, she was there in spirit and would no doubt have been 'full of beans' as we toasted her as well as other absent friends.

Portside Taverna, Argostoli

Earlier, on that first day a cruise ship had steamed into port and Rosa, who had been run off her feet all morning, reckoned she had served three hundred cups of coffee to the 'swarming' passengers.

'Stop complaining,' I told her, 'look at it as being a good omen for the rest of the season.'

Taking the P**s

When it came to haggling over the prices of paintings, I'd got it down to a fine art! There was no point in bothering with price lists, because as soon as a painting sold it was immediately replaced with another, which meant any sort of list would have been out of date the moment a painting left the wall.

Although the majority of visitors were happy paying the full price, which for most was affordable, especially for an original oil painting, occasionally there was the odd bod who wanted something for nothing, well, almost nothing, and who was really trying it on; putting it bluntly they were taking the p**s.

They were easy to spot and when I did, the price of the painting went up to compensate for the inevitable drop once the haggling started. I was more than happy to do a deal and drop the price accordingly, which was usually half way between the asking price and the one being offered, and as long as it was a sensible offer then everybody was happy.

A couple of days after opening the May exhibition a couple came in, selected three paintings, all costing the same, then after finally selecting one asked, 'Is 125.00 euros your best price?'

'Make me an offer,' I said, at which they dropped to 100.00.

'112.50,' I countered. Then something happened that completely threw me; they pleaded poverty. 'OK, if you're really that hard up and you honestly want the painting it's yours for 110.00.' A bargain I thought.

But no, still not satisfied with my gesture they offered 105.00, whingeing that if they had to pay any more, a massive five euros more, it would leave them short for the rest of the holiday. Not only had I heard enough, I'd had enough.

'Listen, I have to make a living selling paintings and there are only six months of the season in which to do it, I'm not dropping the price any further, you take it or leave it.'

'OK, we'll have to leave it then,' and frankly I was glad they did.

Thankfully I can honestly say, people like them were rare and I might have been fortunate enough to meet less than a handful in the course of a season.

Pam's Sunrise

On a number of last summer's early morning walks along the Fanari coast road there had been some beautiful soft and subtle sunrises. Pam had been inspired and during the winter tried her hand with the brush and painted one on a small canvas. It was remarkable how she'd captured the special atmosphere as the light hit the water and the rays of the sun threaded through the trees.

For a bit of a laugh I hung her painting in the Bell Tower to see if people would pay it any attention, which they did. Amazingly, that lovely little sunrise could have sold many times to a lot of genuinely interested would-be buyers.

And there were no smart alecs offering silly prices, not that it would have mattered anyway; Pam decided her sunrise wasn't for sale.

Different Answers

For several days road works had disrupted the normal flow of traffic around the south east corner of the square. Narrow, shallow trenches had been dug and I wanted to know why, so I asked a few people, while at the same time suspecting that I'd receive different answers from each one.

'Peter, it's for water pipes.'

'It's for electricity cables, 'another said.

'Drains,' somebody else suggested, but they were all wrong because the trenches weren't deep enough for any of those. As work continued they were half filled with a concrete foundation onto which heavy kerbstones were placed and cemented into position, the top of which was raised slightly above the level of the existing paved patios where the cafés' tables and chairs were. In reality the kerbstones were a boundary, and any café owners venturing over that boundary would risk incurring the wrath of the ever vigilant and observant Municipality Police.

Oddly though, nothing was done to restrict the 'café overspill' in the opposite corner of the square, where the problem was far worse.

The kerbstone project was another classic example of how to pour taxpayers' money down the drain, proving to be a costly and unnecessary hare-brain scheme. Surely it would have been cheaper, quicker and equally effective to have painted a coloured line on the road round the perimeter of the square. The raised kerb was thought by some to be idiot proof, and was there to assist the patrolling Municipality Police in their fight against straying café furniture.

And a coloured line wouldn't?

The Municipality Police

Four different Police Forces operate in and around Argostoli: The National Police, The Harbour Police, The Tax Police and The Municipality Police; with each one having a different responsibility for enforcing law and order.

The National Police enforce the law generally, and like many other Police forces around the world carry guns, but mostly they ride round in cars smoking cigarettes and trying to look mean and scary.

The Harbour Police not only check sea traffic in and out of Argostoli, but also patrol the vicinity of the harbour and port, usually on foot. During the summer they can be seen along the waterfront road doing their best to control traffic, but often failing miserably. They wear white uniforms and do a lot of whistle blowing.

The Tax Police are notorious for hassling businesses, especially in the summer. They are anonymous in their plain-clothes and don't carry guns or whistles.

The Municipality Police are, in effect, streetwalkers and roam the town in pairs checking for hazardous obstacles, such as 'A' boards, racks of clothing, of which there are many, postcard and gift stands of which there are many more, and of course, the tables and chairs that in places stretch as far as the eye can see and are outside every café in the town.

I was unfortunate enough to fall foul of their powers of observation one evening as they nonchalantly strolled past the Bell Tower. At the time I was unaware that my 'A' board was positioned further than it should have been, protruding by a staggering five centimetres over the boundary line. One metre was the legal distance and as a guide the Lithostroto paving had a continuous line running along it exactly one metre from the front of all buildings, thus forming the boundary in fact (at least that's what I was told). After taking a severe tongue lashing I thanked them for pointing out the error of my ways and moved the board back to the correct distance.

I was obviously a targeted man, because a few days later two more streetwalkers came into the Bell Tower demanding to see the licence for the 'A' board. Licence, what licence? The Lithostroto, they were quick to point out is a public road and everything on it has to have a licence.

'Are they serious?'

It seems they were. Lena however was on the ball and had everything under control within a matter of hours. The licence was hastily applied for and issued, but in the meantime, while the application was being processed the board stayed where it was and I carried on as though nothing had happened. After all, the Bell Tower and *kafeneion* was a municipality enterprise, and they, the Municipality Police, couldn't be seen giving grief to 'their own' people; or could they!

It Takes All Sorts

The spiral staircase in the Bell Tower was, in some people's eyes, daunting but as long as it was treated with caution there was no problem going up or down, although going down could be a bit tricky, especially with a bag full of paintings, or if it came to that, a bag full of anything. But it was rare that anyone had ever flatly refused to go up, and more often than not by the time most of the more nervous ones had, they were happy enough to carry on to the top of the tower. It was a confidence thing and merely a matter of taking those first few steps, which I suppose was a bit like me and my swimming.

Spiral staircase at The Bell Tower

One morning a woman with a walking stick struggled her way up the spiral to the first floor and sat for a few minutes to get her breath back.

'Are you OK?' I asked.

'Oh yes' she replied with a big smile, 'I'm fine, but you know, in this life it's not what you can't do, it's doing what you can, and looking at the paintings on these walls I'm glad I made the effort.'

What a compliment! We spent some time talking about nothing in particular before she had one last look round and then made her way back down.

About an hour later a man came up, totally ignoring me before carrying on to the next floor. On the way back down he stopped and asked for a price list.

'I'm sorry, but because the paintings constantly change it's not worth printing one.'

'Ah yes, but it's for my friends, they're downstairs.'

'Bring them up then,' I said.

'No, you don't understand, they're tired, they would never get up the stairs.'

I was gobsmacked, because in all honestly I couldn't believe what he was saying. It was in total contrast to the lady with the stick and I felt like telling him so, but there was no point so I said nothing and kept my thoughts to myself.

There's No Such Thing as an Ordinary Day

For some reason known only to themselves, George was helping Erik on the day shift at The Bells, and one morning took it upon himself to cut the grass between the chairs and tables and the small playground in the square. Thankfully there were no customers or children around at the time because George and his strimmer not only cut the grass, but whipped up the bone dry soil to create a serious cloud of dust. Erik looked on in total disbelief from the steps of the *kafeneion* as it settled on everything, including the unfortunate George.

After brushing himself down he disappeared indoors, from where, shortly after, one of the young lads working there appeared with a cloth and a bucket of water. Within minutes everything had been washed down and things were back to normal for yet another unpredictable day in the Bells *Kafeneion*.

When using the words 'normal' and 'Bell Tower' in the same sentence I always had to remind myself to expect the unexpected, because there was no such thing as an ordinary day there. Being out-of-the-ordinary was what made The Bell Tower such a wonderfully unique experience, but that summer the guys lost a little thread of their individuality and uniqueness. The male staff were issued with burgundy coloured polo shirts with 'The Bell's Café' printed on the back, whereas the girls looked radiant in pink.

Not all visitors who came up the spiral were visiting the exhibition, some were just passing through on their way to the top floor. Prints of old Argostoli, as well as other interesting information were fixed to the walls of the upper floors giving visitors a glimpse into the history of the tower and the Cabana neighbourhood, which in itself was fascinating. Then upon reaching the top there was the added bonus of an amazing roofscape of Argostoli.

It was just before two o'clock one day, and I was waiting patiently for a couple to come down from upstairs when suddenly the silence was broken by the sound of the front doors of the café slamming shut and a key turning in the lock. Realising we were about to be locked in jolted me into action, and like a shot I was down the spiral just in time to see Spyros and Lena walking across the Lithostroto towards the tables and chairs. Quickly opening the windows I called to them, whereupon they turned and looked back in disbelief. Smiling, Lena said, 'Sorry Peter, we didn't realise you were still up there.'

I told them about the couple upstairs, called them down, gathered my belongings, and went home for lunch.

No, there was no such thing as an ordinary day at the Bell Tower.

Return To The Gallery

Nick Edwards was visiting the island again on Rough Guide duties, and Tony was enjoying one last holiday while Pam and I were still living there.

I'd spent some great evenings relaxing with them under the sun umbrellas in the Cabana square, as I had with other friends, some who I'd got to know over the years, and others who, relatively speaking, I'd known for only a few minutes. Sipping chilled ouzo on hot summer evenings was a perk of the job and the longer the summer went on the more of a perk it became, it was in fact a very enjoyable occupational hazard.

If I was socialising under the sun umbrellas, should it happen that anybody went up into the Bell Tower then one of the *kafeneion* guys would be quick to let me know, usually by sticking a finger in the air and pointing in the direction of the spiral; a rude gesture to some, but I knew what it meant.

On one particular balmy evening after finishing work, Tony, Nick and I went for a lads' night out! There was a selection of good tavernas to choose from but Nick suggested eating at 'The Gallery' (although it wasn't called that then) which was conveniently close to the pub which was where we would end up after the meal for the obligatory nightcap.

Since I'd left, the gallery had changed hands more than once and had become a busy souvlaki joint. Customers had no choice other than to eat outside, in and out of season, but the roll down plastic walls were protection against any inclement weather that winter might bring. Prices were cheap and the menu minimal. There wasn't one. The other novelty was that diners didn't eat off plates, but instead used a plastic substitute.

'What have you got for vegetarians?' I asked the waitress.

'Salad,' she smiled, and that was it. It wasn't the most adventurous of salads either, there was more nourishment in the nuts Linda put out on the tables at the pub. Long gone were the days of the traditional English pub when there had always been a variety of crisps to choose from, but Linda's nuts were better than nothing.

Returning to the gallery hadn't been the best evening out for me, and with such a lousy menu I never went back, but Nick and Tony, being meat eaters, were happy enough.

Building Regulations

For well over a year a huge apartment block had been slowly rising out of the ground close to the rear of our apartment, then suddenly all work on it stopped. It didn't take us long to get used to the silence until we forgot about it altogether. Then one morning our dreams were shattered as the sound of heavy machinery rumbled into action again, but they weren't resuming work on the building. Exactly the opposite in fact; huge skips had been positioned around the bottom of the building as demolition on a grand scale began. The roof came off first. Timber joists, battens and tiles, the whole thing was stripped completely before the serious and unenviable task of demolishing the top floor began. A gang of navvies with large pneumatic drills broke up the reinforced concrete into manageable chunks before lowering them into the skips with hydraulic cranes.

Because of constant seismic shift, the height of all new buildings in Kefalonia was restricted to three storeys at a given height. The large buildings on either side of the new one had however become dwarfed by it, it was clear something had gone seriously wrong.

As a consequence, and to comply with the island's Building Regulations it was being cut down to size; literally.

Prevention Is Better Than Cure

The stretch of coast between Argostoli and the lighthouse is delightful, and because of its many different moods and colours was where Pam and I, along with other locals, and scores of tourists, walked in either direction all year round. But over a period of time this beautiful walk had become littered with every kind of debris, from ordinary household waste to used condoms, and was particularly bad at the Maistrato end where illegal camping and fly tipping, especially during the season, had become a regular practice. Two summers ago, close to Maistrato I'd met a local man named Spyros, who, with his black bin liner was acting as an unofficial litter collector.

'Good afternoon,' I said, 'you've got a job for life there.'

'Yes I have,' he replied, 'and it saddens me when people abuse my town in this way.'

We were on the same wavelength and could have talked forever, agreeing the problem was real, but that it wasn't exclusive to Argostoli, or even Kefalonia. It was a Greek problem, and until Governments, National and Local, educated people into becoming aware of it, litter pollution in all its forms would only get worse.

I was sitting downstairs in the Bell Tower one hot July morning when two streetwalkers came in.

'Whoops,' I thought, 'now what have I done, and what haven't I got a licence for this time?' But I breathed easy, because they were only handing out leaflets and left me alone.   Due to increasing pressure from the European Union, protecting the environment had become a big issue in Greece and was being raised on a regular basis in the National Parliament. It was a political hot potato and the government was receiving adverse publicity through the media nationwide.

The majority of Kefalonians, certainly the Argostolians, were aware of the problem and voiced their concerns through local media channels, so much so that the Municipality appealed for volunteers to clean up the verges along the coast road between Maistrato and Fanari.

However, not only did the coast road get a 'spring clean', but around the same time the shore and footpath along the lagoon got one too. The Town Hall provided the garbage truck, tools, plastic bags etc. for both projects, while the volunteers did the tidying and cleaning. The sad thing was that, within a matter of days, all the good work started to come undone, especially under the pines at Maistrato. It was July, and as the convoys of camper vans rolled off the ferries once more, fresh litter appeared in all the usual places.

In all fairness it was a great initiative by the *Dhimos*, but I was slightly confused as to why it had been left until just before the hordes arrived; was it to impress them? And why rely on volunteers to clean it up when there was a ready made work force? And why only clean up once in a blue moon?

The fact of the matter was they didn't have the foresight to stop the blight happening as often as it did, when after all, prevention is better than cure.

Incidentally, the clean up campaign was what the streetwalkers were handing out the leaflets for that morning in the Bell Tower.

A Summer of Fires

It was during the height of summer, when the weather was at its hottest, that some of the worst forest fires on record destroyed thousands of acres of forest land throughout Greece. As well as the natural environment, millions of euros worth of damage had also been caused to property.

Kefalonia too was affected as large areas of the landscape became charred desolation. Many local people had a fire related tale to tell, either from first hand experience, through family, friends, or just hearsay, and comments such as 'totally destroyed', and 'almost' or, 'we were very lucky' were not uncommon .

Parts of the south, especially around Skala were some of the worst hit, where strong winds fanned the fires which spread rapidly down towards the village from the lower slopes of the mountains. Tourists and locals were forced to evacuate their holiday accommodation and homes to seek refuge on the beach, watching in helpless horror as the flames threatened to engulf everything before them.

I listened to stories from some of the holidaymakers who had been through it all. But it would have been interesting to have heard from some of the unsung heroes, the crews of the fire fighting planes who often risked their lives to save others. It was incredible to watch as they flew in low, scooping up hundreds of gallons of water from Argostoli harbour, itself a hazardous manoeuvre, before heading for the fire zones and dropping it onto the flames below.

It was after the fires had been finally extinguished that the recriminations began. There were those Kefalonians who believed that the fires were started intentionally, as a ploy by crafty landowners of getting round the intricate web of planning regulations governing construction work on the island.

Building on forested land anywhere in Greece was illegal, but if those forests had been destroyed, for example, and very conveniently by fire, there was nothing to stop the owner of the land from submitting a building application, which, if the right palms had been greased was usually granted.

There was no doubt the summer fires were catastrophic, not only because of the overall destruction they caused, but also because of the cost involved to a country that just couldn't afford it. The estimated national bill for the fire fighting equipment alone was somewhere in the region of forty million euros!

But nature is resilient, and despite a blackened landscape it would quickly regenerate.

Kefalonian Meat Pie

I wanted a pair of comfortable jogging bottoms for lounging about in, and didn't want to pay much for them. In the same street as the Tax Office there was a cluster of small clothing shops, and the one that caught my eye was 'The Stock Center', whose sign oddly enough was written in English. Like most other Argostoli clothes shops a selection of garments hung on rails outside which appeared to be reasonably priced, so I went in and was welcomed by a guy with a friendly face and a big smile.

'*Kalimera,*' I said.

'Good morning, what can I do for you?' he replied (yes, in English!).

I told him, and ended up buying a claret coloured pair with two black stripes down the outside of each leg, although I would have preferred them to have been light blue, the stripes that is. Claret and blue are the colours of an English Premier League football club's strip who are Birmingham based and shouldn't be confused with the east London club who wear the same colours.

Such was the value-for-money clothing that I became a regular visitor to The Stock Center. It was also a convenient stop off on the way to work, whether at The Studio or the Bell Tower. Dimitris, the guy with the big smile, enjoyed talking about anything and everything, partly as a way to improve his English, but also because there was a wide range of topical conversation which was never boring, and from my point of view it was good to enjoy a coffee with him to start the day and also to pick up on local knowledge. He had lived in Athens before returning to Razata to look after his elderly parents, then one morning as we discussed the Kefalonian way of life and in particular the diet, he completely, and out of the blue invited Pam and me to join him and his parents for lunch. We were always glad to sample local homemade cooking, and because it would give us the chance to make new acquaintances I gladly accepted his invitation.

Knowing there would be mountains of food we worked up an appetite by walking across the bridge, where Dimitris was waiting at the Dhrapano side to drive us the short distance to the village. His parents were delightful and as we'd expected weren't English speakers. Not that it mattered, because Dimitris, who spoke it well, translated and made sure everything went smoothly and that the language barrier didn't become an embarrassment for hosts or visitors.

As we'd entered the house an aroma of everything good about Kefalonian cooking drifted in the air, and we didn't have to wait long before the food reached the table. Along with the customary salad was a selection of other vegetables and a huge fish pie that had been specially baked for me; the carnivores on the other hand tucked into the most amazingly large Kefalonian Meat Pie, which Pam said was the best she'd ever tasted.

After an afternoon of eating, drinking and talking we looked forward to a casual stroll home, it was after all, downhill and no real distance. Dimitris however, insisted on driving us, which we thought would be to the bridge, but ignoring our protests he drove us all the way home.

Later in the year Dimitris left the Stock Centre to open his own clothes shop in the Lithostroto, just across from the Bell Tower.

Confused

Having lived in the UK for over fifty years I'd been used to weekly rubbish collections, where the guys came along, emptied the bins, took it away and that was that. Should there have been anything to re-cycle we took it to the nearest point, either by car or on foot.

That though was all in the past and we soon got used to the refuse collections in Argostoli, which, except for Sundays, holidays, and the odd strike, was daily; but it wasn't the most hygienic collection system I've come across. Because of the small diameter of toilet plumbing, and to avoid serious blockages, toilet tissue had to be put into pedal bins lined with plastic bags, which when full(ish), along with the rest of the ordinary household refuse was deposited in the wheelie bins. It was a messy business (and was why Nikos was so proud of his western plumbing at Vivian Villa) but one the Greeks had been using for decades.

It was though easy, because all we had to do was take our waste to one of the three large green 'wheelie' bins, which were conveniently located only a few seconds walk from our apartment. Nothing needed sorting because re-cycling was in its infancy (so much so it didn't exist) and any larger items, such as household goods and even furniture, were left next to the bins where they too were collected, or taken by anyone who could use them - I guess recycling did exist after all!

As well as being rubbish containers, the bins provided a never ending source of food for the scores of cats that lived locally, and who thrived on the unwanted edibles of their human benefactors.

I left the apartment one morning with the intention of 'binning' our plastic bag only to find the wheelies gone. 'Who on earth would want to nick three garbage containers?'

I thought, and carried on walking. Once I got round the corner the bin mystery was solved - they'd been moved to one of the car parking bays adjacent to the boundary wall of Napier's Garden.

Later that morning one of the hydraulic cranes that was being used on the demolition of the new apartment block rumbled into Piniatorou street and positioned itself in the space where the bins had been.

The neighbourhood cats meanwhile were totally confused and for a short time wandered around aimlessly (being careful to avoid mobile cranes that might be on the move) looking for their next meal, but they didn't have to wait long. There were those people in the neighbourhood who couldn't be bothered to walk the few extra yards round the corner and left their rubbish on the ground just as though the bins were still there; were they blind or just lazy? But at least the cats were happy, and happier still once the demolition had finished and the bins were back in the normal place.

Moving Ahead of The Grapevine

Out of respect for our closest Kefalonian friends we told them about our move before the grapevine got the news and blew it up out of all proportion; Stathis and Irini were the first to know.

They wished us all the best, and Irini said, 'You never know you might change your mind, but if you don't we'll understand.' Then on our behalf they told Makis and Soula.

When I told the Icon his response was one of surprise. 'Peter you can't go, you're one of us now, but don't worry my friend within six months you'll be back.'

I smiled and replied, 'I don't think so Nick, but you never know.'

Rosa was upset, almost to the point of tears; but once we'd

explained all the whys, wherefores and ifs and buts she fully understood.

It was Nick's 'you're one of us', which was probably the greatest compliment a Kefalonian could ever pay to a non-Greek, although it was a sentiment echoed by most of the local people who knew us well.

The Kefalonians love their island and found it difficult to understand why we, of all people, were leaving, especially as we'd lived there for so long.

Acclimatising

Living in a different climate to the one you're used to for any length of time plays havoc with the body's thermostat which means adjusting through a period of acclimatisation.

For Pam and me that meant suffering the searing heat of summer, the temperate dampness of winter and everything in between, but despite never completely acclimatising we somehow managed, even when the summer heatwaves were almost too much to bear. We weren't the only ones to suffer however, because in July and August everyone did, even the Kefalonians, but they didn't react the same way we did, by sweating gallons. They appeared not to sweat at all, which gave the impression they were comfortable, but they weren't and moaned and groaned just as we did.

Despite the high temperatures and blistering heat the Kefalonians had perfected ways of keeping cool which I quickly adopted. Like them I walked, wherever and whenever possible, slowly... in the shade, and drank plenty of water, but I did draw the line at wearing black clothing and using a brolly as a mobile sun shade!

It sounds crazy but the best way of keeping the apartment cool during the hot spells was by closing everything, windows, doors, shutters, the lot. At night to stand a chance of getting some decent sleep the shutters were opened slightly and the windows opened fully. It was the only way to circulate the air, which although sometimes warm was always cooler than during the day. Some air movement was better than none.

In those two excruciatingly hot months our body clocks adjusted to the afternoon siesta, and then as September arrived and with it the end of summer (according to the Greeks that is) the body clocks automatically re-adjusted back to normal 'night only' sleeping patterns; and that was it, no more siestas until the next year.

There were afternoons when I woke after sleeping with the feeling that I hadn't slept at all, so I mentioned it to Costas. He was a local guy who had recently taken to drinking an early evening coffee at the Cabana Square, and because there were rarely any exhibition visitors that early I sometimes joined him.

'How long do you sleep for, Pete?'

'Oh, between two and three hours.'

'That's your problem, you're sleeping far too long, you should siesta for the most, about an hour and a half, try it.' So I did, and he was right, I felt a lot fresher after waking from the shorter sleep.

As the heat of summer faded altogether our bodies became accustomed once again to the cooler evenings. At first we wore more layers, then at the end of October Makis filled the tank with oil and switched the central heating on.

General Election

Polling day for the general election clashed with Aston Villa's Premier League game at Manchester City; light blue against claret and blue. I'd supported Villa from childhood, and since living on the island tried to watch their matches on television. It hadn't been difficult because most of the bars in Argostoli broadcast live English Premier League matches on one of the many satellite channels.

The latest in a long line of 'viewing venues' was the fast food restaurant, Pizza Pizza, situated at the top end of the square which, unlike some of the other bars and *kafeneions* I'd previously frequented didn't get fogged out with tobacco smoke.

The television there was huge and watching it was a bit like being in a small cinema, with food as an added extra if I wanted it. Canello and his staff were friendly and soon got used to seeing me on match days, but gave me awful stick if Villa lost, which is what happened on that General Election day. The election shared central stage with the football, and Canello, being Greek, and judging by his behaviour, a wannabe politician, annoyingly flicked back and forth between channels for the latest news from the election exit polls.

That same evening Pam and I settled down in front of our own television with no distractions or interruptions, but there wasn't much to watch, not of any interest anyway. Fifteen out of seventeen channels covered the election results, leaving a choice of the ballet or French football on the other two.

In the election New Democracy were re-elected but with a much reduced majority and Petros lost his seat. Despite being the current Member of Parliament he wasn't the only candidate from the Government contesting the seat, and bizarrely was defeated by one of two opponents from within his own party. His only consolation, if there was one, was that New Democracy held the seat.

Although Nick (the icon) had explained how the candidate selection process and voting system worked it was far too complicated for me to understand, but as with the election of the Prefect I couldn't vote anyway, so it didn't really matter.

Their Grand Entrance

In the years Pam and I had lived in Kefalonia we'd only been to one wedding and that was a civil one, but with only five weeks before we left the island we were invited to another, a traditional Greek orthodox one. Menos's daughter Emilie was marrying Pete, her American boyfriend, who she brought to the Bell Tower and broke the happy news, while at the same time giving me the invitation.

The ceremony took place at Kouvalata, Menos's village on the Paliki, and because the weather was so nice on the day Pam and I drove the long way round, arriving at the church with plenty of time to spare. The weather was glorious as was the setting for the wedding, the small orthodox chapel nestled amongst the olive trees on the hillside commanding spectacular views across the gulf of Argostoli.

View from Kouvalata

As is the custom the bride and her father arrived last, by which time the church was not only packed to the walls, but it was also steaming hot and very loud. Their arrival was a signal for the congregation, who were already pushing and shoving to get as close as possible to Emilie and Pete as they stood before the priest vowing to love, honour and obey, at least I think that's what they said; it was after all a Greek ceremony.

The evening reception was held further along the peninsular at a very spacious taverna overlooking Xi, the red 'walkabout' beach. As the tables slowly filled, everyone waited in anticipation for the newly-weds, and what an arrival. Their grand entrance was made on horseback, emerging slowly from the darkness of the beach to appear like ghostly shadows in the night, and as they approached the gathered guests, spontaneous applause broke out in warm welcome.

For the second time that day I was celebrating, because earlier I'd received a phone call from my son-in-law Neil telling me that Clare had given birth to a son who they named Oliver Nigel.

As the grand toast of the evening was raised to the bride and groom, my own private one was to my daughter, my son-in-law and my new grandson.

'No It's Not the Same Peter'

Two women appeared at the top of the spiral, and upon seeing me the first one turned, looked down to her friend and with a shake of the head said, 'No it's not the same Peter.'

'What's all that about then?' I wondered, but once we got talking I soon found out.

As the story unfolded it transpired she was referring to Prue's Peter, who they'd met along with Prue on a visit to the island some years before. I brought them up to date with events and was naturally interested to find out how they'd tracked me down. It turned out they'd been to Portside, and seeing my name in the menu had asked Rosa,

'This Peter, does he drink?'

Rosa thought carefully before answering, then without batting an eyelid told them, 'No'.

Nonetheless they were on the scent and followed the trail.

And they weren't the only people with a Prue connection to visit me. A few days later another couple who had also known her, but in totally different circumstances to the two women, came to the Bell Tower.

There was a polite good morning, a formal introduction then the man said, 'Peter, we're from Worthing, and I conducted Prue's funeral service.'

What was I supposed to say? He knew of our friendship but I didn't ask how, it didn't really matter, however, it was very thoughtful of him to look me up.

A Clear Out

During the middle of October I started packing, but there were other things to do first. I dismantled the exhibition for the last time and as a token of thanks and appreciation I gave a painted stone to each of the guys and girls who worked downstairs in the *kafeneion*. One by one, just as thousands of summer visitors had done, they climbed the spiral and took their pick, but Spyros, who had always had his eye on a small Zola painting, Zola being his village, took that; Erik and George also chose from a selection of other small canvases.

Once everything was off the walls and packed away I stood in the middle of the empty room, looked round it, and with mixed emotions, left. Leaving the Bell Tower with its oddities and eccentricities had been sad, but as with Prue, there would always be many happy memories to fall back on to keep me smiling.

Having emptied the Bell Tower I focused on clearing the Studio. The fridge, which had stood the test of time since those distant days of The Gallery had been sold, and anything else that wasn't going to France was 'wheelie binned'.

And so came the time to start the ultimate clear out of the apartment. Removals and local storage had been arranged with an English guy who made frequent trips to the UK via France.

Finding packing boxes wasn't a problem because the main streets of Argostoli were full of them, most of which had been flat packed down and left at different points by businesses, for collection by the municipality, so for me it was a question of taking what I wanted, when I wanted.

Pam's friend and colleague Sue offered to drive us to the airport and came to do a luggage check, just to make sure everything fitted into her small but deceptively spacious Fiat Siecento.

Our Panda was sold almost before the ink had dried on the For Sale sign that Pam put in the back window, written in Greek of course. She parked on the road near the office in Lassi where the ad. immediately caught the eye of a young man named Yiannis who had recently returned to the island after living in the UK. He test drove it, gave the thumbs up, paid a deposit and collected it a couple of days before we left.

Parting with our white Panda was like losing a close friend. We'd been all over the island on journeys of exploration and discovery that had coloured our lives and given us pleasure and happiness that we would treasure forever.

Due to the complicated procedure of selling anything in Greece, we were, or rather Pam was (after all it was her car) reminded once again of the tangled web of bureaucracy; the paperwork was, as it always had been, horrendous. Eventually though, as with everything else, the I's and T's were dotted and crossed and the documents signed and stamped.

On one of those last days a big and pleasant surprise came from upstairs. Makis knocked on the door, and with a big smile handed me a wad of euro notes. It was the original deposit and advance payment for the apartment which over the years I'd completely forgotten about, but obviously he hadn't.

I don't know why, but somehow it seemed appropriate that he was holding his name day celebrations on the evening before we left, but because we had to be up at five the following morning it meant we couldn't stay late. There had been so many goodbyes and good luck wishes over the past few days, but emotions that evening were running high.

The final farewells echoed on the stairs as we made our way down them for the last time. It had been almost six years to the day since we'd first wished Makis 'Chronia Polla', and now he and our other Kefalonian friends were wishing us the same 'Many Years' for our future well-being.

A few short hours later we were up before the sun, and after loading our luggage into Sue's car, I locked the apartment for the last time and dropped the keys into Makis's letter box.

And that was it… the end of a six month painting holiday.

Assos
Painting, oil on canvas by Peter Hemming

I dreamed I saw the seas of turquoise again

And the deep green of Ionian pines.

I dreamed of shimmering, silver olive leaves

Dancing in the sun,

And of burnt sienna earth.

I dreamed of friendship and warmth.

I was dreaming of Kefalonia

Peter Hemming 2013

18568313R00204

Made in the USA
Charleston, SC
10 April 2013